T0330208

Enhancing Global Competitiveness through Sustainable Environmental Stewardship

NEW HORIZONS IN INTERNATIONAL BUSINESS

Series Editor: Peter J. Buckley
Centre for International Business,
University of Leeds (CIBUL), UK

The New Horizons in International Business series has established itself as the world's leading forum for the presentation of new ideas in international business research. It offers preeminent contributions in the areas of multinational enterprise – including foreign direct investment, business strategy and corporate alliances, global competitive strategies, and entrepreneurship. In short, this series constitutes essential reading for academics, business strategists and policy makers alike.

Titles in the series include:

Enhancing Global Competitiveness through Sustainable Environmental Stewardship

Edited by

Subhash C. Jain

University of Connecticut, USA and Graduate School of Business, Zurich, Switzerland

and

Ben L. Kedia

University of Memphis, USA

NEW HORIZONS IN INTERNATIONAL BUSINESS

Edward Elgar

Cheltenham, UK • Northampton, MA, USA

Published by
Edward Elgar Publishing Limited
The Lypiatts
15 Lansdown Road
Cheltenham
Glos GL50 2JA
UK

Edward Elgar Publishing, Inc.
William Pratt House
9 Dewey Court
Northampton
Massachusetts 01060
USA

A catalogue record for this book
is available from the British Library

Library of Congress Control Number: 2010929036

ISBN 978 1 84844 874 2

Typeset by Servis Filmsetting Ltd, Stockport, Cheshire
Printed and bound by MPG Books Group, UK

Contents

PART I   PERSPECTIVES ON SUSTAINABILITY

PART II   UNDERSTANDING SUSTAINABILITY
          CONCERNS

PART III   STRATEGIC APPROACHES TO
           SUSTAINABILITY

Figures

Tables

Contributors

Alexander, John, Grand Valley State University, USA.

Brown, Darrell, Portland State University, USA.

Brown, Halina Szejnwald, Clark University, USA.

Clampit, Jack, University of Memphis, USA.

Dowell, Glen, Cornell University, USA.

Gaffney, Nolan, University of Memphis, USA.

Henriques, Irene, York University, Canada.

Jain, Subhash C., University of Connecticut, USA.

Kedia, Ben L., University of Memphis, USA.

Levy, David L., University of Massachusetts, USA.

Lewis, Ben, Cornell University, USA.

Marshall, R. Scott, Portland State University, USA.

Paquin, Raymond, Concordia University, Canada.

Plumlee, Marlene, University of Utah, USA.

Shivarajan, Sridevi, Rutgers University, USA.

Shrivastava, Paul, Concordia University, Canada.

Abbreviations

BBC	British Broadcasting Corporation
BRIC	Brazil, Russian, India, China
CDP	Carbon Disclosure Project
CER	Corporate Environment Report
CIBER	Center for International Business Education and Research
CME	coordinated market economy
CO_2	carbon dioxide
CSR	corporate social responsibility
EKC	Environmental Kuznets Curve
EMS	environmental management system
EU	European Union
FCC	Federal Communications Commission
FASBI	Financial Accounting Standards Board Interpretations
FDI	foreign direct investment
GAAP	generally accepted accounting principles
GDP	gross domestic product
GRI	global reporting initiative
HCCPBL	Hindustan Coca-Cola Beverage Company Private Limited
IEA	International Energy Agency
IPCC	Intergovernmental Panel on Climate Change
IRRC	Investor Responsibility Research Center
KGWB	Kerala Ground Water Board
KSPCB	Kerala State Pollution Control Board
LME	liberal market economy
MNC	multinational corporation
MNE	multinational enterprise
NFR	non-financial reporting
NGO	non-governmental organization
OECD	Organisation for Economic Co-operation and Development
PPMV	parts per million per volume
S&P	Standard and Poor's
SEC	Securities and Exchange Commission

SME	small- and medium-sized enterprises
SRI	socially responsible investment
UK	United Kingdom
UNEP	United Nations Environment Programme
VED	voluntary environmental disclosure

Preface

In recent years, the concept of climate change has received growing recognition. It is no more a reserve of scientists and political activists. It has become a mainstream discussion. It is now widely accepted that Earth is warming; to a large extent it is a result of the emission of greenhouse gases resulting from mankind's activities; and it has significant impact for Earth's environment. It is recognized that climate change is a global problem that requires a global approach to resolve it.

In the world of global business, climate change has evolved from being a fringe issue to a strategic concern that requires high level deliberations and decision-making. More and more multinational enterprises (MNEs) have come to accept that the issue of climate change goes beyond the focus on a firm's brand and its social responsibility. While climate change could pose enormous problems for some MNEs, it also offers huge potential for innovation leading to new products and services. Firms that recognize the challenge early, and respond imaginatively and constructively will create opportunities for themselves and thereby prosper. Others, slower to realize what is going on or electing to ignore it, will likely do markedly less well.

Considering the importance of the climate change issue, the Centers for International Business Education and Research (CIBERs) at the University of Connecticut and the University of Memphis decided to organize a two-day by-invitation-only conference from 14–16, May 2009. The conference was held at the main campus of the University of Connecticut in Storrs. The CIBERs at the University of California at Los Angeles (UCLA), University of Maryland, Temple University, University of South Carolina, and University of North Carolina at Chapel Hill co-sponsored the conference.

Thirteen faculty members from different parts of the world made presentations at the conference. Since it was a by-invitation-only conference, it offered the participants a unique opportunity for intensive discussion and interaction. Thirteen presenters submitted nine papers for publication in this book. Collectively these papers provide deep insights into the climate change issue, its negative and positive impacts on different industries, and in different geographic regions of the world. The book is useful for both practicing managers as well as academics. It reinforces the thesis that climate change is a tectonic force that changes the economic landscape. MNCs must act fast to face the problem, make investments in new technologies and processes, and thus gain global competitiveness. For academics, the book introduces different frameworks and conceptual schemes to tackle the climate change challenge, and indentifies areas for scholarly inquiry.

We are grateful to Ms Susanna Easton at the US Department of Education for her encouragement in this endeavor. We sincerely thank CIBER directors Christopher Erickson, UCLA; Kislaya Prasad, Maryland; Arvind V. Phatak, Temple; Lynne Gerber, North Carolina; and William R. Folks, Jr, South Carolina for their support through co-sponsoring the conference.

We thank our deans Chris Earley at the University of Connecticut and Rajiv Grover at the University of Memphis for their advice and counsel in making the program successful. Kelly Aceto, associate director and Michele Metcalf, program assistant at the University of Connecticut CIBER deserve our appreciation for all their administrative support and for managing day-to-day details in organizing the conference.

We also want to thank Dr Dan Esty for his willingness to serve as our keynote speaker. Finally, we want to thank our acquisition editor, Alan Sturmer, and the desk editor, Bob Pickens at Edward Elgar Publishing for their help in seeing the book to completion.

Subhash C. Jain
University of Connecticut

Ben L. Kedia
University of Memphis

This book is University of Connecticut and Memphis CIBER-supported research intitiative. CIBER is a program of the US Department of Education. The CIBER program's mandate is to enhance US competitiveness in the global business arena through activities involving US businesses, educators, and students.

PART I

Perspectives on sustainability

1. Climate change and global business: challenges, opportunities and research guidelines

Subhash C. Jain

Kogut (2003) has identified 'context' as the key component of international business (IB) inquiry and research. Although the twenty-first century is still young, recently a variety of events and concerns have surfaced that suggest re-defining the context of international business to accommodate them. Buckley and Ghauri (2004) and Peng (2004) suggest broadening the context in response to the emerging globalization of national economies, since it affects the strategy, structure and performance of multinational corporations (MNCs). After the debacle of the WTO meeting in Seattle in 1999, non-government organizations (NGOs) assumed a significant role in influencing the global perspectives of nation states and MNCs. According to Teegen, Doh and Vachani (2004), the IB field should be redrawn to include NGOs, since they impact MNCs in their endeavors to create value through resource transformation and exchange.

In the aftermath of 9/11, terrorism has become a substantial phenomenon, presenting a new type of risk for companies that conduct business internationally. Jain and Grosse (2007) propose adding post-9/11 security measures as another core element in examining the field of IB for theory development and research.

In recent years, climate change has developed from being a fringe concern within the corporate world, addressed primarily through a company's corporate and social responsibility (CSR), to an increasingly central topic for strategic deliberation and decision-making by executives and investors around the globe.

The driving force behind this change in corporate outlook is an emerging consensus on three broad points: that Earth is warming; that this is largely the result of greenhouse gas emissions; and that this will produce significant consequences for Earth's environment. In this context, this chapter takes a hard look at global warming. We begin by examining the relevant scientific and climatological evidence. We then proceed to the economic consequences and policy implications, followed by a discussion of the potential impacts on major business sectors globally and the steps that MNCs might take to prosper under these conditions and to make positive environmental contributions. The chapter concludes with suggestions for future academic research.

GLOBAL WARMING: SCIENTIFIC AND CLIMATOLOGICAL EVIDENCE

With widespread industrialization, the environmental impact of fossil fuels (such as coal, oil, and natural gas) has taken center stage in an international debate over the phenomenon known as global warming. Fossil fuels provide roughly 84 percent of the energy consumed in the US and make up 80 percent of the energy produced worldwide (International Energy Agency, 2006). The question is: does the use of fossil fuels which emit carbon dioxide (CO_2) lead to deleterious global warming?

Analyzing historical data, Mann et al. (1998, 1999) have concluded that there has been a sharp increase in Earth's mean temperature in the second half of the twentieth century. The 2001 report of the Intergovernmental Panel on Climate Change (IPCC) noted that over the course of the twentieth century, Earth's average temperature rose by about 0.6 of a degree centigrade. According to Brumfiel (2006), 2005 was the warmest year over several millennia. Furthermore, nine of the last ten years have been the warmest since the end of the nineteenth century, when temperature records were first kept (Shaw, 2006).

Changes in Earth's temperature are caused by the concentration of greenhouse gases in the atmosphere, which increase the amount of energy reflected down to earth. There is a positive correlation between Earth's temperature and the concentration of greenhouse gases. Thus, greenhouse gas emissions add significantly to atmospheric greenhouse gas concentration.

Under natural conditions, the Earth goes through gradual cycles of cooling and warming. But excessive emissions disturb the natural cycle. Thus, the actual warming resulting from human fossil fuel emissions might be 15–78 percent higher than the natural warming (Scheffer et al., 2006). If the status quo continues, the atmospheric concentration of greenhouse gases could reach 500 ppmv (parts per million per volume) by 2050 (Shaw, 2006).

Tables 1.1, 1.2 and 1.3 show the rising trend of CO_2 emissions. The carbon emissions generated by nations in the Organisation for Economic Co-operation and Development (OECD) declined by 25 percent during

Table 1.1   Rising CO_2 emissions (in millions of metric tons)

1751	1775	1800	1825	1850	1875	1900	1925	1950	1975	2000
0	4	8	17	54	188	534	975	1630	4613	6611

Source: Oak Ridge National Laboratory, NASA Goddard Institute for Space Studies

Table 1.2   Carbon emissions by region

Region	Carbon emissions (1973)	Carbon emissions (2004)
OECD	66%	49%
Former USSR	14%	9%
China	6%	18%
Asia except China	3%	9%
Latin America	3%	3%
Africa	2%	3%
Middle East	1%	5%
Others	5%	4%
Total	100%	100%

Source: World Resources Institute, 2006.

Table 1.3   Carbon emissions by sector

Sector	Carbon emissions
Power	24%
Land use	18%
Industry	14%
Transport	14%
Agriculture	14%
Buildings	8%
Other energy-related	5%
Waste	3%
Total	100%

Source: World Resources Institute, 2006.

the 31-year period between 1973 and 2004. On the other hand, the share of carbon emissions by Asian nations increased three-fold over the same time period. In 2000, industry, transport and agriculture generated equal amounts of carbon emissions. Industry can be subdivided into sectors, among which power accounted for the highest share of carbon emissions (almost a quarter) followed by land use.

In the future, the global primary demand for fossil fuels is expected to grow by 50 percent from 2004 to 2030, about 1.6 percent annually, since fossil fuels are likely to remain the predominant source of energy, accounting for 83 percent of the overall increase in energy demand. Coal is predicted to register the largest increase in demand driven by power generation. Four-fifths of the incremental demand for coal will occur in China and India (International Energy Agency, 2001).

The International Energy Agency (IEA) went on to predict in 2006 that developing nations would account for over three-quarters of the increase in emissions by 2010 or shortly thereafter, likely overtaking the OECD nations. According to their predictions, China and India will be responsible for almost 60 percent of the rise in global emissions due to steady economic growth and heavy reliance on coal (IEA, 2006).

Global warming impacts our planet in various ways. First, increases in temperature affect Earth's biological systems through such phenomena as glacier shrinkage; ice on rivers forming later in the year and breaking earlier; lengthening of growing seasons at high altitudes; reductions in some plant and animal populations; and earlier flowering of trees and shrubs (IPCC, 2001). For example, the ice cap over the Arctic is retreating. One study has estimated that Greenland is losing 20 percent more ice each year than it receives from new snowfalls (British Broadcasting Corporation, 2006). Arctic perennial sea ice, which in the past did not usually melt during summer months, was reduced by 14 percent during 2004 and 2005. Holland (2006) predicted that the retreat of Arctic ice might result in ice-free summers in the Arctic by 2040. Briefly, increases in global temperatures impact water resources, agriculture and forestry, marine systems, animal life, and human health.

Second, global warming impacts the world's hydrological systems and water resources. For instance, some regions might experience higher rates of evaporation due to an increase in the water-holding capacity of air, resulting in drought conditions. Other areas might receive violent and intense rains, leading to insurmountable flooding. Furthermore, water quality may suffer due to increased pollutants brought in by intense precipitation. Third, climate change from global warming adversely affects food production due to excessive heat and drought. Flooding caused by global warming affects food production as well.

Fourth, climate change impacts plant and animal populations by disturbing the terrestrial and freshwater ecosystems, which, in turn, leads to the extinction of certain species that are unable to adapt to change. Further, seasonal patterns are disturbed which produce changes in flowering and egg-laying. Also, hotter and dryer summers destroy fauna and flora and increase the risk of forest fires. Fifth, climate change affects coastal zones and marine ecosystems due to flooding, erosion, and damage to coral reefs and mangroves, for example. Lastly, warmer climates, exacerbated by humidity and pollution, can increase illness and death in humans, particularly in urban areas.

Changing climate affects the entire world. However, the intensity and nature of the impact varies from one region to another. Africa is especially vulnerable to climate change because of extreme poverty and poor governance. Asia could face an acute shortage of the drinking water due to reduced river flow from the Himalayas, which provide over half of the drinking water for 40 percent of the world's population. Impact in Europe, North, Central, and South America will vary by region. For instance, some areas will experience drought while others are prone to flooding, producing different effects on agricultural systems (Stern et al, 2006). Eventually, global warming/climate change is expected to endanger all of Earth's inhabitants through flooding, ocean disruptions, shifting storm patterns, reduced farm output, animal extinctions, and droughts (Carey, 2004). This is what one school of thought led by such luminaries as Al Gore (2006) leads us to believe about the devastating impact of climate change. The IPCC (2005) has concluded with 90 percent agreement among scientists that emissions of greenhouse gases were affecting the climate, and that the emissions should be reduced by 2020 to avoid calamitous consequences.

However, there are those in the scientific community who maintain that such concern is exaggerated. Avery and Singer (2007) argue that human activities do not affect global climate in any significant way. According to them, 'Climate will continue to change, as it always has in the past, warming and cooling on different time scales and for different reasons, regardless of human action. I would also argue that – should it occur – a modest warming would be on the whole beneficial.'

Some scholars feel that natural factors should be simultaneously considered. Geological records indicate a continuous pattern of warming and cooling over a 1500-year cycle extending back over one million years. Yet most politicians and environmentalists have accepted the burning of fossil fuels as the primary reason for global warming based on what they claim to be *scientific consensus*. The major source of that consensus is the United Nations' IPCC (2005). According to Avery and Singer (2007), the majority of the panelists have no scientific qualifications. In addition, they claim the evidence that fossil fuels cause global warming is scant and drawn out of context. For example, Gore (2006) pointed out that glaciers are melting and sea ice shrinking, suggesting a correlation between CO_2 levels and global warming. But correlation is not causation. Throughout most of the last century, the climate was cooling while CO_2 levels were rising. Therefore, one cannot scientifically conclude that industrial activities lead to global warming. This conclusion is supported by the climate change science program report 1.1 issued by the US government (climatescience. gov, 2006). It shows the disparity between observed and predicted patterns of global warming. To summarize, this view argues that increases in CO_2 levels caused by human activities have insignificant effect on climate change.

Some scholars believe that the best current measurements of climate suggest no catastrophic effects resulting from human activities. They cite that the life expectancy, health, welfare and productivity of humans have improved with the use of fossil fuels for energy, and the resulting economic growth has allowed for the production of environmental improvements beneficial to health. They also point out that CO_2, the primary greenhouse gas produced by burning fossil fuels, is not a toxic pollutant. On the contrary, it is essential to life on Earth. Plants have flourished as well – agricultural experts estimate a 10 percent increase in crop growth in recent decades – due to the fertilization effect of increased CO_2 in the air. It has been argued that over the next several decades, fossil fuels will be important in maintaining local economic integration and improving the human condition. In their view, current scientific evidence shows the effects of carbon emissions on the climate to be relatively minor and slow to develop, affording us an opportunity to continue to improve observations and computer simulations of the climate. These findings will serve to better define the magnitude of warming caused by human activities and allow development of a beneficial and cost-effective response.

The above arguments attempt to address the question of whether, and to what degree, human activities are responsible for global warming. It is generally accepted that burning of fossil fuels (for energy generation) releases large quantities of CO_2 into the environment. Since the beginning of the industrial revolution, over 200 years ago, the level of CO_2 in the atmosphere has been gradually increasing, and has risen by 35 percent during that time period. Further, it is scientifically accepted that CO_2 is a greenhouse gas capable of absorbing significant amounts of infrared or heat radiation. It can be argued then that burning of fossil fuels leads to enhanced greenhouse effect.

The debate about global warming and its effects has been highly emotional. Concerned agencies and individuals recommend strong government action to enhance energy security and reduce CO_2 emissions. They urge governments around the world to enact measures to improve efficiency in energy production and use; increase reliance on non-fossil fuels; and sustain the domestic supply of fossil fuels within net energy importing countries. An example of such measures would be the production of more efficient cars and trucks, as well as electrical appliances, such as lights, air conditioners, and industrial motors. Efficient fuel production involves renewables and biofuels. For such measures to be viable, they must yield financial savings for all concerned that far exceed the initial extra invest-ment. Proponents of government action argue that each year that passes without implementation of such policies will see more harmful pollutants emitted into the air.

The responsibilities of MNCs, in relation to global warming, are a subject of controversy. To ignore the potential dangers could be risky but, on the other hand, there is still some question as to whether the scientific evidence is strong enough to demand costly measures at the present time. After all, efforts that contain climate change require huge investments, necessitating a global consensus among business leaders on whether or not to commit such resources to the issue.

RESOLVING THE PROBLEM

As discussed above, scientific evidence of the impact of global warming on our environment is mixed. Yet, on balance, it is compelling enough to suggest examination of the global warming problem from different perspectives. This chapter probes the issue as it applies to international business.

Global warming involves economic externality, in other words it finan-cially impacts parties other than the one taking the action. Such impact could be positive or negative. An example of positive externality is a new invention, which benefits the public at large. On the other hand, industrial pollution is an example of negative externality since it harms those affected by the pollution, not the polluter. Emission of CO_2 into the environment heavily affects present and future generations while the emitter bears a fraction of the cost. The principle of fairness, however, requires that the entity causing the problem should be fully responsible for its action. In other words, the party emitting greenhouse gases into the atmosphere should be obliged to pay the full costs of the consequences of the harm done by these gases.

We argue that individuals, firms, governments, and NGOs can all play a role in addressing the emission problem (Figure 1.1). Individuals and firms make choices that increase or reduce emissions of greenhouse gases. NGOs play a unique role in the implementation of policy. Governments impose costs and penalties that are designed to discourage practices that cause global warming. The global warming phenomenon has three unique

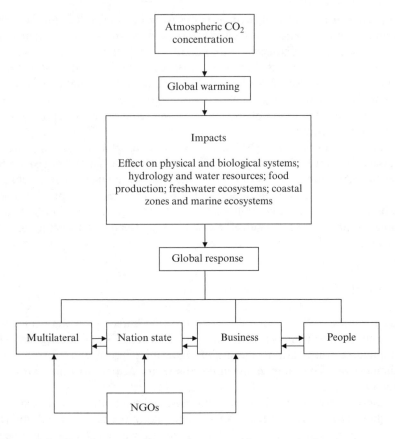

Figure 1.1   Resolving the climate change problem: parties involved

characteristics. First, it is a global problem since its causes and consequences compromise the entire planet. Second, the impact of greenhouse gases emitted in the present might last for centuries into the future. This requires computing the cost of consequences on future generations. Third, it is full of uncertainties. Is the problem really as big as it is made out to be? Is it wise to challenge Mother Nature? Should the huge level of money and resources required be used elsewhere to more effectively aid huge numbers of people?

Global warming can affect gross domestic product (GDP), either negatively or positively, relative to what it would be if the climate did not change. The impact varies from nation to nation. Nordhans (2006), for example, estimated that a warming of 2.5 degrees Celsius would result in a net benefit of 0.7 percent of GDP for Russia and a net loss of almost

5 percent of GDP for India in 2100. The global average would be a net damage of 1.5 percent of GDP with a warming of 2.5 degrees Celsius. Overall, developing countries are likely to lose more than developed nations.

Cost Consideration

Essentially, there are two ways of resolving the climate change problem: abate or adapt. Abate implies lowering the rate of emission of greenhouse gases. Adapt refers to the steps nations undertake to adjust to the effects of global warming.

Cost of abatement

The cost of abatement is influenced by three variables: (i) the target level of atmospheric carbon concentration; (ii) the discount rate used; and (iii) technological progress. Stern et al. (2006) suggest a target level of 450–550 ppmv (the current level is about 380 ppmv which is growing annually by 2–3 ppmv). According to him, a target level below 450 ppmv would be extremely costly, while one above 550 ppmv could be catastrophic for the environment.

The present value of abatement costs depends on the discount rate applied. To illustrate the point, using a discount rate of 4 percent, a damage of US$1 million in about 100 years time is worth US$20,000 today. A discount rate of 8 percent, on the other hand, gives a figure of only US$500. The pace of technological development may result in implementation of significant new techniques and tools to reduce carbon emissions, which should help in cutting costs.

Abatement costs are also impacted by the methods used for abatement, such as forestry, fuel switching, renewable energy, energy saving and efficiency. In developed countries forestry, such as planting trees, would be expensive, given high labor costs; while energy saving and efficiency would be more expensive in developing nations, given their more limited access to technology.

Economically speaking, abatement should be pursued to the extent that the resulting benefits of emissions reduction are equal to the cost of doing so. It is reasonable, therefore, to spend up to US$1 million to avoid losing US$1 million of GDP. Any cost exceeding US$1 million to reduce emissions to save US$1 million of GDP would be economically irrational.

An optimal abatement policy would have to consider two factors: the quantity dimension, that is the emissions target, and the cost dimension. Designing such a policy is very difficult because of uncertainty about the actual level of climate change and the desirable emissions target.

Nevertheless, a marginal analysis could be made using appropriate assumptions that are based on existing knowledge in order to determine the abatement policy. The marginal benefit of abatement is a decreasing function of the abatement level and an increasing function of the abatement level targeted. Thus, it would cost less to reduce the greenhouse concentration from 550 to 500 ppmv than from 500 to 450 ppmv.

According to Nordhans and Boyer (1999), the optimal policy should target a decrease in atmospheric carbon concentration from a projected business-as-usual figure of 586 ppmv in 2100 to 532 ppmv, which should reduce the degree of global warming from 2.15 degrees Celsius to 1.96 degrees Celsius. They estimated that the cost of carbon produced by the above figures would rise from US$6 per ton of carbon in 2000 to US$38 in 2100. Based on their calculations, the net gain would likely be 0.7 percent of global GDP per year by 2100. Their estimates can be questioned on two grounds. First, more recent scientific findings suggest that the cost implications of global warming on the global economy could be significantly higher than the past calculations. Second, their computations do not consider the range of uncertainty. Therefore, additional work is needed before their estimates can be used to design a policy. But their endeavor is commendable in its logic and provides a pedagogical basis for future scholarly pursuits, and policy-making.

Cost of adaptation
Even if abatement policies are designed and implemented forthwith, climate change will still occur, that is Earth's mean temperature will continue to increase. A further rise of 1 degree Celsius or so will occur over the next 50–100 years due to delayed and feedback effects. In any event, greenhouse gas emissions are not likely to vanish anytime soon. Thus, in addition to abatement efforts, there is a definite need for adaptation policies to control the damage. The costs of adaptation are inversely related to abatement success. If the abatement efforts to reduce emissions are successful, the adaptation will cost less, and vice-versa.

Adaptation is feasible either through voluntary measures on the part of individuals and corporations, or through legislation by nation states. Adaptation measures, whether voluntary or legislative, include emergency responses to climate change via early warning system; investments in infrastructure projects such as large reservoir storage and sea-walls; vaccination programs; reduction in energy/resources usage.

Globally, different adaptation steps are already in place both in developed and developing countries. For example, the United Kingdom (UK) government has established the Thames Estuary 2100 project to design a tidal flood risk management plan for London and surrounding areas.

Similarly, among developing nations, Bangladesh has, in recent years, made investments to reduce monsoon flooding.

It is difficult to perform a cost-benefit analysis of adaptation due to lack of information on the economic costs of climate change separately. All that have been reported to date are the overall costs of climate change, and the costs for particularly vulnerable areas (such as the cost of coastal protection against rising sea-levels). This means adaptation policy has to be made on as rational a basis as is feasible, using the best data available, making appropriate assumptions, and providing for likely margins of error.

Multilateral Policy Action

Although different nations have been concerned about global warming for several decades, the first concrete step toward reducing global emissions took place in 1997. Delegates from both developed and developing countries gathered in Kyoto, Japan, in December 1997, to negotiate a global treaty to reduce greenhouse gas emissions. The end result was a global accord called the Kyoto Protocol that came into force in February 2005. As of January 2007, 166 countries had ratified the accord. The ratifying nations committed themselves to reduce their emissions by 5.2 percent below their 1990 levels by 2008–2012. The accord was underwritten by nation states and is governed by global legislation enacted under the UN.

The accord stated that the developed nations ratifying it are obligated to reduce gas emissions. But developing countries are not legally bound by the greenhouse gas caps. They are, however, required to monitor and submit their annual greenhouse gas inventory. The US and Australia are the two major developed countries that did not ratify the Kyoto Protocol.

Toward the end of 2007, the US indicated a change in its approach to global warming. President George W. Bush proposed to hold a Whitehouse meeting of the nations considered the biggest emitters. In addition, at the UN Climate Convention in December 2007, held in Bali, Indonesia, all nations including the US agreed to negotiate a global climate agreement as a successor to the Kyoto Protocol beyond 2012. The new post-2012 protocol is likely to be finalized by the end of 2011.

Essentially, nations consider two ways to control the damage done by carbon emissions: cap-and-trade systems, and carbon taxes. The UN Development Program recommended the carbon tax system, since taxes create cost certainty for polluters, forcing them to invest efficiently in reducing emissions. The cap-and-trade system sets carbon emission standards for different industries. If a company in an industry is unable to meet the target, it can buy the permission to emit more from those who have exceeded their targets in reducing carbon emissions. Politically, carbon taxes are difficult to levy. The cap-and-trade scheme has a limitation as well. It is based on quotas granted to different industries in different geographic areas and, thus, their equitability can be questioned. Besides, trading, based on demand and supply conditions, makes carbon price volatile, creating cost uncertainty for the polluters.

In addition to the multilateral Kyoto Accord, governments around the world have resorted to technology-related measures to reduce emissions, primarily through the development of non-fossil fuels. For example, government subsidies have encouraged the development of alternative fuels, such as corn-based ethanol in the US. At the end of 2006, there were 110 ethanol refineries in the US; many more were being built and the existing ones expanded. Unfortunately, this industry has flourished due to generous government subsidies, but it has yet to play any significant role in reducing the demand for imported oil. In addition, production of corn-based ethanol has a side effect: the price of corn, a staple grain for billions of people around the world, has increased many times over, from less than one US dollar a bushel in 2000 to US$4.49 in July 2010. The prices of other staples, such as wheat and rice, have increased to decade highs since farms allocate more land to corn farming in place of other crops, particularly in the US, where subsidies for producing ethanol are high. Thus, with the US producing over 40 percent of the world's corn and over half of its corn exported, the burden of the development of corn-based ethanol has fallen hardest on the poor (Runge and Senaur, 2007).

Governments have also funded a variety of projects to develop alternative fuels. One example is hydrogen-based energy for transportation. To date, however, no practical solution has been found to replace fossil fuels.

Individual Government Steps to Reduce Emissions

By and large, governments have come to believe that the emissions of greenhouse gasses have been altering the climate and that such emissions must peak by 2020 to avoid calamity. As mentioned above, the US is now on board and encouraged discussions on a possible successor to the Kyoto Protocol at the 2007 Bali submit. Australia, which had also rejected the Kyoto Accord, started considering setting up a carbon trading system in 2007. Japan has been pushing its companies to pursue environmentally-friendly policies in their energy-usage. The European Union (EU) has long been fully convinced of humanity's role in causing global warming, and has been in the lead to enforce a cap-and-trade system. Several other nations, including Norway and Iceland, have joined the EU carbon trading system, showing their commitment to reduce greenhouse gases.

Developing nations, however, present a different perspective. First, China and India are big emitters of greenhouse gases since they use coal, a dirty fuel, in large quantities, and coal produces more carbon emissions than other sources of energy such as gas or nuclear power. (In 2008, China became the world's biggest emitter of greenhouse gases.) Second, developing countries insist that developed nations take the lead because, they claim, rich countries have been responsible for the current stock of emissions in the atmosphere. Third, developing nations expect the rich countries to pay for reducing global warming. As a matter of fact, under the Kyoto Protocol, developing nations have received a few billion dollars from developed countries to establish carbon reduction projects such as wind farms and equipment to remove industrial gases from manufacturing facilities.

Industry Position

Different industries and firms within an industry have responded to the global warming problem in various ways. Consider the energy industry: Shell would like industry to be fully involved in cutting greenhouse gas emission in the near term. ExxonMobil, however, sees climate change as a century-long issue, a problem that should be handled over the next hundred years rather than requiring any immediate attention (Packard and Reinhardt, 2000). Overall, practically all industries agree that carbon emissions must be controlled, but they have adopted different measures to accomplish this, measures they consider environmentally-friendly and socially responsible. Chemical industries have taken steps to realize energy efficiency. The food industry, on the other hand, still struggles to figure out what might be done about global warming. This is because the industry has a supply chain that is long and consists of diverse entities such as agribusiness, food processing companies, supermarkets, and transportation firms. Further, some agricultural commodities (such as coffee) are sourced from far away, produced by farmers who have been accustomed to conduct their operations in a certain way for hundreds of years. In addition, rising commodity prices have forced food and agricultural businesses to introduce carbon reduction programs sparsely.

It would be reasonable to assume that, sooner or later, governments will impose taxes on the emission of greenhouse gases. This will present a challenge for each industry: is it preferable, economically, to pay the tax or invest in projects that reduce emissions? Irrespective of government action, businesses in many industries may be forced to reduce carbon emissions to protect their brand image, and their market shares.

Citizens' Actions

There are a variety of steps that individuals can undertake to reduce green-house gas emissions, such as buying green products, driving hybrid cars, avoiding waste and planting trees, *Time* (2007) listed 51 things that individuals could do to reduce global warming but individual action will not be sufficient since the most powerful players are government and industry, which must take the lead.

Overall, resolution of the global warming problem requires that society adopt fundamental changes: the way we conduct different businesses, our lifestyle (how we move around, what we eat and consume, and what we buy, how we buy, and when we buy). Our dependence on fossil fuels will have to change – something that has not been done for 250 years.

CLIMATE CHANGE AND INTERNATIONAL BUSINESS

Let us reiterate the global warming phenomenon. Gases, such as CO_2, methane and several others (called greenhouse gases), trap heat in the atmosphere that should bounce off the planet into space. To an extent such trapping is useful since without this greenhouse effect, the earth would be too cold to support life. The problem is that since the days of the industrial revolution, we have added much to the heat-trapping capacity. For example, the level of CO_2 in the atmosphere has increased from about 280 parts per million by volume (ppmv) to 380 ppmv currently. If humans continue to live as we have, the level of CO_2 in the atmosphere is likely to increase to 500 ppmv in the next 50–100 years, giving rise to further increases in global temperatures.

The effect of climate change on international business is examined using a baseline rise in global temperature of between 2 and 5 degrees Celsius. Following the findings of the IPCC, such a rise will happen by 2100, and will lead to changes in seasonal patterns, shrinkage of glaciers, rising sea levels, extreme weather conditions (such as tropical storms, cyclones, droughts and unusual precipitations), increasing heat waves, and decline/extinction of some plants and animals. The damage caused by climate change is likely to increase progressively to a rate of 3 percent of global GDP annually as the global mean temperature rises by 2–3 degrees Celsius. With larger increases in temperature, the impact will be higher. Climate change is a slow-moving phenomenon, like demographic shifts and globalization of economic activity. It will inexorably impact behavior of firms engaged in international business through production structures, geographic relocations, product mix, and so on.

Firms may act voluntarily to take measures that help to reduce emissions and hence global warming. Otherwise, governments may be forced to legally require companies to adopt specific measures. For example, auto companies may be required to produce cars that travel at least 30 miles on a gallon of gas. In fact, MNCs are more likely than local firms to be closely scrutinized by their host countries. For example, Coca-Cola was charged for excessive water use in its south Indian plant, while the Indian-owned Kingfisher Brewery was spared even though it used far more water (Esty and Winston, 2006).

It should be mentioned that climate change does not necessarily invoke a penalty on firms; it also provides an opportunity for competitive advantage. Consider Toyota's Prius, a car with a hybrid gas-electric engine which has been a success story of eco-advantage leading to a changed profile and substantial shareholder value.

Firms are impacted by various domains such as government through regulatory measures, physical exposure to rising temperatures, competitive pressure due to cost increases of energy-intensive measures, reputational impact from customers' and investors' perceptions of climate change endeavors, and technology impact from business opportunities provided by low-carbon goods and services. Different firms in the same region and/or industry are likely to be affected differently. Definitely there will be winners and losers.

Regulatory Measures

Regulatory action has affected some industries more prominently, such as the automobile industry (not transportation in general), utilities, oil and gas, and the building, construction and cement industries. For example, in the case of the automobile industry, firms are required to meet emission standards regulated by the government. Other industries are also exposed, albeit indirectly, to regulatory requirements. In 2001, Sony Corporation's Playstation game systems were refused entry into the Netherlands because a small amount of the toxic element cadmium was found in the game control cables; although the amount was small, it was above the legal limit. Sony ended up spending US$130million to fix this 'little' global warming problem (Masaki, 2003). The bottom line is that in today's environment, the business world is closely linked to the natural world. Thus, even the best-managed company is affected by global warming issues.

Physical Impact

Such outcomes of climate change as the melting of glaciers, rising sea levels, and the intensity of violent weather expose the infrastructure of companies in different industries to risk. Among these are the oil and gas, insurance, building and construction, and real estate industries. In addition, the physical impact of climate change increases the incidence of certain diseases, which affects the healthcare industry including pharmaceutical companies.

The nature of the physical impact may be illustrated with reference to the insurance industry. Climate change impacts companies in property, life and health insurance. For example, increased precipitation, droughts, tropical storms, hurricanes, and flooding affect insurers through heavy payouts, which may also result in liquidity problems. In addition, human miseries due to natural disasters may result in thermal stress, vector-borne diseases and other disorders, leading to huge losses for health insurance firms (Mills and Lecomte, 2006).

Always there are indirect impacts of climate change on other industries. For example, food companies in the fisheries business, such as Unilever, are affected if the aquatic environment is disturbed by global warming and leads to the extinction of certain species.

Competitive Pressure

Competitive pressure impacts business in two ways. As consumers shift to products that are more energy efficient and leave a smaller carbon footprint, firms must make investments to develop and market new products. This is both a challenge and an opportunity that firms must grasp. Firms must also bear the costs of installing new capital equipment and undertaking new procedures to meet regulated standards for energy efficiency and carbon reduction.

Even smaller firms are not exempt from competitive pressures. For example, small firms that service large firms may be required to undertake environmental management measures if they wish to remain on the list of preferred suppliers (Murray, 2007a).

Reputational Concern

The nature of a firm's business will determine how its implementation of protective measures against global warming is perceived by the public. Firms that service retail markets will be viewed positively by most people if they adopt such measures. Further, hearsay is another element that influences consumers' views on which industries cause environmental degradation. For example, airlines are regarded negatively even though the industry accounts for only 2 percent of global CO_2 emissions (Llewellyn, 2007). The information technology industry, on the other hand, is regarded favorably because it facilitates long-distance communication, thus avoiding the use of transportation and, in turn, carbon emissions.

Differences in reputation can also occur within the same industry, favoring firms that adopt pro-active measures. For example, a few years ago, General Electric (GE) announced a new program it called Ecomagination, which committed the company to double its investments in environmental products, from energy-saving light bulbs to large water purification systems to jet engines. The announcement, followed by an ad campaign launching Ecomagination, has created a positive image of GE as an environmentally-friendly company. Similarly, Wal-Mart Stores has committed US$500 million annually to cut energy use by 30 percent, to use 100 percent renewable energy (for example, from wind farms and solar panels), and to double the fuel efficiency of its shipping fleet (*Time*, 2007). As a result, Walmart's reputation registered a tremendous boost.

In today's world no company can afford to ignore concern for the environment. Any misstep on this matter could hurt a company's reputation badly, and might lead to share loss in the market and reduce the value of the company by billions. No wonder awareness of carbon foot printing has been gaining popularity among companies of all sizes. Carbon footprinting is the amount of CO_2 emitted in the process of producing goods and services and it provides a measure of a company's impact on the environment (Harvey, 2007). There are different steps that companies can take to cut emissions. Nike, for example, has arranged with Delta Airlines to assign a portion of the ticket price of business trips of US-based employees to a fund that invests in projects designed to reduce emissions (Murray, 2007b).

Effect of New Technologies

On the face of it, the concern for global warming (and reducing emissions) requires companies to make investments in developing new technologies, new processes, and new programs. In other words, commitment to protect the environment involves costs. But such costs also have a positive side, in terms of generating new business opportunities for the firm. For example, development of new technology to produce low-carbon products and services may open new markets. Similarly, measures to reduce carbon emissions may make the firm more efficient in using inputs with a positive impact on manufacturing costs.

The point may be illustrated again with reference to Toyota's Prius. Toyota made investments to produce a hybrid gas-electric car for over ten years. Finally, the effort paid off. In 2004, Prius was named 'Car of the Year' by *Motor Trends*, opening the door for Toyota to a new profit stream. Customers were willing to wait six months to get delivery of the hybrid car (Liker, 2004). Companies that look ahead and make investments in developing new technology to reduce emissions in their operations add new degrees of freedom to grow and to increase profits.

Firms that proactively foresee the importance and inexorability of climate change and adopt appropriate measures ahead of their competitors will prosper. A firm's future prospects require adaptation to climate change. It is a new force that a firm can ignore at its own risk.

WHAT CAN COMPANIES DO?

Climate change is the big issue of the moment, and it is likely to remain important for a very long time. Indeed there is no choice for firms but to take actions that protect the environment if they are to ensure their own prosperity. It is no wonder that currently over 75 percent of big, global companies regularly monitor and report on their climate impact and the strategies they plan to implement to reduce their greenhouse gas emissions. By and large, companies agree that actions to address climate change are necessary and that it is possible to implement them without destroying the world's economies (Harvey, 2007).

A question may be raised: are all companies equally susceptible to the global warming issue? The answer is that while it is desirable for all firms to be sensitive to the effects of climate change on their businesses, some companies face greater risk than others, and such companies must act with determination to protect the environment (Packard and Reinhardt, 2000). This includes companies with: (a) high brand value (Coca-Cola, Lever Brothers, Procter & Gamble, McDonald's, for example); (b) big environmental impact (companies in extractive industries such as ExxonMobil, BP, and Shell, and those in heavy manufacturing such as Alcoa, LaFarge, and others); (c) dependence on natural resources (such as Cargrill, Nestlé, and International Paper); (d) operations that generate hazardous materials (for example DuPont and Dow Chemicals); (e) operations that are heavily regulated (such as utilities); (f) increasing potential for regulation (such as automobile companies and electronics firms); (g) competitive markets for talent (for example Citigroup, Google and Microsoft); (h) low market power (those dependent on big customers who may require them to examine climate change issues and take necessary actions); and (i) low environmental reputation (those that have had problems relative to the environment in the past and might be scrutinized more intensively).

Before specifying the initiatives that companies may undertake to become more eco-friendly and gain eco-advantage, two basic principles must be stated. First, companies must go beyond the legal requirements. All automobile companies, for example, comply with emissions standards set by governments. But smart ones go beyond complying with the law. Second, environmental considerations should be phased into all aspects of the firm's operations. Specifically, corporate response should relate to practically all areas of a firm's activities.

Essentially, companies may adopt the following steps as they move to reduce global warming:

(a) Develop new and innovative products to help customers resolve their climate change problems.
(b) Create new, eco-defined market spaces, for example find segments in the marketplace that are willing to buy (and, even pay more, if necessary) for eco-friendly products.
(c) Require suppliers to set and meet environmental standards in their different operations.
(d) Take measures to achieve efficiency in supply-chain operations.
(e) Work with NGOs and other stakeholders to determine new and innovative solutions.
(f) Create awareness of climate-change issues in the organization, and infuse a new eco-friendly culture among all employees.

As mentioned above, a number of companies have already adopted measures to reduce emissions in different ways. In the US, for example, the US Climate Action Partnership was established in 2007 and included many large companies and big energy users such as Alcoa, BP America, Duke Energy, GE, Caterpillar, and Proctor & Gamble (*Time*, 2007). The partnership has asked the federal government to move aggressively on climate change and to set legal limits on the permissible industrial CO_2 emissions. Companies are convinced that it is safer to go green, but they want to see regulatory action before they commit massive investments. They hope that in the long run such investments will pay heavy dividends.

Companies always look for opportunities to gain advantage over their competitors, and the emerging concern of global warming provides a unique opportunity for firms to leapfrog their rivals. The growing call for green products – such as organic foods, unbleached filters, and natural cosmetics – show that green goods are slowly making inroads globally.

In the successful marketing of green products, different aspects of the marketing mix must be properly examined. First, the market must be segmented. Not all consumers or customers are ready to go green. It is a new idea that is likely to become commonly accepted over time. But for now, for various reasons (such as the basic rationale of buying green products, whether their quality and functionality are comparable to existing products, and their price), not everyone is interested in green products. Genetically modified products, for example, were acceptable in the US but flopped in EU nations.

Second, the product positioning must be thought through. What works in one country may not in another. Shell's experience is relevant here. Shell developed a new fuel with the brand name Pura for the Thai market. It was marketed as a new blend that reduced pollution and made engines run cleaner and last longer. Pura did very well in Thailand. When launched in the Netherlands with the same positioning, it fell flat. Post-launch examination showed that Dutch customers saw no connection between cleaner burning fuel and engine protection. In Thailand, drivers care about gasoline quality and the effect of impurities on engine performance, but not in the Netherlands. Subsequently, Shell re-launched Pura in its home market with a new brand name, V-Power, which emphasized engine power. This attempt was successful (Esty and Winston, 2006).

A third consideration is that people prefer to buy green products only if they do not have to pay a price premium and if they do not have to compromise on quality. In other words, firms cannot expect a large market to develop for green products unless all the dimensions of price and quality with the existing products work out to be a better deal for the consumer.

Fourth, as far as promotion is concerned, third-party testimonials work effectively. For example, the US government's energy star label on electronic goods and home appliances communicates that these are energy-efficient products. In addition, where feasible a partnership with an NGO is helpful in promoting green products. For example, Chiquita works with the Rainforest Alliance which certifies how naturally its bananas are grown. Certification by an independent third party is very useful in legitimizing the green claims of a product.

While some companies are developing green products on their own, others are forced into it by the buying power of their major customers. For example, Walmart's buying power led to the shift to double-concentrate laundry detergent when it insisted that its suppliers take steps to reduce packaging. Since Walmart praised Unilever for developing a triple-concentrate of its detergent, Proctor & Gamble, Henkel, and Church & Dwight took the hint and all of them introduced a double concentrate detergent sometime in 2008. This is an interesting industry-wide change that occurred without regulation and shows the impact of buying power on the greening of household lives (Birchall, 2007a).

Thus, companies seek competitive advantage by introducing green products and processes. They gain cost advantage through eco-efficiency (that is improved resource productivity), eco-expense reduction (reduced environmental cost and regulatory burden); value-chain co-efficiency (lower costs upstream and downstream); and eco-risk control (improved management of environmentally-driven business risk). The end result is increased revenues via eco-design (designs that meet customers' environmental needs); eco-marketing (improving product positioning and building customer loyalty to green attributes); and eco-defined new market space (promoting value innovation and developing breakthrough products). In addition, the intangible value of the company goes up through the enhancement of its corporate reputation as a trusted brand.

It has become fashionable for companies to talk about their environmentally-friendly measures. GE spent a multimillion-dollar corporate advertising budget on Ecomagination, extolling its green products, even though they account for only about 8 percent of its sales. Yahoo! and Google are committed to making their offices and computer centers carbon neutral by the end of 2010. The question is: is this just a hype or reality? Green endeavors do not provide the same return on investment as other projects competing for corporate money: either they aren't as swift or as large as alternative uses (Elgin, 2007).

In November 2007, Walmart issued its first green report. The company claimed that its carbon footprint was growing, and that it was reducing waste slowly but definitely. Critics felt, however, that Walmart had not made the extent of progress it claimed. They blamed the company for offering isolated details, without context (Birchell, 2007b). Elgin (2007) noted that in a program in Paris, Sony, Nike, and Lafarge (a French cement company) were proclaimed as climate savers while in reality the carbon emissions from the three companies had increased by 17 percent, 50 percent, and 11 percent respectively.

Companies face the dilemma of allocating scarce resources to an issue that requires huge sums of money, while the payoff is undefined and the results may not be seen for decades. In addition, available technology limits the amount of feasible reduction in emissions. For example, Dow spent US$1 billion to obtain 19 percent reductions between 1994 and 2005. However, the company did not expect any additional reductions to happen before 2025. Conceptually, corporate environmentalism makes sense, but the short-term orientation of companies forces the issue of global warming to the backstage. Companies do talk about it, but their misleading statistics merely make them look good in the media (Elgin, 2007).

RESEARCH AGENDA

Based on scientific evidence, global climate change is real and its effects are worldwide. This suggests that business across the world should be concerned about it. But concern about climate change is a slow-moving trend. This is despite the fact that a company's response or lack of response to climate change is an important determinant of its longevity and success.

There is widespread recognition among firms and individuals of the fact of climate change and how it might lead to insurmountable problems. Yet there is still confusion about what it means at a practical level. It has often been said that companies which are responsive to the changing economic, social, and environmental trends brought about by climate change will find new growth opportunities. (Of course, these opportunities would be accompanied by challenges.) This, in turn, would create wealth for shareholders. But what challenges, what opportunities, from which markets (business to business, business to government, or consumer markets), in what time frame, are all speculations. There is some anecdotal evidence but nothing else. In other words, there is a lack of conceptual, empirical and analytical work related to climate change. International business scholars can play a significant role in filling this gap.

Climate Change Frameworks

While there is no doubt about climate change, its impact on different sectors of human society and its environs is understood only via various unpredictable permutations. International marketing and international business scholars can make a substantial contribution by developing conceptual models of climate change from international business perspectives. Consider Tables 1.1, 1.2 and 1.3. We know the problem of climate change is global and its impacts are widespread. Its mitigation requires worldwide effort. Multilateral agreements such as the Kyoto Protocol or the Bali Agreement can lay out the parameters for all nations to work together. But the first stage of implementation begins with a nation's government (or a regional body like the EU) that has the authority to regulate different measures. Thereafter, the problem-mitigation action takes place at the level of business and people. Businesses may take voluntary steps or may simply do as much as legislation requires. Individuals may, on their own, behave in an eco-friendly way (for example, saving energy in their day-to-day living, by buying local products, by avoiding waste) or they may be lured into changing their lifestyles in response to actions that businesses take (such as the introduction of eco-friendly products and services). Finally, NGOs may work with governments, businesses, and individuals servicing as outside parties to encourage resolution of climate change problems and to monitor programs that business undertake.

There is a need to develop nation-specific or area-specific conceptual frameworks. Although the climate change problem is global, its resolution takes place in different regions and nations with differing political, economic, and social perspectives. For example, Japan was a signatory to the Kyoto Protocol but the US was not. China generates the most CO_2 (it took over from the US toward the end of 2007), but it is not willing to commit resources toward the problem as European nations have been doing. People in Nordic countries are generally more favorably disposed toward environmental protection than in the US All these differences present a challenge to international business academics to undertake different types of studies in different parts of the world to shed light on the climate change problem and what roles different entities might play.

International Business and Multilateral Actions

How are multinational firms affected if some nations become signatories to a multilateral response, such as the Kyoto Protocol, and some do not? Consider Toyota. Does it need a different green strategy in the US than in the EU? How about China and India? International marketing and international business scholars need to examine these questions and make practical recommendations.

To make matters more difficult, in the US, the state of California has passed legislation to develop state regulatory and market mechanisms designed to reduce the emission of greenhouse gases in the state by 25 percent by 2020. Globally speaking, California is the world's seventh largest economy. Business has to subscribe to the state legislation in order to continue doing business there. But the research question is: should a business apply California standards to other parts of the US in developing, for example, new products, or should that business divide the US market into different segments and work out a different climate change strategy for each segment?

Pro-Active Measures by Firms

Some firms have adopted pro-active climate change-related measures on their own. DuPont has, just by changing one process – the production of adipic acid – reduced its contribution to global warming by 72 percent. This was accomplished by eliminating the emissions of nitrous oxide, which causes more warming than CO_2. The company has also taken other steps, such as keeping its energy use constant, and thereby getting the same output with lower inputs. In the period from 1995–2005, these measures have saved the company US$2 billion (Esty and Winston, 2006).

Similarly, 3M's 3P program (Pollution Prevention Pays) resulted in an environmental reduction of 2.2 billion pounds of pollutants, which amounted to a saving of US$1 billion in the project's first year (Esty and Winston, 2006). By installing energy-efficient lighting systems in its branches at a cost of US$3,000 to US$10,000 per branch, FedEx Kinko broke even in lighting costs within 12 to 18 months (Esty and Winston, 2006).

The above examples illustrate how different pro-active measures may be launched to reduce emissions without creating any financial burden on the firm. Before voluntary measures are adopted, firms of different sizes in different industries must establish the cost-benefit relationship of these measures. In this regard, international business scholars can be of immense help by developing models for undertaking cost-benefit analyses to determine the financial impact of a particular measure in the short as well as the long run.

Seeking Competitive Advantage

It has been hypothesized that innovative and entrepreneurial companies are more likely to adopt voluntary programs to cut global warming. Such companies are able to generate revenue growth, lower operational costs (including lower interest on borrowings from banks), and increase the wealth of their owners. Toyota's hybrid gas-electric car, the Prius, is an example of such an innovative program from the viewpoint of global warming.

Academic research is needed to explore the relationship between innovative action and performance. Under what circumstances does innovation pay off? What are the underlying risks involved? Are there different kinds of innovations? Are some innovations more conducive to better performance? Under what circumstances is it better to be a follower than an innovator? Does culture play a role in the matter of innovation? Do companies from some parts of the world innovate more than others? What factors explain such behavior of firms? International business researchers can play an important role in encouraging global firms to examine these questions.

Global Supply Chain Management

In a globalized world, supply chains play a crucial role in carrying out business transactions. Companies with long supply chains both upstream and downstream can effectively help in reducing global warming by scrutinizing their chains. In this regard, IKEA's flat packaging program has been exemplary. By squeezing millimeters out of every box, IKEA has been able to pack its trucks and trains much tighter, saving up to 15 percent on fuel per item (IKEA, 2005).

Here, different research questions require probing. Which part of the supply chain, upstream or downstream, has the potential to realize an eco-advantage? Is it significant enough to be of value? Which functions of the supply chain impact global warming (such as transportation, packaging, material handling, warehousing)? Can a model be developed to determine whether a reduction in global warming as a result of change in one area justifies application of that change to another area? Can a systems approach be applied to minimize global warming for the entire supply chain? International business research in this area may encourage firms, even firms in developing countries, to adopt programs that reduce global warming.

Impact of Market Power in Reducing Emissions

Wal-Mart Stores is the largest company in the world. Due to its sheer size and market share, it has the market power to implement an environmental program much more effectively than other firms. For example, if Walmart sets an environmental standard beyond those that regulators require, it can steer environmental change through 50,000 companies (Birchall, 2007b). Not only Walmart's suppliers would be willing to go along with its greening effort, even its rivals would have no choice but to follow its lead. International marketing scholars can make a unique contribution by developing an index of market power and ranking major companies on it. Such an index could become the hallmark for conversation on environmentalism. After all, endorsement of a program by a company with huge market power gives it a level of credibility.

Consumer Studies

Despite increasing recognition, there is still confusion among consumers over what 'going green' means, particularly at the practical level. Impractical schemes to remake a person's entire life carbon footprint are often proposed, and they are supported by perplexing statistics on different aspects of day-to-day living such as power usage and efficiency (Smith, 2007). As far as the consumer is concerned, all this information is confusing.

Scholarly international marketing studies can help determine which populations should adopt what kind of emission-reduction lifestyle. Such studies may deal with things that people do: how they heat and cool their homes, their use of electrical appliances and energy efficient devices, their water usage, decisions regarding purchase of locally grown foods and goods that are manufactured nearby, transportation choices and so on.

Going green will be demanding for some consumers. Can such consumers be profiled in developed as well developing countries? What compromises will people need to make in order to live 'green'? Perhaps in developed countries people will need to make sacrifices in their lifestyle while in developing countries the challenge will be to prevent people from following in the footsteps of their counterparts in rich nations. For example, in a country like the US, people may be asked to share car rides as much as possible, while in China the suggestion may be not to buy a car but to continue using a bicycle in the greater interest of the environment. Under what circumstances would consumers in developed nations be willing to live a simpler life? Comparative studies of this nature will help identify workable strategies that could convince people to adopt greener lifestyles.

Other Types of Research

Accepting the reasoning that the real causes of global warming are natural and cannot be controlled, a number of policy issues become relevant which require examination by international business scholars. First, would regulation of CO_2 emissions be productive? If not, what can international business executives do to convince governments that mitigating regulations would be expensive but would have no significant impact on global warming. What kind of lobbying or other efforts would be effective?

Second, information is needed to determine the usefulness of developing non-fossil fuel energy sources such as ethanol and hydrogen considering they have to be produced with huge capital inputs and great amounts of ordinary energy. The same reasoning applies to substituting natural gas for coal in electricity generation. Research is required to examine the economies of wind power and solar power for individual companies. Despite the subsidies from the government, would these sources of energy effectively replace fossil fuel energy sources?

Another area of research centers on the outcome of the Kyoto Protocol, which was ratified by all industrialized nations but the US and Australia. For example, consider a feature of the Kyoto Protocol called the Clean Development Mechanism, which permits a CO_2 emitter (that is an energy user) to support a CO_2 reduction scheme in developing nations in exchange for the right to continue unabated emissions of CO_2 in developed nations through emissions trading. Emissions trading among the countries that have signed on to the Kyoto Protocol permits the sale of certificates of unused emission quotas. The initial quota was distributed by governments to power companies and other organizations which in turn collected a high price for the quota from consumers. How do MNCs view emissions trading? Is the scheme fair? Is it working to move them toward reducing CO_2 in a cost-effective manner?

An interesting stream of research related to global warming looks at the role played by NGOs. NGOs such as Greenpeace, the Sierra Club, and the Environmental Defense Fund, have collected billions of dollars from private foundations and ordinary citizens through the global warming scare. What have NGOs done to mitigate global warming?

Many knowledgeable people express the opinion that a slightly warmer climate with more CO_2 is in many ways beneficial. Since CO_2 is an essential plant food for the growth of crops and trees, international business scholars might examine the positive impacts of global warming in improving agriculture and forestry. There are other positive aspects as well: northern homes could save on heating costs; Canadian farmers could harvest bumper crops; oil and gas might be found in Greenland; shippers could save by using the Arctic shortcut between the Atlantic and Pacific; forests could expand; Mongolia could emerge as an economic superpower (Mendelsonn et al., 2008). Much academic research is needed to validate such conjectures.

CONCLUSION

Fossil fuels were first used to create energy at the beginning of the industrial revolution. These fuels contain an abundance of latent energy but have one problem: they generate carbon emissions. These emissions build up in the planet's atmosphere, where they act like panes of glass on a greenhouse, letting the sun's heat in, and keeping it in. Thus, the heat does not radiate off into space but is once again reflected back toward the planet's surface. Temperatures then rise and the earth begins to warm.

Based on scientific evidence, it can be safely said that the issue of global warming is the biggest challenge of the twenty-first century, one that affects all human beings in every corner of Earth. As a matter of fact, the effect extends to our children and their children.

Governments around the world will most likely adopt legislative measures to cut global warming, measures with which companies and individuals must comply. But companies must go beyond responding to regulations if carbon emissions are to be reduced to an acceptable level. A few smart companies have already shown that investments in reducing global warming are not merely an expense, but a sound strategy on which to build competitive advantage.

To make an environmental green strategy work, a company requires long-term thinking, careful planning and adherence to the following principles (Knauer, 2007):

a. Integrate the green strategy throughout the business (that is make reducing emissions a core of the business).
b. Collaborate across industries and the public sector (for example by leveraging partnerships for the right choices of processes and products to reduce costs; and by cooperating with government's big research labs for help in spurring scientific advances).
c. Bring the supply chain along (buyers with their market power can demand suppliers to provide products that use less energy).
d. Develop technologies that are part of the green effort (such as new materials).
e. Have all stakeholders on board to support the green endeavor (employees, suppliers, and consumers should embrace it).

The global warming problem is universal and affects all facets of human life and its environs. It is not limited to a particular nation or region. In principle all entities accept the problem and agree that steps must be taken to reduce global warming. But as an individual company moves ahead to design and implement programs to cut emissions, a variety of questions arise. International marketing and business scholars can play a crucial role in defining the underlying issues, identifying alternative routes to address the issues, and developing workable solutions.

REFERENCES

Avery, D.T. and S.F. Singer (2007), *Unstoppable Global Warming: Every 1,500 Years*, New York: Rowman & Littlefield.
BBC (2006), interviews with experts, 4 December.
Birchall, J. (2007a), 'Soft soap', *Financial Times*, 10 September, p. 7.
Birchall, J. (2007b), 'Mixed response to Walmart's "green" Report', *Financial Times*, 16 November page 6.
Brumfiel, G. (2006), see the National Academies Website at http://www.national-academies.org.
Buckley, P. J. and P. Ghauri (2004), 'Globalization, economic geography, and the strategy of multinational enterprises', *Journal of International Business Studies*, **35** (2): 81–98.
Carey, J. (2004), 'Global warming', *BusinessWeek*, 16 August, pp. 60–69.
climatescience.gov (2006), 'Temperature trends in the lower atmosphere: steps

for understanding and reconciling differences', a report by the Climate Change Science Program and the Subcommittee on Global Change Research, Thomas R. Karl, Susan J. Hassol, Christopher D. Miller and William L. Murray (eds), Washington, DC.

Elgin, B. (2007), 'Little green lies', *BusinessWeek*, 29 October, pp. 45–52.

Esty, D.C. and A.S. Winston (2006), *Green to Gold*, New Haven, CT: Yale University Press.

Gore, A. (2006), *An Inconvenient Truth*, New York: Rodale.

Harvey, F. (2007), 'Winds of change beginning to blow', *Financial Times*, 12 October, special report, p. 7.

Holland, M.M. (2006), 'Future abrupt reduction in the summer Arctic sea ice', *Geophysical Research Letters*, **33**: L23503.

IKEA (2005), 'Social and environmental responsibility', IKEA's report, Stockholm, Sweden.

International Energy Agency (2006), *World Energy Outlook*, Washington, DC.

International Energy Agency (2001), *World Energy Outlook*, Washington, DC.

IPCC (2005), *Carbon Dioxide Capture and Storage*, New York: United Nations.

IPCC (2001), *Climate Change: Impacts, Adaptation and Vulnerability*, New York: United Nations.

Jain, S.C. and R. Grosse (2007), 'Impact of terrorism and security measures on global business transactions: some international business guidelines', working paper, University of Connecticut CIBER.

Knauer, K. (ed.) (2007), *Global Warming*, New York: Time Inc.

Kogut, B. (2003), 'Globalization and equity/democracy of capital and globalization', a keynote address at the First Annual Conference on Emerging Research Frontiers in International Business, Duke University.

Liker, J. (2004), *The Toyota Way*, New York: McGraw-Hill, Inc.

Llewellyn, J. (2007). *The Business of Climate Change: Challenges and Opportunities*, New York: Lehman Brothers.

Mann, M.E. et al. (1998), 'Global scale temperatures patterns and climate forcing over the past six centuries', *Nature*, **392**(4): 779–87.

Mann, M.E. et al. (1999), 'Northern hemisphere temperatures during the past millennium: inferences, uncertainties, and limitations', *Geophysical Research Letters*, **26**(6): 759–762.

Masaki, T. (2003), 'Keynote II', speech at *Business for Social Responsibility*, Los Angeles, CA, 11 November.

Mendelsonn, R. et al. (2000), 'Country-specific market impacts of climate change', *Climate Change*, (45): 553–69.

Mills, E. and E. Lecomte (2006), *From Risk to Opportunity: How Insurers Can Proactively and Profitably Manage Climate Change*, CERES Report, New York: US Government, available at www.climatescience.gov.

Murray, S. (2007a), 'Food chain is complex', *Financial Times*, 12 October, special report, p. 7.

Murray, S. (2007b), 'Companies taking the road less traveled', *Financial Times*, 12 October, p. 4.

Nordhans, W.D. and J. Boyer (1999), 'Role of the DICE again: the economics of global warming', working paper, Yale University.

Nordhans, W.D. (2006), *The "Stern Review" on the Economics of Climate Change*, Washington, DC: National Bureau of Economic Research.

Packard, K.M. and F. Reinhardt (2000), 'What executive needs to know about global warming', *Harvard Business Review*, July–August: 129–35.

Peng, M.W. (2004), 'Identifying the big question in international business research', *Journal of International Business Studies*, **35**(2): 99–108.

Runge, C.F. and B. Senaur (2007), 'How biofuels could starve the poor', *Foreign Affairs*, **86**(3): 41–53.

Scheffer, M. et al. (2006), 'Positive feedback between global warming and atmospheric CO_2 concentration inferred from past climate change', *Geophysical Research Letters*, **33** (L10702).

Shaw, J. (2006), 'Fueling our future', *Harvard Magazine*, May–June: 40–48.

Smith, R. (2007), 'A consumer guide to going green', *The Wall Street Journal*, 12 November, R1.

Stern, N. et al. (2006), *The Stern Review on the Economics of Climate Change*, London: Cabinet Office/HM Treasury, Ch. 2 and Ch. 6.

Teegen, H., J.P. Doh and S. Vachani (2004), 'The importance of non-governmental organizations (NGOs) in global governance and value creation: an international business research agenda', *Journal of International Business Studies*, **35**(3): 463–83.

Time (2007), 'Global Warming', 9 April pp. 51–109.

PART II

Understanding sustainability concerns

2. Sustainable enterprises: addressing management challenges in the twenty-first century

Paul Shrivastava and Raymond Paquin

'There are many things we do not know about the future. But one thing we do know is that business as usual will not continue for much longer. Massive change is inevitable. Will the change come because we move quickly to restructure the economy or because we fail to act and civilization begins to unravel?'

Lester Brown (2008) in *Plan B 3.0: Mobilizing to Save Civilization,* p. 265

Lester Brown's point that the time for 'business as usual' is over comes at a very appropriate time. As we embark on the twenty-first century, the world faces challenges that are truly epic in size and scope. Business managers and management educators need to understand what is so different about the coming century from the previous one. Why is business as usual not adequate? Why are massive changes inevitable? Is the choice really between restructuring the economy and societal unraveling?

One way of examining business challenges of the twenty-first century is to understand the socio-ecological context in which business enterprise operates. By looking at the big picture of how the world is shaping up around us, we can identify many issues with which businesses need to be concerned. In this chapter, we approach this task by focusing on the many crises facing the world. These crises in the economic, social, political and ecological spheres are persistent, repetitive, and ubiquitous. We suggest we are living in a 'crisis society' in which most major global systems are in crisis and in need of restructuring. These crisis conditions are rooted in our current systems of production, consumption, and wealth creation. Crises are an unintended side effect of these systems. As we discuss below, our crisis society manifests itself through global environmental, financial, social, and identity crises facing our world today.

Yet, when addressing these crises we find national and international governments are incapable of resolving them alone. Economically, most governments at national, state and local levels run on deficit financing.

They lack the resources needed to cover the costs of services expected by the public. Many of these services involve dealing with externalities of production. That is, the negative environmental and social impacts that accompany the industrial production of goods and services. These include but are not limited to pollution, waste, unemployment, and harm from product usage. Deficit financing is also requiring governments to cut back on social services such as health care, education, defense security, and social security. Politically, liberal democracies in Western industrial nations seem to be stuck in inter-party gridlock with conservatives and liberals increasingly at loggerheads over every major policy issue. There is rarely consensus over any major concerns, and even the processes and mechanisms for building consensus seem to be eroding. This leaves countries largely incapable of making the necessary dramatic changes for the future. This loss of governmental political power coincides with the rise of political power among global MNEs. The outcome is that governments are no longer the most powerful institutions in the world. Through direct lobbying, industry groups, campaign contributions, personal favors, and so on, businesses have often shown themselves to be both more powerful and more astute at wielding political power than governments. We can infer this in part from the United Nations' various calls over the past few decades for cross-sectoral collaboration and business involvement in addressing environmental issues (for example, the 1972 Stockholm Conference on the Human Environment and 1992 Rio Summit on Environment and Development). More explicitly, we can see this in the primacy of business interests in recent national and international attempts at reform including current US healthcare reform efforts and preparations for the UN's 2009 Copenhagen Conference on Climate Change. In short, governments alone lack the knowledge, political will, or resources needed to bring about the necessary regulatory and structural changes to address our crisis society (Brown, 2008; Stern, 2006).

Existing management approaches have not alleviated these crises, rather they have likely exacerbated them. Managers often appreciate neither the scope and scale of these crises nor their own impact on promulgating them. Some are simply ignorant, not having read the emerging science of climate change, ecological degradation, and social and economic decline. Most are likely to know something of these concerns yet simply lack the time in their hyper-busy schedules to keep up-to-date and address these issues strategically (Mintzberg, 1975). Those who do take the time to learn of emerging social and ecological problems are often not compelled to act given the uncertainty of how to address such issues through corporate action, ideological convictions impeding meaningful action, or simply organizational inertia.

More insidiously, traditionally unidimensional profit-driven management approaches reward narrow sets of behaviors and perspectives. This orientation becomes more corrosive when individual managers are more motivated by personal gain and profit than organizational and community interests – as evidenced in the mortgage finance and investment banking sectors during the global financial crisis. Some progressive companies have taken a more enlightened approach pursuing stakeholder goals, though even then the primacy of corporate profitability often remains unquestioned. Truly integrative corporate social responsibility often plays only a secondary role here. Such internal organizational structures and reward systems encourage maximizing short-term profit over long-term health of either the organization or its broader stakeholders in a number of ways. Lucent's total fixation on quarterly revenue targets eventually brought itself down and also much of the telecom industry (Burrows, 2003; Endlich, 2004). Enron, Andersen, and WorldCom showed outright malfeasance and fraud by taking such profit obsessions too far (Eichenwald, 2005; Jeter, 2004; McLean and Elkind, 2004). GE's 30-year battle to avoid cleaning up pollutants it dumped into the Hudson River (NRDC, 2007) shows an aggressive fight over having to re-internalize previously externalized environmental and social costs, rather than addressing these broader issues head on.

Confounding these points is the perspective of most managers that the natural environment is just another set of resources or assets that can be bought and sold as commodities. Such commoditization places no value on the holistic integrity of natural ecosystems themselves. Rather, individual resources are chopped up, used, and discarded in service to organizational goals. Climate science research, though, shows natural ecosystems as highly interdependent complex and subtle systems, with only finite capacity to regenerate naturally. Once exploited beyond their natural carrying capacities, natural ecosystems will collapse. Examples of commercial overfishing provide just one example of natural ecosystems collapsing (Economist, 2009).

Returning to Brown's opening comment, this is the business as usual attitude which is outdated. The managerial approaches valorizing short-term profits over longer-term, broader, and more integrated social, ecological, and economic performance measures encourages individual greed over community welfare, commoditizes nature, and ignores the multiple interdependencies connecting these issues. If we are to create the necessary and meaningful changes needed for our collective future we need to change this perspective and, more fundamentally, we need to develop new models for business success.

We propose that to tackle this crisis society, we need to move beyond addressing the symptoms of any individual crisis (fiscal, environmental, social) and towards addressing their underlying and interrelated root causes. We need to develop sustainable enterprises that seek long-term prosperity for their investors *plus* other stakeholders, including the natural environment. Such organizations will create economically viable strategies which successfully balance short-term profits with long-term sustainability of the organization, its communities, and our global ecosystem. These organizations will have socially and ecologically sensitive visions, inputs, throughput systems, and outputs. In visioning a sustainable enterprise, we must also rethink our current ideas of personal development, and individual identity creation; and encourage the building and rebuilding of the interconnections of individuals with themselves, their families, local communities, and to global society.

This chapter continues as follows. First, we describe the four key crises – environmental, societal, economic, and personal – which together create our crisis society. Second, we discuss the necessity of adapting to the impacts of these crises while at the same time seeking to build new social systems to alleviate some aspects of our crisis society. Third, we propose the sustainable enterprise as an ideal-type organization, one involving a more robust approach to conceiving of and successfully managing for the future. We then conclude with some research directions around how to better understand and support sustainable action and develop sustainable enterprises.

THE EMERGING CRISIS SOCIETY

Earth – this third rock from the sun we call home with its natural eco-systems and resources – and our world – the sum total of our individual societies and the global society in which they exist – are both in crisis. This situation is not new. It has been brewing over the past century of industrial development. The many early warning signs (such as smaller, more local-ized economic, political and social crises) have been interpreted as local anomalies or minor disasters (Hoffman and Ocasio, 2001). In our view, these signals are symbolic of more global and systemic crisis problems (Shrivastava, 1996). Earth, and our human world, are today in a systemic crisis. We are living in an emerging crisis society. Crisis here means a condition where systems that produce value break down in structure and process; and are accompanied by extensive damage and harm to stake-holders. It is a time for making critical strategic decisions and for restruc-turing. Below we touch on four major crises – environmental, economic, societal, and individual – currently manifest in our crisis society.

Before doing so, we note much work has been done discussing the need for sustainable development to balance environmental, economic, and societal needs (Adams, 2006; Brown, 2008; Marcus and Fremeth, 2009; World Commission on Environment and Development, 1987). While we agree with this work, that each of these areas are in crisis suggests at least two points. First, that each of these pillars of sustainable development are in crisis shows how far removed actual business practices are from sustainable business practices – or what is necessary for our long-term societal health. Second, the traditional western paradigm of industrialization, competitive capitalism, cost externalization, and so on. has created and exacerbated our current economic, environmental, and societal crises. As well, they have impacted and uprooted the individuals which make up our societies. This individual perspective, what we propose is an individual/development crisis of its own, also needs to be explored and understood as we continue to develop ideas and practices around sustainability.

Environmental Crisis

Resource crisis

Though some may dicker over the minutiae of particular calculations or findings, the science is clear and overwhelming – we are using our Earth's renewable resources faster than Earth can replenish them; and we have almost exhausted many of Earth's non-renewable resources. Increased environmental regulation and enforcement has slowed the pace of our renewable resource exploitations, yet many renewable resources such as fisheries, forests, safe drinking water, and arable land are nearly exhausted in many parts of the world. The continued loss of arable land (land which can be productively used for agriculture) combined with current population projections, suggest per capita arable land will fall from 0.23 hectares in 1950 to 0.07 hectares in 2050 (Brown, 2006). In other words, between 1950 and 2050, the average amount of land available to support the food needs of a human being will shrink from around two-fifths of a soccer field to an area the size of the penalty box.

The situation for key non-renewable resources is similarly bleak. As Brown stated in summarizing work of the US Geological Survey, 'Assuming an annual two percent growth in extraction . . . current economically recoverable reserves show the world has 18 years of reserves remaining for lead, 20 years for tin, 25 years for copper, 64 years for iron ore, and 69 years for bauxite' (2006: 109). Oil, a uniquely critical resource for our everyday industrial-urbanized lives, is no exception. While the politics of oil is a complex topic of its own, it is clear that we are exhausting economically feasible oil reserves globally; and that it is only through government subsidization that many of us are not more aware of our current overuse of oil in everyday life (Brown, 2008; ICTA, 1998).

Climate crisis

Accumulation of carbon in Earth's atmosphere has grown rapidly since the beginning of the industrial revolution. Currently, the level of carbon in Earth's atmosphere is 389 ppm and rising. Climate science projections suggest that continuing on our current path of industrial development will increase carbon levels to 475–500 ppm over the next century (IPCC, 2007). Climate research suggests atmospheric carbon levels in excess of 400 ppm are highly risky for the stability of Earth's climate. Carbon in the atmosphere acts as a heat trap and is the cause of global warming. This, in turn leads to arctic ice melting, sea levels rising, and biological and agricultural disloca-tions. As Lord Stern summarized in his ubiquitous *Stern Report*, 'the sci-entific evidence is now overwhelming: climate change presents very serious global risks, and it demands an urgent global response' (2006: i). Among other points, Stern concluded that Earth's average global temperature will likely rise 2–3 degrees centigrade by mid-century. Yet, this seemingly simple global measure does not manifest itself uniformly or calmly. Rather, it comes in the form of traumatic localized and regional weather and climate upheavals. We have already seen many such changes – desertification of formerly arable land; severe and longstanding droughts; frequent and severe flooding; increasingly intense coastal storms – and can expect to see more frequent and intense examples of such localized upheavals in the future.

Societal Crisis

As of 2006, the global population was estimated at 6.7 billion and pro-jected to rise to over nine billion by mid-century (Brown, 2006). This growth is not uniformly distributed. In recent decades, population growth in poor and developing economies has outpaced industrialized economies, some of which have even stagnated. By 2025, the UN's World Commission on Environment and Development estimates the global population will be 1.4 billion people in industrialized economies and 6.8 billion in develop-ing ones (1987). However, individuals in industrialized societies continue to live longer and healthier lives than those in the poorest societies. Currently, two-thirds of the world live in poverty, with 20 percent living in deep poverty (defined as living on USD$1 per day or less). The poorest 10 percent of the global population consume 2.5 percent of annual global GDP, while the richest 10 percent consume 29.8 percent. In the USA and the eight largest industrial economies, 10 percent of the population holds 50–71 percent of wealth.

This widening schism between the poorest and richest populations can be seen in differences in life expectancy, educational levels, rate and treatment of infectious disease (such as malaria, tuberculosis, HIV), and nutrition (c.f., Brown, 2008; Stern, 2006; World Commission on Environment and Development, 1987 for more detail). These disparities are increasingly seen as socially unjust and are becoming a source of social and political unrest. The extremely poor are susceptible to ideological manipulation around these disparities and being inducted into violent means for capturing basic resources. Political upheavals, revolutions and terrorism can emerge out of these unjust and extreme conditions of poverty as ideologues are able recruit the poor to their causes. We have seen elements of this in the Maoist guerillas' takeover in Nepal, Naxalite movements in Western India, and the rise of Al-Qaeda fundamentalism in the Middle East and Southeast Asia (Pape, 2006).

Economic Crisis

As of 2009, the collapse of the real estate bubble in the US, UK, and elsewhere has led us into arguably the most serious global economic crisis since the Great Depression. The US government initiated several costly bailout and stimulus programs attempting to mitigate the worst impacts of this collapse (such as the $700 billion Trouble Asset Relief Program (TARP); $94 billion in direct taxpayer stimulus checks; 'cash for clunkers'; and homebuyer tax credits). Finance ministers and central bankers in many other countries have likewise initiated stimulus programs attempting to mitigate the worst of the economic crisis in their respective countries. To understand this situation, we need to know something of the underlying actions and influences leading to the crisis – namely over-leveraging in the banking industry and reduced regulatory oversight from government agencies. With these changes, lenders introduced new types of mortgage products where individuals – who traditionally required 20–30 percent down payments for house purchases – could buy homes with little or no down payment. This left many new homeowners with little or no financial stake in their homes. Meanwhile, lenders aggregated and securitized these mortgages into new types of investments for sale. Thus, the lenders had no stake in these properties either. As well, decreased regulatory oversight allowed US banks to increase their leverage (a ratio of assets borrowed to assets owned) – from historical levels of 12:1 to over 30:1 (Sirota, 2009). As housing prices began falling in 2006 the result was many owners finding themselves with houses worth less than their mortgages and simply forfeiting their homes to the banks. The banks meanwhile, having increased their leverage (or rather decreased the proportion of assets they actually owned) could not absorb the losses from these forfeited mortgages and properties. The result was the halting of the global credit market, severely hampering the ability of individual businesses and economies to function; hence the need for several governments to engage in economic stimulus programs.

Individual Crisis

With population increases, we are becoming more crowded – both physically and psychically. Technological innovations allow us to travel and communicate more frequently, with greater ease and to more diverse places than ever before (Friedman, 2008; Gergen, 1991). The result is access to a greater volume and diversity of information. Our world is figuratively shrinking or 'flattening' (Friedman, 2008). Paradoxically, for many, our increasingly information-based world has eroded more traditional forms of social support – church, community organizations, nearby family (Putnam, 2000). Traditional 'Western' economic development (that is mainstream capitalism) has exacerbated these changes, further eroding traditional values and societal structures in which individuals live (Neef, 1992). With the increased mobility of the 'professional class' (one far reaching effect of Western economic development), individual identities become more fractured, multifaceted, and difficult to manage as individuals are stretched farther afield in their personal and professional lives (Gergen, 1991; Kegan, 1994). Without traditional values and social anchors mooring ones' values and norms, individuals are often left more overwhelmed and isolated than in previous generations (Gergen, 1991; Kegan, 1994; Putnam, 2000).

That said, many have argued that the benefits of economic development – such as rising standards of living, increased opportunity, and poverty reduction – outweigh the social, environmental, and individual costs discussed here. As well, prior work in areas of micro-finance and social entrepreneurship make strong cases for ways to approach economic development which create wealth by supporting economic self-sufficiency in ways which complement existing community structures and values. We find some hope in these approaches as we feel it a moral obligation to enhance individual and community-level economic self-sufficiency in these more integrative manners. At the same time, we are also wary of the potentially detrimental changing values and perspectives which may occur as a result of more traditional Western capitalism. While traditional management approaches focus on the supremacy of individual wealth creation over environmental, social, or individual concerns, research suggests that after meeting basic food, shelter, and health needs increased wealth does not translate in to increased happiness or emotional well-being

(Kahneman et al., 2006; Lane, 2001). Even more concerning is related work showing that individuals with materialistic aspirations and values tend to be less satisfied with their lives (Nickerson et al., 2003) and more prone to mental disorders (Cohen and Cohen, 1995) over time than those with non-materialistic values and aspirations for their lives.

ADAPTING TO A CRISIS SOCIETY

We are living in a crisis society. That is, globally we face multiple, inter-related types of crises in all spheres of life. Individual manifestations of these crises may be localized, but their impacts ripple out to regional and global levels. More formally, we consider the crisis society we live in to be global. In other words we are in a time and place where every major system is one-step away from crisis. Many of Earth's natural resources are harvested at or beyond capacity. The disparities between the industrialized and developing economies are widening and increasingly contentious as developing countries demand change. While the phenomenon of families living 'paycheck to paycheck' is not new, this recession has shown that many businesses and even governments have also been operating in this short-sighted manner. As uncertainty mounts for individuals around their personal and professional lives and the future state of our world, they are increasing left to manage these stresses alone, often without the commu-nity and family support structures available to previous generations.

These crises are man-made. Our reason for discussing them is simple: the traditional Western paradigm of industrialization (that is competitive capitalism, resource exploitation, cost externalization) has created and exacerbated these crises and risks collapsing under our feet. Most exist-ing organizations and institutions do not have the resilience or capacity for dealing with these crises. They are surviving on their last innovation, rather than seeking their next one. Whenever that runs out, or becomes obsolete, they will be in crisis as well. As business scholars, we need to move beyond the traditional paradigm of Western capitalism and become more than mere catalogers of business action. We need to become engaged in improving our global society by helping businesses under-stand, adapt and eventually prosper under the new resource-constrained, carbon-constrained world we have entered. Business, for its part, needs to acknowledge its responsibility in creating these crises. Then, it needs to get to work fixing them.

Part of stepping up requires that businesses adapt to a new paradigm of economic development that honestly addresses and internalizes the full costs of its impacts on the environment, including climate change. The global climate crisis is not simply an academic concern for scientists – it is real and has already negatively affected the lives of millions globally. Current science suggests mitigation to avert climate change is no longer an option – we have waited too long. Future managers will be unlikely to succeed with unidimensional profit orientations which ignore the necessary full-cost accounting of human action. Businesses and their leaders need to see more clearly the relationship between their local actions and the broader and more complex global context (Hoffman and Ocasio, 2001; Sharma, 2000; Shrivastava, 1995). As scholars, we also need to change our perceptions of business to be more attuned to, and more strategically engaged with, the changing world around us.

The bright side, for both managers and scholars, are the opportunities arising from crisis. While traditional models of economic development may no longer be viable for the future, new models are emerging. Recent work involving multi-sector partnerships between for-profit firms, NGO's, and government agencies (Austin, 2000; Steger, Ionescu-Somers, Salzmann and Mansourian, 2009), hybrid organizations (Boyd, Henning, Reyna, Wang and Welch, 2009), and social enterprises (Borzaga and Defourny, 2001), suggest just a few ways in which organizations are creating environmental and social, as well as economic benefit. Another, perhaps more clearly defined opportunity involves the anticipated and emerging $500 billion US annual market around climate adaptation. This will affect many, if not all, business sectors and offer great opportunities for those poised to take advantage of them (Stern, 2006).

VISIONING SUSTAINABLE ENTERPRISES

In 1996, I (the first author) concluded my book *Greening Business* with a discussion of an organizational ideal-type – BioCorp. I envisioned BioCorp as 'an ecologically stable entity' which would 'maintain the ecological balance within its bioregion . . . preserv[e] eco-resources and socioeconomic security . . . contribute to socially equitable improvements in the quality of life' (Shrivastava, 1996: 225–6). We propose the sustainable enterprise as an extension of BioCorp – one integrating the maturation of thought and research on sustainability in the intervening years. We define a *sustainable enterprise* as an organization able to account for and transcend the surface-level contradictions of reducing environmental impact, creating social benefit, and competitively creating economic value. Whether technically for-profit, not-for-profit, or some other configuration, a sustainable enterprise embraces an integrative vision of its engagement with and impact on surrounding societal and natural environments

(Wirtenberg, Lipsky and Russell, 2008). Such a perspective is not unidimensionally profit-driven but takes the triple-bottom line approach of integrating economic, environmental, and social value into its measures of success (Elkington, 1999).

The oft-used phrase 'doing well by doing good' encapsulates this key perspective of sustainable enterprise. Sustainable enterprises begin with a vision that goes beyond producing profits for investors, to creating economic, social and cultural value for a wider community of stakeholders. They do not treat inputs (such as energy, natural resources, and people) as commodities to be bought, converted and used. Instead, they take a cradle-to-cradle view of resources and production (McDonough and Braungart, 2002). They seek to minimize the use of virgin resources, minimize their resource footprint and restore resource ecosystems to their natural regenerative capacities. They design products, operations and logistical systems to a scale and efficiency most consistent with their ecological context (McDonough and Braungart, 2002). In this way, sustainable enterprises are ecocentric, and maximising their ecological efficiency in all aspects of organizing.

Recent work on environmental management and corporate social responsibility shows how this idea of sustainable enterprise is not only economically viable, it can be competitively superior to traditional business practices (King and Lenox, 2002; Sharma and Vredenburg, 1998; Waddock and Graves, 1997). The competitive advantages here accrue in planned and unplanned ways as firms engaging a broader sustainability perspective increase their ability to see new ways to create new value through previously un- or under-valued organizational practices or resources (Baker and Nelson, 2005; Paquin, 2008; Sharma and Vredenburg, 1998). However, we also believe meaningful change requires moving beyond the 'doing well by doing good' perspective. Below we use some recent examples of business activities to articulate some of the ways sustainable enterprise can competitively differentiate itself from a more traditional business.

Full Accounting of Business Impacts

A sustainable enterprise should have a full and honest accounting of the impacts of its actions – economically, environmentally, and socially (Brown, 2008; Shrivastava, 1996). Over the past decade, increased interest in developing accounting-style metrics for non-financial business impacts has led to the development of triple-bottom line accounting (Elkington, 1999), social and environmental accounting and reporting (Deegan, 2002; Hopwood, 2009), the Global Reporting Initiative, as well as several other approaches to capture these impacts. Various stakeholders – institutional investors, individual shareholders, insurers, and NGO's, for example – have led these efforts by demanding more non-financial information directly from firms, or indirectly through the development of socially responsible investment funds and public firm rankings based on environmental and social performance (such as the FT4Good index). These demands have led to an increasing number of firms publishing environmental and social metrics. One clear signal of the increased attention paid to such metrics was the June 2009 launch of Deutsche Bank's carbon counter (Deutsche Bank, 2009). Placed near Penn Station in New York City, this counter displays cumulative global carbon emissions into the atmosphere.

Such activities are clear signs of progress in developing more robust accounting systems for business. Yet, at the same time, it is just a start. Unlike the Generally Accepted Accounting Principles (GAAP) there are no such standards for measuring and tracking environmental and social impacts. Despite the increasing number of CSR and sustainability reports coming from businesses, the widely varied approaches – from detailed quantitative metrics to anecdotal cases and even vague rhetoric – makes objective interpretation and analysis difficult. Such vagaries also provide ample cover for firms to engage in greenwashing, or decoupling their environmental and social rhetoric from their actions. One notable example is British Petroleum (BP) whose 'Beyond Petroleum' tag line and strong pro-environment message helped it cultivate a relatively positive reputation in recent years. However, a comparison of BP's 2005 CSR report with the firm actions as reported by news outlets shows a wide discrepancy between what the firm actually did and what it reported in its CSR report (Ruffing, 2007).

Second, and more important, is our systemic lack of an honest accounting of firm impacts (Brown, 2008). That is we know of no firm that has yet created a full and complete accounting of the economic, environmental, and social costs of its activities. Considering the full-cost of oil is instructive here (ICTA, 1998). In 1998, the retail price of gasoline for the US consumer was roughly US$1 per gallon. Yet, this retail price hid the myriad additional costs of securing, refining, providing, and using gasoline – including government subsidies to oil firms to extract and provide the product; military, diplomatic, and security costs of protecting US oil interests around the world; and environmental, health, and societal costs through pollution, land degradation, auto infrastructures, and lifestyle changes. If these costs were transparently calculated and directly incorporated into the price of gasoline, retail gasoline in 1998 would have cost somewhere between US$5.60 and US$15.14 per gallon (ICTA, 1998).

Yet even in 2007, only in a handful of countries was the retail price for gasoline US$5 per gallon or more; and US consumers paid on average only US$3.10 per gallon (de Sousa, 2007).

Organizing for Positive Change

Entrepreneurship is a key aspect of capitalism, one involving the ability to create value through new opportunities others have not seen (Aldrich and Fiol, 1994; Baker and Nelson, 2005; Hughes, 1979). A sustainable enterprise should embrace an ethos of social and eco-entrepreneurship, seeking out new opportunities for creating economic value while simultaneously creating environmental and societal value. One way to approach this is for sustainable enterprises and their leaders to pursue investments in renewable energy, waste management, clean technology, eco-design, and eco-niches in conventional industries. They can also embrace opportunities provided by constrained global resources and population growth. The 'fortune at the bottom of the pyramid' (Prahalad, 2007) is spawning business opportunities to fulfill needs of historically underserved populations. There is also an opportunity for value creation through personal development and social change; increasing living standards among the world's poorest without increasing environmental burdens; and value creation which complements rather than competes with local communities and economies.

Though not mutually exclusive, another approach would be to explore deeper level questions around organizing for the future. How do we design business to create long-term value in ways that restore the health of Earth and the ecosystem (McDonough, 1995)? How do we build business to simultaneously support itself, our ecological communities, and our employees (Shrivastava, 1996)? How can we engage in business competition in ways that improve our natural and societal ecosystems? How do we build business in ways that can create economic value and environmental value (Hawken, 1993)? How do we use business to support the sustainability of our societies so that they may flourish, potentially forever (Ehrenfeld, 2008)?

Embracing these types of questions within an organization, would direct attention away from a more unidimensional short-term profit orientation to one focused on the long-term health of, and impact on, the communities and natural ecosystems with which the organization resides. This broader perspective is not just about finding ways to create green value (Marcus and Fremeth, 2009; Siegel, 2009), though green value is clearly an aspect of this perspective. Rather, this is a broader view of sustainable value creation. Our view of sustainable value creation is one involving continual engagement with, and efforts to improve an organization's eco-system – which includes, but is not limited to its communities, employees, customers, other stakeholders, and the natural environment (Shrivastava, 1996; Torbert and Associates, 2004).

RESEARCH DIRECTIONS

Embracing sustainable enterprise as a future model of sustainable organization and value creation suggests a number of interesting questions for future research. For simplicity, we close this piece by exploring two areas of interest. First, how can we more fully account for and track the impact of firms' actions on societies, economies, natural ecosystems, and ourselves? Second, how might we organize sustainable enterprise for long-term health and success?

Accounting for the Full Impact of Business Activity

Many scholars cite innovation – creating value by integrating and recombining existing knowledge in novel ways – as a key aspect of developing more sustainable practices (Hart, 1997; McDonough and Braungart, 2002; Prahalad, 2006). This perspective mirrors that of strategy and innovation scholars more broadly for developing competitive advantage (Hargadon and Sutton, 1997; Obstfeld, 2005; Porter and van der Linde, 1995). Building from here, the argument that firms can create lasting value through more strategic attention to their environmental and social impacts is also well-established (Berchicci and King, 2007; Porter and van der Linde, 1999; Sharma and Vredenburg, 1998; Shrivastava, 1996; Waddock and Graves, 1997). Despite this, businesses do not account for nor track the full impacts of their actions (Brown, 2008; Gore, 2006; Stern, 2006).

As discussed above, there are a number of avenues scholars and practitioners are pursuing to develop more robust measures of impact including the social and environmental accounting discipline; increased CSR, environmental and social reporting among firms; and developing reporting standards such as the Global Reporting Initiative. Each of these approaches is moving business towards a more robust triple bottom line approach of measuring firm performance on economic, environmental, and social measures (Elkington, 1999). Yet such ideas are still little more than lip service in most businesses. Even among leaders wishing to understand the true costs of their business, such information is difficult to come by.

Given some of the gaps in what information firms and investors use, how they use such information to guide their firms towards more positive impacts, and the relative incompleteness of the non-financial data currently collected, there are a number of interesting questions to consider. For one, how can we instigate firms to develop a level of standardization of metrics and measurements across environmental and societal levels similar to economic levels? While it may be too much to consider regulatory changes to existing GAAP standards, prior work on industry self-regulation and adoption of new standards and practices may lend some insight into how broad-based changes occur through industry (Guler, Guillen and Macpherson, 2002; Howard-Grenville, 2002; King, Lenox and Terlaak, 2005; Terlaak and King, 2006). With this, there is also the question of how firms and investors would use this additional data. While industry self-regulation primarily focuses on environmental practices, this work suggests that firms are more likely to engage in these activities when (a) external forces, such as industry associations or primary customers, demand it and (b) when firms are attempting to rebuild their reputations from previously detrimental actions.

This situation provides another conundrum in need of further exploration. As discussed above, one strand of research suggests that firms who strategically engage in environmentally and socially responsible actions can develop long-term competitive advantage over firms who do not. Another strand suggests firms engaging in overt actions such as adopting industry-level certifications or publishing social and environmental reports are not necessarily developing increased environmental or social benefits and may simply be decoupling their sustainability rhetoric from their actions (greenwashing). Yet this suggests that at least some firms are actively acquiring and interrogating environmental and societal information to create value. Thus, future work might invert the question of what we should hold firms accountable to (that is the triple bottom line perspective), and instead ask what types of information are most beneficial to firms seeking to develop competitively viable sustainable practices over time. How do leaders in these organizations use and integrate the knowledge generated from such information into their decision-making, strategic planning, and daily operations in ways that create long-term value and positive environmental and societal impact?

Last, while environmental and climate change scientists have long stated businesses and consumers pay only a fraction of the full cost of their activities (Brown, 2008; Gore, 2006; Stern, 2006), most businesses have yet to fundamentally restructure their approaches or their strategies here. One likely reason for businesses not integrating more accurate environmental and societal costs is the structure of our international markets, which discount the price of many production inputs through direct or indirect government subsidies, including never accounting for the full impact of extracting natural resources from their natural ecosystem in the first place. Yet, these costs are not unknowable. Research from disciplines such as materials engineering, environmental and physical sciences, and sociology have provided much insight into the often externalized costs of business – those costs which business scholars and practitioners have so often systematically ignored. Given prior work suggesting that firms who strategically address environmental and societal issues can develop long-term competitive advantage over their peers, there are a number of questions to consider. Why are more firms not engaging in such action? How can firms reorganize or restructure themselves to become more sustainably focused while also remaining economically competitive? How can firms more quickly move from managing pollution (meeting regulatory requirements) to becoming environmental and social stewards (Hart, 1997) – that is being on the leading edge of developing new organizational processes and practices which actually benefit and support environmental and societal restoration (Hawken, 1993)?

New Ways of Organizing

Embracing this additional level of information will likely require firms to go beyond questions of developing local opportunities and extensions of existing products, to fundamentally rethinking how they engage in their activities and with their customers, employees, and broader communities. This level of change likely requires firms to restructure themselves to address these issues more fully. Work on stakeholder management and engagement (Freeman, 1984; Hart and Sharma, 2004; Post, Preston and Sachs, 2002; Sharma and Henriques, 2005) has long provided guidance on how firms can engage with their various stakeholders and communities to competitively improve their actions over time. More recently, positive organizational scholarship (Cameron, Dutton and Quinn, 2003) has studied how organizations engage in organizational and community-level activities which positively support the organization, its employees and its community.

As primarily firm-centric perspectives, stakeholder management and positive organizational scholarship are not well suited to addressing many of the more complex and pressing issues such as community erosion, environmental degradation, poverty, and health care. Addressing issues of this complexity requires rethinking not just the organization but the limits and boundaries of organizations as individual entities within broader social and environmental contexts. For this, we need to explore more recent areas of research which focus more directly on the inter-organizational environments in which these issues might be more effectively addressed. Two interesting areas of research here include cross-sector partnerships and hybrid organizations. Cross-sector partnerships are partnerships between some combination of private, NGO, and governmental actors formed to explicitly address key social or environmental concerns which the individual actors could not successfully address on their own (Austin, 2000; Steger et al., 2009). Research here has shown that firms can be both economically successful while also supporting community and environmental development. Work on bottom-of-the-pyramid issues also provides insight into potential opportunities, as well as pitfalls, of integrating social and environmental goals with economic ones in developing economies (Hart and London, 2005; Prahalad, 2006). More recently, work on hybrid organizations – organizations who govern themselves and who define success by explicitly integrating environmental or societal value creation with economic value creation – provides some insight into alternative business models for the future (Boyd et al., 2009).

In all four of these areas – stakeholder management, positive organizational scholarship, cross-sector partnerships, hybrid organizations – research has moved beyond traditional firm-centric economic value creation perspectives offering us glimpses of what the future of business may indeed look like. What are successful business models for sustainable enterprises and how can they successfully develop competitive advantage to support long-term economic, environmental, individual, and societal value creation? How do such organizations integrate and align their cultures, operations and production activities, and managerial incentives to support long-term health and success at this level?

CONCLUSION

As we have discussed, our world is one of a 'crisis society'. We have reached a state where most of our major systems – economic, environmental and societal – in are crisis and in need of restructuring. Our current approaches to consumption and production – which are embedded in and supported by our current business practices – have led us to this point. One outcome of past business success is that business has become one of the world's most powerful institutions and has facilitated the increasingly blind acceptance of a unidimensional, economically driven measure of success in our societies, economies, and among ourselves as individuals. Yet, as the detrimental impact of this approach – economically, environmentally, socially, and individually – has become clearer, it has become more pressing that we as business scholars and practitioners find new ways of practicing business. We need to find ways to structure business and conceive of business activity to support the long-term health and success of our economic, environmental, and community systems. As one way to do this, we propose the idea of a sustainable enterprise as an organization which is economically competitive and also environmental and socially beneficial; and suggest avenues for future research towards this end.

REFERENCES

Adams, W.M. (2006), 'The future of sustainability: re-thinking environment and development in the twenty-first century', report of the IUCN renowned thinkers meeting, 29–31 January 2006, p. 19.

Aldrich, H. and C.M. Fiol (1994), 'Fools rush in? The institutional context of industry creation', *Academy of Management Review*, **19**: 645–71.

Austin, J.E. (2000), *The Collaboration Challenge: How Nonprofits and Business Succeed through Strategic Alliances*, San Francisco, CA: Jossey-Bass.

Baker, T. and R.E. Nelson (2005), 'Creating something from nothing: resource construction through entrepreneurial bricolage', *Administrative Science Quarterly*, **50**(3): 329–66.

Berchicci, L. and A. King (2007), 'Postcards from the edge: a review of the business and environment literature', *Academy of Management Annals*, **1**: 513–47.

Borzaga, C. and J. Defourny (eds) (2001), *The Emergence of Social Enterprise*, London: Routledge.

Boyd, B., N. Henning, E. Reyna, D.E. Wang and M.D. Welch (2009), *Hybrid Organizations: New Business Models for Environmental Leadership*, Sheffield, UK: Greenleaf.

Brown, L.R. (2006), *Plan B 2.0: Rescuing a Planet under Stress and a Civilization in Trouble*, New York: W.W. Norton.

Brown, L.R. (2008), *Plan B 3.0: Mobilizing to Save Civilization*, New York: W.W. Norton.

Burrows, P. (2003), *Backfire: Carly Fiorina's High-stakes Battle for the Soul of Hewlett-Packard*, Hoboken, NJ: John Wiley & Sons.

Cameron, K.S., J.E. Dutton and R.P. Quinn (eds) (2003), *Positive Organizational Scholarship: Foundations of a New Discipline*, San Francisco: Berrett-Koehler.

Cohen, P. and J. Cohen (1995), *Life Values and Adolescent Mental Health*, Mahwah, NJ: Lawrence Erlbaum.

de Sousa, L. (2007), 'The cost of gasoline around the world', The Oil Drum: Europe, available at http://europe.theoildrum.com/node/2653 (accessed 15 January 2009).

Deegan, C. (2002), 'Introduction: the legitimizing effect of social and environmental disclosures – a theoretical foundation', *Accounting, Auditing and Accountability Journal*, **15**(3): 282–311.

Deutsche Bank (2009), 'The Carbon Counter, available at http://www.dbcca.com/dbcca/EN/ (accessed 4 September 2009).

Economist (2009), 'A tale of two fisheries', *The Economist*, 10 September.

Ehrenfeld, J. (2008), *Sustainability by Design*, New Haven, CT: Yale University Press.

Eichenwald, K. (2005), *Conspiracy of Fools*, Broadway.
Elkington, J. (1999), *Cannibals with Forks: Triple Bottom Line of 21st Century Business*, Capstone.
Endlich, L. (2004), *Optical Illusion: Lucent and the crash of telecom*, New York: Simon & Schuster.
Freeman, E.R. (1984), *Strategic Management: A Stakeholder Approach*, Boston: Pitman Publishing.
Friedman, T.L. (2008), *Hot, Flat, and Crowded*, New York: Farra, Straus & Giroux.
Gergen, K. (1991), *The Saturated Self*, New York: Basic Books.
Gore, A. (2006), *An Inconvenient Truth: The planetary emergency of global warming and what we can do about it*, New York: Rodale Books.
Guler, I., M.F. Guillen, and J.M. Macpherson (2002), 'Global competition, institutions, and the diffusion of organizational practices: the international spread of ISO 9000 quality certificates', *Administrative Science Quarterly*, **47**(2): 207.
Hargadon, A. and R.I. Sutton (1997), 'Technology brokering and innovation in a product development firm', *Administrative Science Quarterly*, **42**(4): 716–49.
Hart, S.L. (1997), 'Beyond greening: strategies for a sustainable world', *Harvard Business Review*, January/February: 66–76.
Hart, S.L. and T. London (2005), 'Developing native capability', *Stanford Social Innovation Review*, **3**(2): 28–33.
Hart, S.L. and S. Sharma (2004), 'Engaging fringe stakeholders for competitive imagination', *Academy of Management Executive*, **18**(1): 7–18.
Hawken, P. (1993), *The Ecology of Commerce*, New York: Harper Collins.
Hoffman, A.J. and W. Ocasio (2001), 'Not all events are attended equally: toward a middle-range theory on industry attention to external events', *Organization Science*, **12**(4): 414–34.
Hopwood, A.G. (2009), 'Accounting and the environment', *Accounting Organizations and Society*, **34**(3–4): 433–39.
Howard-Grenville, J. (2002), 'Institutional evolution: the case of the semiconductor industry voluntary PFC emission reduction agreements', in A.J. Hoffman and M.J. Ventresca (eds), *Organizations, Policy, and the Natural Environment: Institutional and Strategic Perspectives*, Berkeley, CA: Stanford University Press, p. 489.
Hughes, T.P. (1979), 'The electrification of America: the system builders', *Technology and Culture*, **20**(1): 124–61.
ICTA (1998), 'An analysis of the hidden external costs consumers pay to fuel their automobiles', in M. Briscoe (ed.), *The Real Price of Gasoline*, Washington, DC: International Center for Technology Assessment, p. 43.
IPCC (2007), 'Synthesis report on global climate change', Intergovernmental Panel on Climate Change.
Jeter, L. (2004), *Disconnected: Deceit and Betrayal at WorldCom*, New York: Wiley.
Kahneman, D., A.B. Krueger, D. Schkade, N. Schwarz and A.A. Stone (2006), 'Would you be happier if you were richer? A focusing illusion', *Science*, **312**: 1908–10.
Kegan, R. (1994), *In Over Our Heads: The Mental Demands of Modern Life*, Boston, MA: Harvard University Press.
King, A. and M. Lenox (2002), 'Exploring the locus of profitable pollution reduction', *Management Science*, **48**(2): 289–99.

King, A., M. Lenox and A. Terlaak (2005), 'The strategic use of decentralized institutions: exploring certification with the ISO 14001 management standard', *Academy of Management Journal*, **48**(6): 1091–106.

Lane, R.E. (2001), *The Loss of Happiness in Market Democracies*, Yale University Press.

Marcus, A.A. and A.R. Fremeth (2009), 'Green management matters regardless', *Academy of Management Perspectives*, **23**(3): 17–29.

McDonough, W. (1995), 'Industrial Revolution II', *Interiors and Sources*, **38**(1), 22–41.

McDonough, W. and Braungart, M (2002), *Cradle to Cradle: Remaking the Way We Make Things*, North Point Press.

McLean, B. and Elkind, P. (2004), *The Smartest Guys in the Room: The Amazing Rise and Scandalous Fall of Enron*, Portfolio Trade.

Mintzberg, H. (1975), 'The manager's job – folklore and fact', *Harvard Business Review*, **53**(4): 49.

Neef, M.A.M. (1992), 'Development and human needs', in P. Ekins and M.A.M. Neef (eds), *Real-Life Economics: Understanding Wealth Creation*, New York: Taylor & Francis.

Nickerson, C., N. Schwarz, E. Diener and D. Kahneman (2003), 'Zeroing in on the dark side of the American dream: a closer look at the negative consequences of the goal for financial success', *Psychological Science*, **14**(6): 531–36.

NRDC (2007), 'Historic Hudson River cleanup to begin after years of delay, but will General Electric finish the job?', available at http://www.nrdc.org/water/pollution/hhudson.asp (accessed on 1 October 2009).

Obstfeld, D. (2005), 'Social networks, the Tertius Iungens orientation, and involvement in innovation', *Administrative Science Quarterly*, **50**(1): 100–30.

Pape, R. (2006), *Dying to Win: The Strategic Logic of Suicide Terrorism*, New York: Random House.

Paquin, R. (2008), '*Actions of Institutional Entrepreneurship in Managing the Underlying Processes in Diffusing New Interfirm Practices*', unpublished dissertation for Boston University School of Management, Boston, MA.

Porter, M.E. and C. van der Linde (1995), 'Toward a new conception of the environment-competitiveness relationship', *Journal of Economic Perspectives*, **9**(4): 97–18.

Porter, M.E. and C. van der Linde (1999), 'Green and competitive: ending the stalemate', *Journal of Business Administration and Policy Analysis*, **27–29**: 215.

Post, J.E., L.E. Preston and S. Sachs (2002), *Redefining the Corporation: Stakeholder Management and Organizational Wealth*, Stanford, CA: Stanford University Press.

Prahalad, C.K. (2006), *The Fortune at the Bottom of the Pyramid*, Upper Saddle River, NJ: Pearson

Putnam, R.D. (2000), *Bowling Alone: The Collapse and Revival of American Community*, New York: Simon & Schuster.

Ruffing, L. (2007), 'Silent vs. shadow reports: what can we learn from BP's sustainability report versus the *Financial Times*?', *Social and Environmental Accounting Journal*, **27**(1): 9–12.

Sharma, S. (2000), 'Managerial interpretations and organizational context as predictors of corporate choice of environmental strategy', *Academy of Management Journal*, **43**(4): 681–97.

Sharma, S. and I. Henriques (2005), 'Stakeholder influences on sustainability practices in the Canadian forest products industry', *Strategic Management Journal*, **26**(2): 159–80.

Sharma, S. and H. Vredenburg (1998), 'Proactive corporate environmental strategy and the development of competitively valuable organizational capabilities', *Strategic Management Journal*, **19**(8): 729–53.

Shrivastava, P. (1995), 'The role of corporations in achieving ecological sustainability', *Academy of Management Review*, **20**: 936–60.

Shrivastava, P. (1996), *Greening business: Profiting the corporation and the environment*, Cincinnati, OH: Thomson Executive Press.

Siegel, D.S. (2009), 'Green management matters only if it yields more green: an economic/strategic perspective', *Academy of Management Perspectives*, **23**(3): 5–16.

Sirota, D. (2009), *The uprising : An unauthorized tour of the populist revolt scaring Wall Street and Washington*, New York: Crown Publishers.

Steger, U., A. Ionescu-Somers, O. Salzmann and S. Mansourian (2009), *Sustainability partnerships: the manager's handbook*, London: Palgrave-Macmillan.

Stern, N. (2006), *Stern Review on the Economics of Climate Change*, London: Cabinet Office/HM Treasury, available at http://www.hm-treasury.gov.uk/independent_reviews/stern_review_economics_climate_change/sternreview_index. cfm (accessed 11 February 2008).

Terlaak, A. and A. King (2006), 'The effect of certification with the ISO 9000 quality management standard: a signaling approach', *Journal of Economic Behavior and Organization*, **60**(4): 579–602.

Torbert, W.R. and Associates (2004), *Action Inquiry: The secret of timely and transforming leadership*, San Francisco: Berrett-Koehler.

Waddock, S.A. and S.B. Graves (1997), 'The corporate social performance–financial performance link', *Strategic Management Journal*, **18**(4): 303–19.

Wirtenberg, J., D. Lipsky and W.G. Russell (eds.) (2008), *The Sustainable Enterprise Fieldbook: When it all comes together*, Sheffield, UK: Greenleaf.

World Commission on Environment and Development (1987), *Our Common Future*, New York: Oxford University Press.

3. Globalization, environmental sustainability, and system equilibrium

John Alexander

INTRODUCTION: THE PROBLEM OF SYSTEMIC CONSTRAINTS

I think that it is impossible to rationally deny the evidence that, as we evolve into a one-world economic system, we are adversely affecting the environment resulting in normative issues concerning which policies and practices we should pursue. As Peter Singer has effectively argued, we need to understand the normative implications of operating in an interconnected economic/environmental system, where an action in one part has remoter effects in other parts (Singer, 1993, 2001, 2002, 2009). This understanding needs to be reflected in the systematic constraints that are placed on our operating in this system – particularly since so many of these remoter effects are negative. Since these systematic constraints reflect our core values, we must look to what core values we have. Core values are those values that we use to help us define who we are; they play a foundational role in developing our sense of self and social worth, and they help to define our culture or our design for living. In this chapter we will focus on the core values of profit-maximization and environmental sustainability. The core value of profit maximization is one of the primary filtering values through which we interpret the meaning and significance of the other values we hold dear. The normative problem is that if we continue to interpret environmental sustainability through the primarily filtering value of profit maximization, we will continue to make decisions and perform actions that are normatively less preferable than if we adopted environmental sustainability as our primary filtering value and interpreted profit maximization through it.

If we want environmental sustainability to be the primary filtering value, then we need to evaluate our actions in terms of their overall effect on the entire biotic community. A sustainable system needs to be organized so that its component parts – including the market systems associated with the distribution of goods, services and harms – are working in a symbiotic relationship in order to ensure ongoing viability and flourishing resulting in what I refer to as system equilibrium. To accomplish this we need to take what is referred to as an ecocentric as opposed to an egocentric view of our relationship to the natural environment. From an ecocentric perspective, an action would be morally permissible if and only if it maintains or improves the health of the entire system. A system that reflects a symbiotic relationship between its components is one that exhibits system equilibrium.[1]

This chapter takes up the issue of the role systemic constraints play in our decision-making that I introduced in my paper, 'Environmental sustainability versus profit maximization: overcoming systemic constraints on implementing normatively preferable alternatives.' (Alexander 2007). While I still endorse the analysis I gave of the underlying systemic problem, I no longer think the solution offered is satisfactory. I now think that there is a motivational problem that I did not clearly recognize when I suggested a Rawlsian solution – a solution that used the veil of ignorance as a heuristic device to describe impartiality. The problem as I now see it is that assuming, reasonably, that rational persons will not needlessly and avoidably harm themselves, why would those that enjoy privilege in our present societal systems agree to go under the veil of ignorance when they can reason that doing so will harm them? This chapter is an attempt to present an alternative solution that avoids this motivational problem. In this chapter, I will continue the argument that an economic system whose primary systemic constraint is defined by the primary filtering value of profit maximization will lead to overall system disequilibrium characterized by unnecessary and avoidable harm, whereas an economic system whose primary constraint is defined by the primary filtering value of environmental sustainability will promote system equilibrium; as such, if we are truly concerned with pursuing the most normatively preferable actions then we must make environmental sustainability the primary constraint on our economic system. But more is needed than simply presenting sound arguments justifying environmental sustainability as our primary filtering value. We need to formalize a method by which everyone operating in market transactions adopts in practice policies that reflect environmental sustainability and create system equilibrium. In order to overcome the system constraints associated profit maximization, we must create laws that are universal both in scope and in practice, which will ensure the level playing field necessary for true sustainability and to which all participants in the system can be held accountable.

RECOGNIZING AND UNDERSTANDING THE NEED TO SHIFT PRIMARY FILTERING VALUES

Consider the following example of how market decisions are made. There are two companies, Company 1 and Company 2, bidding with a developing nation (DN) to build a manufacturing plant. The companies realize that building a plant in this nation will be a very good investment that will improve opportunities to generate increased profits. The normative question confronting the two companies is whether to build a safe plant (one that exceeds the emissions standards of DN, ensuring environmental sustainability) or an unsafe plant (one that simply meets the emissions standards of DN, jeopardizing environmental sustainability). What presently drives this normative question is the cost associated with exceeding the emissions standards of DN – increasing safety increases costs thereby decreasing potential profits. To understand how the primary present conceptual schema that we use in economic decision-making works, let us suppose that these companies, and the developing nation, are operating in a market where the primary filtering value is profit maximization. The two companies will be motivated to build less safe plants (that is those that merely meet the emissions standards of DN) because the cost of doing so will be less than the cost of building safer plants. Additionally, since increasing safety is a cost that negatively affects potential profit opportunities, DN will be motivated to keep its standards as low as possible, since it is also competing with other developing nations for industrial development. This creates a problem. The system is giving rise to behavior that clearly increases the risk that unnecessary and avoidable harm will be visited upon innocent people – as safety standards fall, risk increases. It is important to recognize that the health of biotic entities is a major component of environmental sustainability. It seems paradoxical to say that the environment is sustainable at a normatively permissible level when being exposed to unhealthy living conditions is harming increasing numbers of biotic entities.

However, while this explains how we presently justify the normative permissibility of our actions, this ultimately fails as an explanation to justify our actions because it lacks normative force when placed within a broader context for understanding our normative responsibility to prevent system disequilibrium that results when we create unnecessary and avoidable harm. In order to understand this we need to understand the implications of a simple thought experiment. Imagine that you are walking along a river and notice that a baby is drowning near the shore. In order to save it all you have to do is bend over and pick it up, but doing so will ruin the US$200 sweater that you are wearing. Are you morally obligated to pick up the baby even though it will ruin your sweater? Most of us will think that we are so obligated. Failure to save the baby would be admitting that we value the baby's life at less than US$200 and this seems to be indefensible from any number of normative perspectives. For example, not saving the baby seems to violate the 'golden rule' that as I certainly would want to be saved if I were drowning, I should save others if I am able to do so. Furthermore not saving the baby seems to violate the Kantian notion that there are certain indirect duties that we have a general obligation to fulfill in our interactions with certain non-persons. Assuming that Kant is correct and babies are not persons in the normatively relevant sense, we still have an indirect duty to save the baby in so far as how we treat the baby is indicative of how we will treat persons to whom we have the direct duty to save, all else being equal. We have a direct duty to save persons who are drowning, therefore we have an indirect duty to save the baby whose treatment influences how we will treat persons. From a conse- quentialist, utilitarian perspective, Peter Singer takes the idea of value and worth as it relates to the sweater and baby and develops what he refers to as the principle of comparable worth and argues that as long as the value of what we are trying to save by eliminating the harm is more than the cost to us of saving it, then we should save it. We know, for example, that approximately 30 000 innocent children die each day from starvation and preventable disease. To pose the challenging normative question raised by Singer and others: are we willing to argue that these preventable deaths are a necessary and unavoidable cost of us living the comfortable lifestyles we presently enjoy? It seems to violate the principle of utility that we should perform the action that results in the greatest amount of good, or the least amount of harm, for everyone affected by the action. Understanding this principle within the constraint that we should not harm someone to create a good for ourselves it seems that we should not think that our comfort- able lives are normatively justified by the harm living these lives causes others, if by lowering our comfort level we could save lives that would otherwise be lost. An interesting and important question is at what level is harming a person less valuable than what we do not want to sacrifice. Is it US$500, US$1000, US$1 million? The point is that, regardless of what figure we choose, we are confronted with the paradox of the heap: why not a dollar more or a dollar less? It is trying to resolve this problem that will be part of the motivation to adopt a solution that requires everyone to agree to some acceptable level of subsistence and safety that must be met by all those participating in the economic system.[2]

It is at this abstract level of analysis that we can understand why we need to change our primary filtering value to one that accurately reflects our normative requirement not to cause unnecessary and avoidable harm resulting in system disequilibrium. Since we, as rational agents, do not want to be unnecessarily and avoidably harmed ourselves, we should incorporate the commonly accepted principles of universalizability and reciprocity (the formalized aspects of what is commonly referred to as the golden rule and which plays an important role in many different normative perspectives) and recognize that we should not cause unnecessary and avoidable harm to others. According to the principles of universalizability and reciprocity, if we think that it is permissible to harm others, then we must think that it is permissible for others to harm us. We need to ask ourselves how we would want to be treated. Do we really want to live in an environment that is less healthy than could have been created had we used a different primary filtering value? Would this be a rational choice for us to make? If we answer "no" (and we should given the discussion above), then we should not think that it is permissible for others to live in those conditions as a result of our choices. While it is one of our goals (maybe our overall goal) to seek our own happiness, we need to follow Singer's argument and recognize that it is impermissible to achieve our happiness by needlessly and avoidably harming others (Singer, 1993, 2001). Furthermore, again adopting an important point that Singer makes, we need to recognize that we are not only responsible for what we do, but we are also responsible for what we could prevent, all else being equal. This being the case, if we can prevent unnecessary and avoidable harm to others, harm that exceeds what is permissible given the principle of comparable worth, we should do so (Singer, 2001).

If it is morally impermissible to behave in a way that increases the risk that unnecessary and avoidable harm will be visited upon innocent people, but such behavior is promoted and positively sanctioned in a system constrained by the primary filtering value of profit maximization, what can we do? Recognizing that using the primary filtering value of profit maximization results in causing normatively impermissible, unnecessary and avoidable harm, we need to change that primary filtering value to environmental sustainability and interpret profit maximization through that core value. It is, after all, not that we want to perform actions that are morally impermissible. It is simply that the present systematic constraints are such that we cannot act in more normatively permissible ways. If these systematic constraints remain unchanged, we will continue to operate at the minimal level of compliance required by the standards determined by the present operational systematic constraints. This will result in increased unnecessary and avoidable harms and increased costs to correct the harms caused. It is important to remember that costs associated with correcting the unnecessary and avoidable harms are external costs; they are passed on to other stakeholders. Thus, while it may seem that profits are maximized, they are actually reduced because of the additional costs being born by the system that needs to be paid for. We see increases in other costs such as taxes, insurance, fines, and clean up costs.[3]

The upshot of this discussion is that, even if we believe that there are normatively preferable ways of doing business, we will be unable to implement these ways of doing business so long as profit maximization remains the primary filtering value. These normatively preferable ways of doing business will, invariably, result in additional internal costs thereby reducing profit opportunities. One company cannot behave in what it views to be a more normatively preferable way so long as other companies are concerned solely with profit maximization and so long as they are positively sanctioned in the marketplace for doing so. (I know this from firsthand experience of having worked for 35 years in the foundry industry; a major environmental bad guy if ever there was one.) The challenge, then, is to determine how we can break free of a systemic constraint that prevents us from implementing normatively preferable alternatives so that we do not cause unnecessary and avoidable harm. What systemic change do we make so that we can create a sustainable environment and also create the wealth necessary to live flourishing lives? We know we need to replace the primary filtering value of profit maximization with the value of environmental sustainability. But, how can we do this at the pragmatic level?

CHANGING THE LEGAL FRAMEWORK

We need to recognize that, when we operate within a system whose primary filtering value is profit maximization, we operate under conditions that resemble the classical prisoner's dilemma. In concrete situations, we make decisions and perform actions that are positively sanctioned by the institutions that are in place for establishing and enforcing the parameters wherein we must act. Within this context, we know that it is necessary that we make decisions that will not needlessly and avoidably harm ourselves. And we do so within the defined parameters of the concrete situation. In the present functioning system, if our choice is to make a decision between two options, one of which will increase, the other of which will decrease our opportunity to maintain a competitive and viable organization, the only rational option is the former even if this option results in harm being caused. In this context, the harm will be viewed as necessary and unavoidable (a cost of doing business). The following Table 3.1 depicts this choice situation.

If, as agents of Company One, we are operating as rational decision-makers whose primary obligation is to promote the viability and flourishing

Table 3.1   Choice situations: profit maximization versus environmental sustainability

		Company Two	
		Follows PM	Follows ES
Company One	Follows PM	PM, PM	PM, ES
	Follows ES	ES, PM	ES, ES

(PM = profit maximization and ES = environmental sustainability)

of our company, then we will make choices that we think will give us a competitive advantage. Similarly, the agents of Company Two will make decisions that give their company a competitive advantage. Because profit maximization is the primary filtering value, the agents of both companies will choose to base their decisions on actions that promote the opportunity to increase profits as long as their actions are in compliance with what is required by the laws of the community in which they are operating. When I started in the foundry business in the late 1960s, environmental issues first began to be voiced in academia and the public media. However, even though some of us were aware of and concerned by these issues, our foundry would not voluntarily increase its costs to reduce harmful emission because we thought other foundries would not follow suit and do the right thing. Besides, we were complying with the laws that were in place. We were not motivated to do the right thing because doing so would have put us at a competitive disadvantage by decreasing our profit maximization opportunities. By the mid 1970s, new laws were being put into effect regulating how businesses dumped their emissions and wastes. But, the new laws were developed using the existing decision-making framework that used profit maximization at the expense of achieving optimal environmental sustainability and system equilibrium. In the terminology of the deep-ecology movement, society is operating from an egocentric normative perspective, when what is needed is an ecocentric normative perspective. We can relate the idea of an ecocentric normative framework to Aldo Leopold's 'land ethic'. Leopold argues that an action is morally permissible if and only if it maintains or increases the overall well-being of the entire biotic system (Leopold, 1966). In this framework, human beings are but one component of the system. Consequently, we need to take into account the effect of our actions not only as it affects us, but also as it affects all other components of the system, including the overall system itself.

The moral of this story is that in order to implement the changes necessary to change the normative perspective defined and constrained by the foundation filtering core value, we need to address the issue of systemic change at the social/political level where sanctioning those who act in the economic sphere actually takes place. The primary social/political institution that governs how we presently sanction actions is the legal system defined by the policies and procedures agreed upon to reach decisions on which laws to enact and which sanctions to enforce. Following the argument of Socrates in *Crito*, as long as a law is enacted following the policies and procedures that were agreed upon, then we have an obligation to abide by that law. This obligation can be understood as a result of an implied act of promising that we make when we knowingly and freely assume the various roles that define who we are (Plato, 2002). This is consistent with the normative position that I have been arguing for: we should not cause unnecessary and avoidable harm. Consider this argument:

Proposition 1: We should not cause unnecessary and avoidable harm.

Proposition 2: Breaking promises knowingly and freely made causes unnecessary and avoidable harm.

Conclusion: Therefore, we should not break promises justly made.

When we break a promise we knowingly and freely made, we cause harm by not acting as we have promised to act, thereby not giving what we have promised to give. The importance of promise-making is well captured by a quote that the President of Vulcan Engineering had on his desk in the early 1990s when I was doing business with his firm: 'I will do what I said I would do when I said I will do it. If I change my mind I will notify you so you will not be harmed by my action'. By knowingly and freely entering into a socially defined role we agree to be bound by the norms and values that define that role. In so far as our economic relationships have legal, as well as normative dimensions, one of our implied agreements is to be governed by the rule of law. This is important in determining how we should change the overall system wherein we make market decisions. In so far as laws (rules, processes, and/or procedures) determine what a system is permitted to do, if we want to effect a systemic change, we need to change the relevant laws to reflect the higher standards that result from our new primary filtering core value of environmental sustainability, than are presently being implemented in practice using the old filtering core value of profit maximization..

Going back to the dilemma created by the companies trying to make the proper normative decision about how safe they should build the plant in DN, it is the legal system that ultimately sanctions them that will determine how they will act. We know that changing the primary filtering value to one that more accurately reflects the normative perspective of unnecessary and avoidable harm (understood through the core value of environmental sustainability) will result in less harm being generated by the system. The primary filtering value of environmental sustainability requires that we internalize all the costs associated with doing business into the operating costs of that business. Because we increase profit opportunities by decreasing costs we will be motivated to reduce the costs associated with not being good environmental stewards by implementing practices designed to promote the overall health of the system resulting in greater system equilibrium. Presently, under the system that results from using the primary filtering value of profit maximization, many of these costs are externalized and therefore hidden and are paid by others even though some of the costs come back to the source in terms of higher taxes, for example.

The only way to pragmatically solve a systemic problem is for people to agree to the rules that will define how they relate to each other going forward. Consequently, it is the legal system that needs to be changed in order to ensure universal systemic equilibrium and environmental sustainability. Following Friedman, the most basic, minimal normative position possible regarding markets and compliance is that organizations should comply with the laws that define acceptable interpersonal interaction and transaction (Friedman, 1962, 1970). This can be made consistent with the normative goal of not creating unnecessary and avoidable harm if we agree that the laws that govern the decision-making framework apply equally to all regardless of location. The justness, or normative permissibility, of a decision is based on whether or not the rules and procedures accepted by all the parties are used correctly and applied equally to all that are affected by the law. If it is agreed that a certain law (or rule, or procedure) will be followed by all regardless of location then this agreement is binding on all members of the community that are affected by this law. [4]

Having recognized the normative imperative to change the primary filtering value to environmental sustainability, it is necessary to pass laws that reflect this higher standard. New laws will need to be passed that require that we build plants to the highest available standards designed to protect the overall health and viability of the system. For example, if environmental and safety laws designed to protect the health of the system require plants to be built that emit lower levels of pollutants than the laws of other nations require, we need to recognize that environmental sustainability requires that we build to the higher standard. Of course this will mean an end to the concept of national sovereignty and will eventually result in a one-world legal system, but that is a necessary result of adopting the new filtering value understood within the consequentialist normative framework I have been defending. If we want to ensure that we minimize, if not completely eliminate, unnecessary and avoidable harm, then we need a system with one set of unified laws that governs and sanctions the behavior of all affected by the activities that take place within the overall system.

CONCLUSION: THE ROLE OF LEADERSHIP AND STEWARDSHIP

In this paper I have demonstrated the following: a system that uses profit maximization as it's primary filtering value will sanction actions that result in unnecessary and avoidable harm. This is morally impermissible given that we should not cause, and should prevent, unnecessary and avoidable harm.

To correct this problem we need to change the primary filtering value to environmental sustainability, understood as system equilibrium, so that the component parts of the system are in a symbiotic relationship working to ensure its overall health and viability and thereby optimally minimizing unnecessary and avoidable harm.

To put the new filtering value into practice within the micro-systems that affect the macro-system, we need to change the present legal system that allows for different sovereign localities to implement laws that sanction different levels of environmental sustainability. We need to establish a single legal system that governs all the various markets and other economic functions so that one agreed upon level of macro-system sustainability can be achieved and maintained.

In closing, I would like to suggest a need for leaders to adopt a philosophy of stewardship that incorporates what Neil Ducoff has called 'no-compromise leadership'. Ducoff argues, as many others have, that leaders need to adopt a high set of organizational objectives and standards that are designed to ensure that their organizations remain viable and healthy. He reasserts the importance of the well-known belief that an organization will mirror the norms and values of its leadership (Ducoff, 2009). In the language of the old-school quality movement, in order for long-lasting systemic change to occur there needs to be 'top down commitment and bottom up involvement' to a set of objectives derived from the norms and values that the leader has committed himself or herself to. These norms and values need to be transparent so that members of the organization, as well as the public, may clearly understand the operating philosophy of the organization. According to Ducoff, success can be achieved only if the leader does not waver in developing and implementing the practices designed to achieve these goals and objectives. An effective leader will not compromise the goals and objects, nor the underlying norms and values that support them, that are in place to ensure organizational success. To compromise is to fail! (Ducoff, 2009).

This requires a philosophy of stewardship that recognizes, and positively sanctions, the transformational nature of leadership that is required to achieve the goal of establishing a system that ensures environmental sustainability. If we simply understand stewardship to mean 'the effective and responsible management of estates or affairs not our own', then we can clearly see the relationship that stewardship and leadership have in common. Leaders are those who have a primary duty to care for the systems they are in charge of protecting. It becomes incumbent upon us, as leaders and educators, to adopt the normative position associated with environmental sustainability and develop an aggressive agenda that pushes this perspective downward through the existing micro-systems. If the overall system is sustainable then the components that make it up will also be sustainable.

ENDNOTES

1. It is important to recognize that we make decisions using a conceptual schema consisting of a coherent system of beliefs that we hold to be true. The truth of these beliefs is established through our experiences using them as we seek to understand the world we live in. As John Rawls has demonstrated, we make adjustments to these beliefs as warranted by our experiences so that we can establish conceptual schemas that reflect what he refers to as a set of 'considered judgments in a state of reflective equilibrium' (Rawls, 1973). Using an important epistemic distinction made by Rudolph Carnap, we can distinguish between external systemic questions and internal systemic questions as they relate to our conceptual schemas. External questions concern the rational validity, or acceptability, of the system itself and are resolved using the pragmatic notion that the truth value of any system of thought is primarily the result of the system working as it is designed to work. Internal questions are questions relating to the truth value, or consistency, of the individual beliefs that make up the system and are settled by how well the beliefs that make up the system cohere with, or follow from, one another (Carnap, 1950, 1956). Those beliefs that are foundational to the system itself serve as its gatekeepers. New beliefs are allowed into the system if they cohere with or follow from these foundational beliefs. Primary filtering values are those beliefs that are deeply imbedded in the conceptual schema. They function as the core values of the system and the system cannot exist without them firmly in place. To understand the epistemic underpinnings of the role that core values play in determining the truth value of other core values it is helpful to imagine that our conceptual schemas metaphorically resemble what Quine and Ullian refer to as a 'web of belief'. If we imagine our web resembling a spider's web with each segment of the web representing a belief that we hold to be true, it is clear that the beliefs that are at the center (core) of the web are foundational to the ones emanating from the core. In this metaphor, we accept beliefs as being true to the extent that they cohere with other beliefs already accepted as being true (Quine and Ullian 1970).

  Using this metaphor, we can see that changing beliefs is more difficult when we need to change our core beliefs. Because of the overall impact such changes have for the rest of the schema, people are reluctant to change their core beliefs or even to accept arguments that demonstrate that (some of) those core beliefs are unwarranted. Relative to our problem, for example, people operating under the primary filtering value of profit maximization will reason that the harmed being caused is, in fact, neither unnecessary nor avoidable, but is actually the cost of doing business. They will reason, as does Milton Friedman, that in order to maximize profits, which is the primary normative responsibility of business people, we need only to comply with the laws of the community we are operating in and not perform fraudulent or deceptive acts (Friedman, 1970). As long as we comply with these minimal requirements, any harm that results is permissible – it is necessary and unavoidable given the legal constraints that are in place. To go beyond what is minimally required is to incur additional costs and results in normatively impermissible harm to the organization and its constituents. From personal experience, working for a corporation operating and trying to survive in a highly competitive market, I can tell you that this is a very compelling argument.

2. Some might want to argue that we are only responsible for what we directly cause. If I take away someone's food and he or she starves to death I am clearly responsible for that person's death. However, limiting our responsibility to this type of action relies on a very narrow interpretation of what it means to be the cause of something. I believe that if we can affect the outcome of a situation we did not cause then we are the cause of that outcome. If I know that I can save the life of a child by sending some excess money that I have to a relief agency and I fail to do so and a child dies, I am part of the causal explanation of that child's death.

3. To understand more clearly the normative importance of changing the primary filtering core value to environmental sustainability, we can schematize the underlying normative issues we have been discussing by incorporating the arguments of Mark Johnson regarding the role that metaphors play in our moral reasoning. Johnson argues that we incorporate normatively rich metaphors in our moral reasoning and that we cannot reason about normative issues effectively without them. An important metaphor that he analyzes is what he refers to as 'morality as health'. He schematizes this metaphor relative to our understanding moral behavior as follows:

Physical health	Moral behavior
Health	Well-being
Sickness	Moral degeneration
Pollution	Cause of evil
Being diseased	Being morally depraved
Physical exercise	Moral training
Growth	Moral improvement (Johnson, 1996)

We can interpret the normative framework that I have been defending as the alternative to using 'profit maximization' as the primary filtering value as an example of another metaphor that we use in our moral reasoning. We can map out the metaphorical implications of what we can refer to as the health of the environment relative to the metaphor of morality as health as follows:

Health of environment	Physical health	Moral behavior
Sustainability	Health	Well-being
System disequilibrium	Sickness	Moral degeneration
Profit maximization	Pollution	Cause of evil
Non-flourishing	Being diseased	Being morally depraved
Problem solving	Physical exercise	Moral training
Continuous improvement	Growth	Moral improvement

Using the metaphor of the health of the environment we can now appreciate the important normative role that the core value of environmental sustainability should play in our overall decision-making schema. In fact the health of the organization and environmental sustainability become normatively equivalent concepts. If we interpret environmental sustainability in terms of the health of the environment then the consequentialist normative framework brought forth earlier becomes clearer and more compelling. We can also see how these concepts nicely overlap with what we have been discussing about the role that conceptual schemas play in understanding the world we live in. These metaphors represent a coherent and self-supporting mechanism that enables us to creatively think about the normative implications of our actions.

4. It is important to recognize that if we are going to convince others to accept our normative position that we argue only for what is minimally required from a normative point of view. Milton Friedman's position regarding a business operator's normative obligation to obey the law and not perform actions that are fraudulent or deceptive is the one that fits this description. There may be more comprehensive normative theories available that reach the same outcome, but adopting the one with the minimum requirements makes it easier to adjust core beliefs in that there are fewer associated core beliefs that need to be readjusted if we change from profit maximization to environmental sustainability. As business people we will still be engaged in maximizing profits, only we will understand how we can best accomplish this through a different core filtering value.

REFERENCES AND SELECT BIBLIOGRAPHY

Alexander, J. (2006), 'Economic instability and the unfortunate, and unavoidable, consequences of acting ethically', *Journal of Business Ethics*, **66**: 147–55.

Alexander, J. (2007), 'Environmental sustainability versus profit maximization: overcoming systemic constraints on implementing normatively preferable alternatives', *Journal of Business Ethics*, **76**: 155–62.

Alexander, J. (2005), 'Metaphors, moral imagination and the healthy organization: a manager's perspective', *Philosophy of Management*, **5**(3).

Brenkert, G.G. (2000), 'Partners, business and the environment', in Patricia H. Werhane and Joel Reichart (eds), *Environmental Challenges to Business*, The Ruffin Series No. 2, Society for Business Ethics.

Carnap, R. (1950), 'Empiricism, semantics, and ontology', in Revue Internationale de Philosophie, 4: 20–40. reprinted in the supplement to *Meaning and Necessity: A Study in Semantics and Modal Logic*, (1956), University of Chicago Press.

Callicott, J.B. (1989), *In Defense of the Land Ethic: Essays in Environmental Philosophy*, Albany: State University of New York Press.

Callicott, J.B. (2002), 'From the balance of nature to the flux of nature: the land ethic in a time of change', in R.L. Knight and S. Riedel (eds), *Also Leopold and the Ecological Conscience*, Oxford: Oxford University Press.

Devall, B. and G. Sessions (1985), *Deep Ecology: Living as if Nature Mattered*, Layton, Utah, USA: Gibbs Smith Publisher.

Ducoff, N. (2009), *No-Compromise Leadership*, Sanford, FL: DC Press.

Freeman, R.E. and J. Reichart (2000), 'Toward a life-centered ethic for business', in P.H. Werhane and J. Reichart (eds), *Environmental Challenges to Business*, The Ruffin Series No. 2, Society for Business Ethics.

Friedman, M. (1962), *Capitalism and Freedom*, Chicago, USA: The University of Chicago Press.

Friedman, M. (1970), *The New York Times Magazine*, 13, September.

Johnson, M. (1993), *Moral Imagination*, Chicago, USA: University of Chicago Press.

Johnson, M. (1996), 'How moral psychology changes moral theory', in L. May et al. (eds), *Mind and Morals*, Cambridge, USA: MIT Press.

Lakoff, G. and M. Johnson (1980), *Metaphors We Live By*, Chicago, USA: University of Chicago Press.

Leopold, A. (1966), *A Sand County Almanac*, New York, USA: Ballantine Books.

McGaa, E. (Eagle Man) (1990), *Mother Earth Spirituality*, San Francisco, USA: Harper Collins Publishers.

McGaa, E. (Eagle Man) (2002), *Native Wisdom*, San Francisco, USA: Council Oak Books.

Merchant, C. (2000), 'Partnership ethics: business and the environment,' in Werhane, P.H. and J. Reichart (eds), *Environmental Challenges to Business*, The Ruffin Series No. 2, Society for Business Ethics.

Merchant, C. (1992), 'Environmental ethics and political conflict,' in *Radical Ecology*, New York, USA: Routledge.

Moberg, D.J. and M.A. Seabright (2000), 'The development of moral imagination', in G. Brenkert (ed), *Business Ethics Quarterly*, October.

Naess, A. (1973), 'The shallow and the deep, long range ecology movements', *Inquiry*, **16**.

Naess, A. (1984), 'Defense of deep ecology', *Environmental Ethics*, **6**(3).

Norton, B.G. (2000), 'Clearing the way for a life-centered ethics for business, in Werhane, P.H. and J. Reichart (eds), *Environmental Challenges to Business*, The Ruffin Series No. 2, Society for Business Ethics.

Parker, K. (1996), 'Pragmatism and environmental thought', in Light, A. and E. Katz (eds), *Environmental Pragmatism*, London, UK: Routledge.

Plato, *Crito*, in *Five Dialogues* (*2nd edition*) (2002), G.M.A. Grube translator and revised by J.M. Cooper, Indianapolis, USA: Hackett Publishing.

Quine, W.V.O, and J.S. Ullian (1970), *The Web of Belief*, New York, USA: Random House.

Rawls, J. (1973), *A Theory of Justice*, Cambridge MA, USA: Belknap Press.

Rawls, J. (1999), *The Law of Peoples*, Cambridge, MA, USA: Belknap Press.

Shrivastava, P. (2000), 'Ecocentering strategic management', in Werhane, P.H. and J. Reichart (eds), *Environmental Challenges to Business*, The Ruffin Series No. 2, Society for Business Ethics.

Singer, P. (1993), *Practical Ethics*, Cambridge, UK: Cambridge University Press.

Singer, P. (2001), *Writings on an Ethical Life*, New York, USA: ECCO Press.

Singer, P. (2002), *One World*, New Haven, USA: Yale University Press.

Singer, P. (2009), *The Life You Can Save*, New York, USA: Random House.

Werhane, P. (1999), *Moral Imagination and Management Decision Making*, Oxford, UK: Oxford University Press.

Westra, L. (2000), 'Integrating the social contract and the ecological approach', in Werhane, P.H. and J. Reichart (eds), *Environmental Challenges to Business*, The Ruffin Series No. 2, Society for Business Ethics.

4. Institutions, MNEs, and sustainable development

Ben L. Kedia, Jack Clampit and Nolan Gaffney

INTRODUCTION

In 1983, Norwegian Prime Minister Gro Harlem Brundtland chaired the World Commission on Environment and Development. Gathered to study links between economic growth, poverty alleviation, and environmental degradation, it coined the term 'sustainable development'.

> Sustainable development is development that meets the needs of the present without compromising the ability of future generations to meet their own needs. It contains within it two key concepts:
>
> - the concept of needs, in particular the essential needs of the world's poor, to which overriding priority should be given; and
> - the idea of limitations imposed by the state of technology and social organization on the environment's ability to meet present and future needs. (WCED, 1987: 43)

MNEs, and the institutional frameworks that guide them, play a key role in determining the likely success or failure of sustainable development-related goals. Critics sometimes claim that MNEs exploit workers and harm the environment, and some fear that the goals of development and environmental stewardship are contradictory. While more optimistic, this chapter is not overly normative regarding the link between economic development and environmental performance, and the role played by MNEs. Our primary goal, rather, is to study the rich, interrelated nature of institutions, MNEs, development, and the environment, focusing on developmental antecedents and environmental implications supported by the literature.

Regarding institutions, this chapter adopts North's definition of institutions as 'the humanly devised constraints that structure human interaction' via 'formal constraints (rules, laws, constitutions), informal constraints (norms of behavior, conventions, and self imposed codes of conduct), and their enforcement characteristics' (1990: 3). Figure 4.1 illustrates how

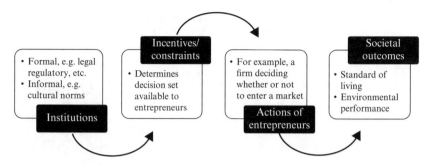

Figure 4.1   Effect of institutions on actions of entrepreneurs and societal outcomes

Table 4.1   Correlation matrix of institutional quality, level of economic development, and environmental performance (sustainability)

	Institutions	Development	Sustainability
Institutions	1.00	0.72	0.55
Development	0.72	1.00	0.62
Sustainability	0.55	0.62	1.00

Source: World Bank (2008 GDP data), Yale University and Columbia University (2008 Environmental Performance Index), Heritage Foundation (2008 Index of Economic Freedom)

institutions within societies dictate incentives and constraints for entrepreneurs (including MNEs) which, in turn, determine the actions of entrepreneurs and subsequent societal outcomes, such as a society's standard of living or environmental performance. A quick example of how powerful institutional incentives can be is illustrated by Nove's (1969: 314) question of how a 'country capable of making an A-bomb (the USSR) could not supply its citizens with eggs?' The answer, quite simply, is that Soviet institutions rewarded conduct aimed at building A-bombs while discouraging the kind of decentralized planning and profit motives that would have resulted in an allocation of resources efficient enough to supply its citizens with eggs.

At a glance, it appears that fears suggesting the world must choose between sustainability and development may be overly pessimistic. For example, Table 4.1 and Figure 4.2 show that correlations between environmental performance, institutional quality, and levels of economic development for 143 countries are fairly high, offering hope that environmental stewardship and economic development may not be fundamentally

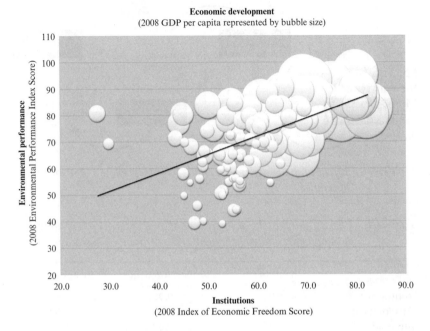

Source: World Bank (2008 GDP data), Yale University and Columbia University (2008 Environmental Performance Index), Heritage Foundation (2008 Index of Economic Freedom)

Figure 4.2   Covariance between development, environmental performance, and institutions

incompatible. Note, however, that the relationship between institutions and environmental performance appears weaker than the relationship between institutions and development. This may, in part, be due to the relatively crude measure of institutional quality employed (an aggregate rating designed to capture formal institutional characteristics such as judicial independence, level of property rights, financial transparency, the right to contract, and so forth). It is quite possible, likely in fact, that economic development alone does not automatically ensure improved environmental performance, and that institutions specific to sustainability-related goals must be employed in order for that link to fully materialize (employment a less expansive measure may have captured). This notion will be explored more fully in a later part of this chapter, but for now we simply note that the goals of sustainable development do seem possible.

We begin this chapter by reviewing literature associated with economic development and the current state of global poverty, followed by a brief overview of environmental concerns and institutions, focusing on the degree of heterogeneity between (and isomorphism within) the boundaries of nation states, and the extent to which this matters.

Next, we examine the links between institutions, MNEs, and development. International business scholars have written extensively about the link between MNEs and economic development (such as Kedia, Mahto, and Perez-Nordtvelt, 2005). While not the sole source of development, MNEs can, and often do, play key roles. Economists, meanwhile, have written extensively about the link between a nation state's institutional framework and economic development (Acemoglu, Johnson, and Robinson, 2001; Barro, 1996). Like international business scholars, economists also have a rich tradition of examining the link between MNEs and development, though economists often focus on a higher level of analysis. While offering numerous empirical studies that sometimes do explicitly take institutions into account, the inclusion of institutions in this context is often as a control variable rather than as an integral part of a holistic conceptual framework exploring the links between institutions, MNEs, and economic development within a given society at once (Borensztein, Gregorio, and Lee, 1998). Drawing on North and in the spirit of Dunning, who often suggested that international business scholars should more fully integrate institutional theory and social concerns into our studies, we explore the relationship between institutions, MNEs, and the standard of living in developing countries, a relationship represented in its simplest form as: Institutions → MNEs → Economic development.

We then examine the relationship between economic development and environmental performance. Sustainability implies Malthusian concern regarding the carrying capacity of nature in relation to human consumption patterns. While Malthus was concerned about our ability to feed geometrically increasing populations in light of arithmetically increasing food stocks, sustainability related concerns are, of course, broader. Predictions regarding the exponential rate of economic development leading to the eventual depletion of natural resources (Meadows, Meadows, Randers, and Behrens, 1972) have, thus far, been thwarted by improved technology. While societies continue to invest in the development of sustainability-related technologies, the truth of the matter is that we simply do not know, ex ante, what the world will or will not invent. Moreover, it is no longer merely resource depletion, whether in the form of overuse or polluted stocks, which worries us. Increasing levels of greenhouse gases, resulting from human activity such as fossil fuel burning and deforestation, seem to be leading to an increase in global temperature levels. Carbon dioxide and methane levels have increased by 36 percent and 148 percent respectively from 1750 to today (EPA, 2008), with global surface temperatures rising approximately 1.3 degrees Fahrenheit between 1900 and 2000 (IPCC, 2007). Many scientists are convinced that this resultant warming will cause sea levels to rise and extreme weather events to increase in terms of both frequency and intensity. As the magnitude of global warming's impact is projected to be quite severe, it becomes even more imperative that we fully understand its relationship with economic development.

Finally, we close this chapter by integrating these topics into a succinct, consolidated model that illustrates the holistic nature of the roles played by institutions, MNEs, and development in relation to each other and, also, to environmental performance. It is our view that conceptualizing the role(s) played by one component in a vacuum, to the exclusion of how it interacts with other components, may lead to unanticipated downstream consequences that may or may not be as favorable as hoped for. In other words, while researchers should undoubtedly drill down and test propositions which spring forth from middle and lower range theory, we should also remember to make every effort to keep the bigger picture in mind.

CONCEPTUAL DEVELOPMENT

Economic Development Overview

According to the World Bank (2008), the number of people living in extreme poverty, (people living on US$1.25 a day or less) has decreased dramatically since the 1980s, falling from 1.9 billion in 1981 to 1.8 billion in 1990 to about 1.4 billion in 2005. The greatest reductions occurred in Asia, where the poverty rate declined from nearly 80 percent in the early 1980s to less than 20 percent in 2005, a decline that translates into an absolute decrease of over 750 million people (World Bank, 2006). Though they still have far to go, India and China are perhaps the two countries mentioned most in terms of poverty reduction, and for good reason: India's official poverty rate has been nearly halved, from over 50 percent in 1978 to 27.5 percent in 2005 (Government of India, 2007), while in China poverty fell from 84 percent to 16 percent, effectively lifting 627 million people above the extreme poverty threshold (World Bank, 2006).

Unfortunately, the rest of the world has not always been as fortunate. For example, the poverty rate in Sub-Saharan Africa fell by just 5 percent during the same approximate time frame, while the absolute number of people living below the poverty line nearly doubled (due to an increase in population). This trend is actually fairly consistent worldwide, in other words excluding Asia from the equation, the number of people living in extreme poverty across the world has nearly doubled as well (World Bank, 2008).

Moreover, after enjoying a decade of strong growth and poverty reduction, due to the global financial crisis the World Bank (2009) predicts that up to one-third of the people who had escaped poverty may fall back in Asia and Eastern Europe alone (where GDP had grown by 67 percent since 2000). As the crisis affects financial, product, and labor markets around the globe, GDP is expected to continue declining, with 5 million people expected to regress back into poverty for each 1 percent decline in GDP.

Even before this recent downturn, however, critics have routinely leveled charges that relative newfound prosperity in parts of the world that have shown impressive levels of economic development has come at the expense of equality. A key point of distinction is whether absolute or relative measures of wealth are used as the basis of claims. For example, Notten and Neubourg (2007) show Ireland's absolute poverty level as having declined from 25.3 percent to 10.6 percent during its ascent from the poorest to the second richest country in Western Europe, while relative measures show rates nearly twice as high; Smeeding (2006), meanwhile, points out that while relative measures show an increase in poverty of 5.4 percent, absolute measures show a double digit decrease. Along similar lines, while Gwartney and Lawson (2008) show that the average income of the poorest 10 percent is nearly three times as high in countries in the top quartile of the EFW Index (Economic Freedom of the World) versus those in the next quartile, and nearly nine times as high as those in the bottom quartile, on the whole the literature is mixed regarding whether higher incomes due to growth-oriented institutions result in more inequality (Barro, 2007; Gwartney and Lawson, 2008; Nolan and Smeeding, 2005). It should be noted that in this chapter economic development, and resultant poverty reduction, will be considered to be an absolute increase in one's income. In other words, we adopt the view that countries with increasing levels of GDP per capita are better off from an economic standpoint than those with stagnant GDPs, and families earning US\$6,000 a year today are better off than when they earned US\$2,500 a year (constant dollars at purchasing power parity), regardless of whether the richest segment of society gained or lost relative to the poor.

The next question, then, is what the best way is to bring about rises in standards of living. A common answer is wealth redistribution in the form of foreign aid. Proponents often claim that a living wage or redistributions of income large enough to offset the gap between actual and living wages is a fundamental human right. Furthermore, they sometimes claim that a 'big push' is needed for countries trapped in poverty to escape, that is aid can serve as the necessary springboard to future growth, serving as a hand-up as opposed to a handout (Krugman, 1991; Sachs & Warner, 1999). Invoking the likes of Descartes, Hobbes, Locke, and Voltaire, critics of aid point to an alleged fallacy of accepting positive human rights as legitimate when they impose claims upon designated duty bearers that directly violate the negative rights of others, while also noting that aid-based strategies have been tried time and time again, with history proving one thing: they do not work. In fact, merely being impotent, according to critics, is often the best case scenario, as in many instances aid has made matters worse by delaying needed reform, fostering a culture of dependency, and facilitating corruption (Chaffour, 2009). Doucouliagos and Paldam's 2009 meta-analysis, examined the results of over 1000 regression equations in nearly 100 aid studies, concluding that despite pressure to publish results favorable to aid-based strategies, and despite recent attempts to tease out effective examples of aid by including contingencies along the lines of good host country governance, 'a clear pattern emerges in the results: after 40 years of development aid, the evidence indicates that aid has not been effective'. Their meta-regression actually showed a small negative effect of aid on economic growth, both with and without outliers included. It should be noted that the stance of this chapter is not necessarily to endorse or disapprove of aid-based tactics to facilitate economic development. We will, however, actively explore an alternative mechanism to aid (whether it be a substitute or complement): the role that MNEs and institutions play in the development process.

Despite condemnation of MNE activities by critics and anti-globalization protestors, the list of scholars noting the role MNEs play in uplifting living standards worldwide is long (Bhagwati, 2007; Kedia et al., 2005; Lodge and Wilson, 2006). MNEs provide jobs where jobs previously did not exist, pay higher-than-market salaries where jobs did exist, often provide positive horizontal and/or vertical spillovers that spur the growth of domestic businesses, help integrate local firms into the global economy, provide political leverage for local governments to embark upon positive institutional change, invest in local infrastructure, and uplift the morale of young people who previously thought there was no hope to escape from poverty.

Regarding the last point, Lodge and Wilson (2006) relay the story of a bishop in Panama who helped establish credit and marketing cooperatives for farmers. Once people realized change was possible, they saw the value of education and built schools teaching vocational skills. Though certain entrenched powers resisted this change and killed the priest, the movement did not die and today runs Central America's biggest chicken factory. Meanwhile, in the neighboring province, Nestlé, following the bishop's lead, organized farmers for the production of milk. While the bishop was a local who did not seek profit, and Nestlé was an MNE who did, in both cases culture was changed from defeatist to optimistic, and productivity and relative prosperity followed.

Bishops of a like mind and capability may be fairly rare agents of such drastic economic change, but MNEs uplift the standards of living of local populations every day; for example Daimler in Brazil constructed a factory manufacturing headrests and seats from renewable domestic fibers, a factory that employs over 5000 people that were formerly impoverished, people who now actively participate in civic affairs and whose children now attend school. Bhagwati (2007) points out that the empirical record regarding MNEs points to higher wages for local workers, better working conditions, and better environmental practices, and claims that MNEs promote positive change that improves the living conditions of domestic populations via reduced corruption, tighter integration into global markets. Moreover, the number of empirical studies showing a link between MNE entry and subsequent economic growth, including an increase in the standard of living of the poor, is large. See Klein et al., 2008, for a review of foreign direct investment (FDI) studies showing a robust direct relationship between MNE investment and per capita income levels, and between per capita income levels and the incomes of the poor, in other words, Smith (1776) may have been correct when suggesting that an invisible hand prompts man to promote societal interests most effectively by pursuing his own interest ('It is not from the benevolence of the butcher, the brewer, or the baker that we expect our dinner, but from their regard to their own interest.') As Lodge and Wilson (2006: 21) note, MNEs 'have the unmatched power and competence to reduce global poverty', and if Smith is right, they may have the motive too.

MNEs may also help improve the institutional framework of countries they operate in, in a manner that helps foster economic development. Dunning and Fourtanier (2007: 34) say, 'The most commonly cited example on how MNEs may contribute to institutions is the financial sector, where for example banks and insurance companies can help establish a structure of financial incentives and thus promote entrepreneurship and enterprise creation'. Critics sometimes argue that large MNEs possess and exploit advantages in bargaining power relative to small, poor countries. This kind of leverage may, however, be used in ways that benefit society as well. For example, Lodge and Wilson (2006: 19) claim 'poverty reduction requires systematic change, and MNCs are the world's most efficient and sustainable engines of change'. They also note the previously mentioned effect of MNEs on informal institutions, such as changing cultural norms that previously convinced people there was no hope for a better life (and thus no reason to try to better their lives), before showing that MNEs, quite often, spend large sums of money on infrastructure and local education.

Environmental Performance Overview

Phenomena such as melting glaciers, earlier growing seasons, and rising heat indexes have led many scientists to conclude that global warming is an unfortunate reality. By the end of the century, land temperatures may increase worldwide by up to 5.8 degrees Celsius, sea levels may rise by up to 0.88 meters, and both the frequency and intensity of extreme weather-related events like hurricanes may increase (IPCC, 2001). Current discourse regarding the relationship between environmental and global poverty reduction concerns seems to be delineated into two distinct, yet related, topics: adaptation, referring to the effects of negative environmental events on developing countries, and mitigation, referring to the effects of countries on the quality of the environment. With the pending expiration of the Kyoto Agreement, and the failure of the 2009 United Nations Climate Change Conference in Copenhagen to produce a legally binding framework for climate change mitigation, this bidirectional relationship is certainly in the public eye today, as policymakers search for an equitable and effective way to balance multiple goals, for example the desire to reduce carbon emissions without undue economic harm that might result in significant job losses or stunted development. Finding the right balance is not necessarily an easy thing, however, as efforts to facilitate the economic development of poor countries may involve building manufacturing facilities that further pollute the environment, while efforts aimed at mitigating the impact of global warming may adversely affect the poor. An example of the latter includes the role of rising food prices, due in large part to biofuel related initiatives, in pushing over 100 million people back into poverty and nearly 300 million more to the brink of it (World Bank, 2008).

Regarding the role played by MNEs, Shivarajan (elsewhere in this volume), documents how framing was used by smaller stakeholders to influence powerful stakeholders to act against Coca-Cola in the face of allegations related to the pollution and depletion of local water supplies in Kerala, India. Again, while critics of MNE activity are numerous (Thornton, 2000), others are quick to note the beneficial effects of MNEs. For example, pollution haven hypotheses notwithstanding (whereby firms are alleged to comply with stronger environmental standards in developed countries by exporting polluting activities to more relaxed global jurisdictions), Bhagwati (2007) and Dasgupta et al. (2002) note that MNEs are actually likely to adopt more stringent, internal environmental standards versus weaker standards required by local law or practiced by indigenous firms, with cleaner technologies and efficient practices regarding resource use sometimes spilling over into local firms.

Konar and Cohen (1997), meanwhile, note that firms whose stock prices have been hurt most by bad press subsequently reduce emissions most. Kolk and Pinkse (2008) note that firms are sensitive to growing public concern regarding environmentally responsible behavior. If firms are self-interested actors, concerned with stock price and the image of their brands, and important stakeholders begin to care more about environmental concerns, it stands to reason that being environmentally responsible is in a firm's best interest. In another example of goal alignment in terms of environmentally conscious conduct and firm performance, Rugman and Verbeke (1998) suggest that firms are more likely to commit to activities that benefit the environment when the activities are reversible and simultaneously create firm-specific advantages in addition to improving environmental performance. A Walmart executive, for example, noted that the first time they sent company engineers into a supply-chain factory, their audit helped reduce electricity bills by 60 percent via the installation of low emissions lighting and other clean technologies (Reuters, 2006).

The popularity of hybrid automobiles and green marketing is undoubtedly due, at least in part, to a desire to increase sales by catering to environmentally conscious consumers. Though the authenticity of claims to environmental concern are subject to skepticism (for example NGO, Corporate Watch, suggesting British Petroleum's 'Beyond Petroleum' ad campaign relabelled as 'Beyond Preposterous'), energy companies are investing in renewable energy research, hoping to diversify via additions to their portfolio of offerings. Kolk and Pinkse (2008) note that firms are also concerned with the strategic impact of security-related issues, such as a disruption of supply lines due to fossil fuel-related shocks. Regardless of their motivations, whether genuinely noble, purely motivated by self-interest, or somewhere in between, examples of environmentally conscious behavior on the part of MNEs seem to be increasing by the day.

Institutional Overview

The exact precision of their mathematical models notwithstanding, neoclassical economists have for years assumed a frictionless and static business environment where transactions are essentially free, and the strategies of firms relatively unconstrained by institutional forces. They have for all intents and purposes confined the role of institutions to that of a bit player in the background, to the extent that they are given a role at all. In reality, however, transactions have very real costs, such as the costs of negotiating, writing and enforcing contracts for each transaction (Coase, 1937; Williamson, 1981). These costs represented 45 percent of US gross national product in 1970 and are getting larger every year as technology enables production costs to drop (Wallace and North, 1986). These costs, and the resultant set of incentives and/or constraints associated with them, are directly influenced by the institutional framework within which firms operate. The heterogeneity among the decision sets available to entrepreneurs in different countries goes a long way towards explaining their behavior and subsequent economic outcomes (Alston, Eggertsson and North, 1996; Bruton, Dess and Janney, 2007; Bueno de Mesquita and Root, 2000; Hill, 2007; Lee, Peng and Barney, 2007; North 1990; Wan and Hoskisson, 2003).

With this in mind, and in order to properly position the role of institutions as it relates to economic development, we will next review the literature that suggests that institutional settings differ, and then review the literature that suggests that those differences matter with respect to determining which societies will grow and which will not.

Heterogeneous, non-ergodic institutional settings
Institutional settings differ, and their non-ergodic nature makes it more difficult for firms to predict or react to differences in those settings, as they are sometimes forced to deal with a moving target (North, 1990). The following two World Bank (2005, 2008) examples illustrate just how much this framework differs in different parts of the world: (1) it requires 124 days and costs more than 20 percent of the property value to register property in Nicaragua and Mali, while in New Zealand it takes two days and costs 0.1 percent of the property value; (2) on average it takes over 200 days and costs 153 percent of per capita income to register a new business in Haiti, while in Australia it takes two days and costs 2 percent of per capita income. On the basis of generalizations drawn from statistics like these alone, one can probably quite accurately guess which countries are more productive and, thus, have a higher standard of living.

Peng et al. (2008) implores scholars to explicitly account for the impact of institutions on MNEs via a three legged stool metaphor, with resource, industry, and institutional-based views of the firm as legs. Hoskisson et al. (2000) also suggest that institutional theory is important and is, in fact, one of the three most insightful theories that exist today when examining MNE activity in developing economies. And while they do also predict that its importance will diminish as isomorphism brings about relative convergence in institutional settings, we might argue that, as recent examples of institutional failure in the US illustrate, institutions will still matter and important differences will still exist between even between even fully developed countries considered to be institutionally similar. One example is France's legally mandated 35 hour work week limit which stands in stark contrast to labor laws in places like the US.

Drawing on research streams from political science and socioeconomics, various studies suggest the existence of multiple varieties of capitalism based on heterogeneous institutional configurations resulting from different histories, cultures, and goals (Albert, 1993; Chandler, 1990; Hall and Soskice, 2001; Redding, 2005; Wade, 1990; Whitley, 1999). Moreover, not only are the institutional matrices different when comparing nations in different regions, for example Asian countries versus the US, they are also different when comparing firms in the same region, such as Asian countries versus other Asian countries (Orru et al., 1997).

Another stream of research introduces the constructs of liberal market economies (LMEs) and coordinated market economies (CMEs), comparing economies where firms adjust to environmental changes on their own, with other firms copying the practices of the more successful firms, resulting in initial heterogeneity but eventual isomorphism, versus economies where aggregate level change is voluntarily implemented or dictated by labor unions, governments, and so on (Albert, 1993; Hall and Soskice, 2001; Witt and Lewin, 2008). This is not the same as centralization or decentralization. For example, the US is a decentralized LME while Germany is a fairly decentralized CME. One key point to be extracted from this stream of research is the idea that CMEs are slow to adjust and prone to 'groupthink' – thus, if the right kind of change is made, all firms benefit, but if the wrong kind of change is made, all firms suffer together. In other words, systemic risk (and reward) seems to be increased, as more eggs are in the same economic basket. Furthermore, due to more limited degrees of firm level experimentation, the odds of stumbling upon a successful strategy may be lower, as society places more faith in the rational ability of technocrats who, presumably, have their best interests in mind.

Further evidence of differing institutional environments, and their non-ergodic nature, comes from the 2007 FDI Confidence Index report that includes the results of surveys of managers with strategic decision-making responsibilities in the Global 1000 (representing 60 countries, 6 continents, and 17 industries). In fact, not only do these surveys suggest differing institutional environments around the globe, they also imply that opinions regarding the institutional makeup may even differ within the same country. For example, while 23 percent of respondents said they had more confidence in the US as a potential environment for FDI versus the previous year, 23 percent had less confidence (A.T. Kearney, 2007). The FDI Confidence Index report also includes updates of important changes in the institutional environments of various countries around the globe. Table 4.2 lists a sample of these recent institutional changes, while Table 4.3 illustrates longer run changes in tax levels.

Table 4.2   Institutional settings update from 2007 FDI Confidence Report

Country	Update
Indonesia	While rich in natural resources and possessing the fourth largest population in the world, Indonesia has had trouble attracting FDI due to institutionally-related issues such as an over-burdensome regulatory environment and security concerns, but is now promising to improve customs rules, labor laws, taxation levels, property rights, and bureaucracy levels.
Thailand	Thailand dropped completely off the 2007 index due to political stability concerns after a military coup.
Germany	In response to concerns that businesses were leaving due to institutional disadvantages, Germany cut corporate taxes from 39% to 30%. Union wage restraint is mentioned as another positive development.
United Kingdom	The UK, with twice as much inward FDI as its closest European rival, continues to benefit from higher transaction costs imposed on US markets by Sarbanes-Oxley, due to a more favorable regulatory environment and skilled workers.
Russia	Survey respondents noted an improved economy, large markets, and skilled labor, but more than half decided to pull back or hold investment constant due to political concerns including the threat of nationalization, poor rule of law, and crime.
France	Outlook improved due to promised reforms including greater labor flexibility, improved education; however the recent US financial crisis seems to have tempered reform. Protectionism concerns remain.
Africa (selected countries)	Concerns remain the same, with 92% mentioning bureaucracy, 80% citing political instability, 69% citing poor public infrastructure, and 58% mentioning the poorly skilled workforce as reasons to avoid Africa.

Source: A.T. Kearney's 2007 FDI Confidence Index Report

Impact of distinct institutional matrices

In order to legitimately insert institutions into our framework, we had to first show that institutional configurations at the nation state level differ and, while certain aspects are remarkably stubborn, those configurations are constantly evolving. Implied in the assertion that they differ is that those differences matter. It is these differences, after all, that provide incentives and disincentives that influence both the decisions of MNEs to

Table 4.3   Change in top corporate tax rates (1980–2007)

Country	1980	2007	Change
Ireland	45.0%	12.5%	−32.5%
Austria	55.0%	25.0%	−30.0%
Netherlands	48.0%	25.5%	−22.5%
United Kingdom	52.0%	30.0%	−22.0%
Portugal	47.2%	36.5%	−10.7%
Germany	56.0%	38.9%	−17.1%
Finland	43.0%	26.0%	−17.0%
Australia	46.0%	30.0%	−16.0%
France	50.0%	34.4%	−15.6%
Denmark	40.0%	25.0%	−15.0%
Belgium	48.0%	34.0%	−14.0%
Mexico	42.0%	28.0%	−14.0%
New Zealand	45.0%	33.0%	−12.0%
Sweden	40.0%	28.0%	−12.0%
Luxembourg	40.0%	30.4%	−9.6%
Italy	40.0%	33.0%	−7.0%
United States	46.0%	39.3%	−6.7%
Canada	37.8%	33.5%	−4.3%
Japan	42.0%	39.5%	−2.5%
Norway	29.8%	28.0%	−1.8%
Spain	33.0%	32.5%	−0.5%

Source: OECD

either enter or avoid a country and its subsequent behavior if it does enter; and economic development prompted by MNE behavior is often a critical channel by which growth-oriented institutions in developing countries alleviate poverty.

The proposition that institutions matter is not controversial. The notion, in fact, can be found at least as far back as 100 BC among various Confucian and Taoist scholars (such as Sima Quin), and as far back as Smith (1776) in the West, who plainly asserts that the state must define property rights and enforce contracts in order for a society to be able to take advantage of the gains associated with division of labor and trade and, thus, collectively improve its material lot. Simply put, rule of law and sound, growth-oriented institutions are a prerequisite for the 'invisible hand' to be able to work its magic. The question to consider, then, is how, and to what degree, institutions matter.

Some have argued that a background role is sufficient in advanced market economies, where vital institutional frameworks such as rule of law can simply be assumed and taken for granted. Increasingly, however, the direct impact of institutions on the firm has been demonstrated to be worth actively considering as more and more evidence surfaces regarding the manner and degree of impact (Lewin and Kim, 2004).

Two brief macro-level examples should confirm that even in a country as advanced as the US, institutions do indeed matter a great deal and are not always efficient to the point of being invisible: first, the role of the Federal Reserve before and during the Great Depression, and second, the catalogue of potential institutional missteps by various actors involved in the US' current financial crisis.

During the Great Depression, America's real output fell nearly 30 percent and the unemployment rate rose from roughly 3 percent to nearly 25 percent (with many of the employed holding only part-time jobs), with recovery over a decade away. Regarding the role of institutions, current Federal Reserve chairman and Great Depression scholar Ben Bernanke, referring to four specific central policy missteps from 1923 to 1933, has on more than one occasion publicly admitted that 'we did it'. Contrary to the image held by some of the Federal Reserve as a white knight who cleaned up the mess of the capitalists and speculative market forces, Bernanke admits the Federal Reserve itself actually played a central role in transforming what would have otherwise been a relatively short downturn into America's most storied and prolonged economic crisis (Bernanke, 2002, 2004). Austrian school economists, of course, begin their examination of central bank conduct even earlier, before downturns ever begin, believing central banks play key roles in promoting unsustainable bubbles that, when popped, may spark downturns which are more severe than they otherwise would have been. Either way, it does seem that institutional failure played a key role.

Institutional influence is prominently on display today as well. Comments made in 2007 by the current president of the Federal Reserve Bank of St. Louis notwithstanding – attesting to the prowess of today's Federal Reserve at fostering real prosperity ('. . .advances in knowledge permit us to say with some confidence that these gains are not just an accident of Alan Greenspan's special skills and intuition', Poole, 2007: 1) – the actions of the Federal Reserve and other US institutional players are currently under scrutiny for their role in the subprime induced financial crisis.

Some point fingers at institutional policymakers who decided to feverishly promote home ownership among people with track records of not paying their debts, while others note the informal constraints preventing politically astute actors from pointing out the danger of those policies. Others point to perverted institutional incentives allowing lenders to lend with impunity as risks were transferred to entities like Fannie Mae, Freddy

Mac, global investors and, ultimately, taxpayers. Still others blame 'easy money' policies of the Federal Reserve that may have helped fuel a real estate bubble, while Alan Greenspan shifts blame towards irrational actors in financial institutions who, based on greed or a desire to placate the never-ending demands of customers for higher returns on their 'safe' investments, over-relied on math experts and finance scholars who suggested there was a new kind of alchemy enabling firms to magically transmute risky mortgages into relatively safe assets via the use of certain derivatives. Regarding these derivatives, many point to failure among regulatory institutions that allowed them to play such a prominent role in the first place, while others claim that contrary to a lack of regulations, rules already on the books actually encouraged their use.

Regardless of who is truly at fault for the economic mess the US is now in, institutional failure does seem to be squarely in the spotlight again. And if perhaps the archetypical model for a sound institutional framework can let its populace down to the degree it has, should it be any surprise that institutions often fail in less established countries?

LINKING INSTITUTIONS, MNEs, AND DEVELOPMENT

Institutions can, of course, do tremendous good. Warts and all, in developed countries like the US they are the bedrock of civilization, providing law and order and the necessary ingredients for prosperity. In fact, the argument has often been made that it is precisely because of America's country-specific institutions that its corporations, and thus the country as a whole, have been so prosperous, and precisely because of their lack of growth-oriented institutions that Third World countries remain poor. In other words, peace and prosperity do not owe their existence to a country's abundant natural resources, large populations, or especially intelligent populations, but rather due to effective institutions. Interestingly enough, the institution of democracy, alone, does not correlate very strongly with prosperity (some have hypothesized a curvilinear effect, with a direct relationship that turns downward once people in mature democracies start voting themselves more and more largesse). Institutions promoting economic freedom, however, do strongly correlate with prosperity, whether they are ensured by a market oriented autocracy or a democracy, for example Taiwan and South Korea jump started growth under authoritarian regimes, while Singapore is a current authoritarian state with a very high degree of economic freedom and an enviable economic record (Alston et. al., 1996; Bueno de Mesquita and Root, 2000; North, 1990, 2005).

Employing a game theoretic context, North (1990) illustrates the logic behind the importance of institutions in a simple and intuitive fashion by relaying the story of how transition from local exchange in a village in centuries past to regional trade was made possible by newly birthed institutions designed to minimize transaction costs. When trade was local, actors had near perfect information about the reliability of others, and as those actors had to continue to live with each other and constantly repeat transactions, there was intense social pressure to live up to one's end of various bargains. The development of impersonal exchange in the form of long distance trade, however, was characterized by: (1) buyers and sellers who knew little about each other and might never deal with one another again; (2) agents hired to deliver goods from villages to far-away markets, to then sell those goods at a worthy price, and finally to return and relinquish the profits from their sale; and (3) hired protection to thwart the efforts of armed bandits. Where societies developed institutions – such as rudimentary forms of contract enforcement and rule of law (such as agreements with local princes for protection or the formation of guilds that provided customers with the promise of a relatively standardized quality of goods) – trade flourished and economies developed. Where appropriate institutions did not develop, however, economic growth did not occur, as the transaction costs in the absence of facilitating institutions exceeded the payoff of economic activity.

Acemoglu et al. (2001) examine over 70 former European colonies and show that in disease free climates such as Australia, New Zealand, and North America, colonists created lasting institutions to protect property rights and curb the power of the state, but when Europeans arrived in areas with high rates of malaria, yellow fever, and other diseases, they did not find as many permanent settlements and thus did not create the kinds of stable, freedom ensuring institutions that make growth possible. They go on to suggest that today's institutional and cultural setting can be traced back to decisions made by colonists back then, decisions that explain much of today's current levels of growth or lack thereof. Similarly, Doucouliagos and Ulubasoglu's (2006) meta-analysis of over 40 studies finds a strong and robust link between institutional quality, as proxied by measures of economic freedom (including rule of law and political factors), and economic growth.

As we have just shown, the theoretical and empirical literature among institutional economists is quite rich. Figure 4.3 contrasts the difference between traditional economic perspectives which sometimes focus on the relationship between institutions and development, international business perspectives which often focus on the relationship between MNEs and development, and an integrated perspective which indicates either perspective alone is incomplete without explicitly accounting for both institutions and MNEs. Perhaps the most prominent link in the chain is the

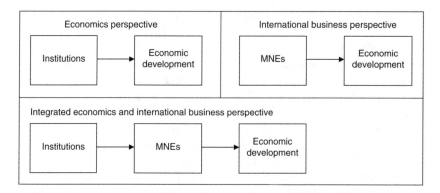

Figure 4.3   Three views of economic development

link between host country institutions and the location choice of MNEs who have made the decision to invest abroad. Much of the study of how institutions impact MNEs involves formal institutions, examples of which include sound political and legal institutions that ensure property rights and an efficient and independent judiciary system, assessments of the threat of government expropriation, regulatory burdens on the opening and operation of businesses, trade barriers, tax levels, the absence of price controls and the presence of sound inflationary policies, the degree of restrictions countries have regarding foreign exchange and capital transfers, the presence of efficient capital markets and private ownership of banks and insurers, the quality of the legal and regulatory framework of a country's labor market, acceptable levels of political risk, and a lack of corruption. Each of these institutions serves as an important determinant of an MNE's location choice. In fact, according to recent A.T. Kearney surveys (2003–2007) of Global 1000 executives, six of the top ten most critical risks to firm operations were related to the performance of a country's institutions, and five of the top six criteria of where to locate research and development operations were also related to institutions.

One of the most commonly studied determinants of location choice is the tax policy of potential host countries. A.T. Kearney (2005) reported that FDI inflows into Germany dropped from US$27.2 billion in 2003 to US$−38.6 billion in 2004 after revisions to the German tax code made it less attractive for foreign companies to retain liquid assets in Germany. Meanwhile, Mooij and Ederveen's (2003) meta-analysis found semi-elasticities ranging from close to zero to as high as 13.75, depending on methodology, with an overall adjusted average of 4.28, meaning FDI drops by 4.28 percent for each 1 percent increase in tax rates.

Another commonly studied determinant, the threat of government expropriation, serves as a constant reminder of the paradox that a government strong enough to protect property rights and enforce contracts is also strong enough to expropriate assets. MNEs will naturally prefer to operate in countries where the risk of nationalization is low. Thus, countries able to provide credible commitments that they will protect the property rights of firms, even from itself – whether it be via the vertical checks and balances of federalism or horizontal competition among different branches of the government – are viewed as more attractive than locations where the commitment is suspect. Brunetti and Weder (1994) and Henisz (2000) go on to note that in some cases, institutions that make it difficult for the government to enact policy changes can further serve to make governmental commitments more credible.

Regarding contract enforcement, in Burkina Faso it typically requires 41 procedures, 446 days, and 95 percent of the debt to collect money owed but not paid. Worldwide, contract enforcement difficulties, crime, bureaucratic regulations and corruption cost firms up to 25 percent of revenue (World Bank, 2005). Regarding corruption, specifically, Stone, Levy, and Paredes (1996) found that 90 percent of small firms, 70 percent of medium firms, and 60 percent of large firms in Brazil admit to paying bribes to government officials and note that Brazil's regulatory quagmire prompts a significant percentage of firms to exit the formal economy and operate in the thriving shadow economy. Consequently, efficiencies related to economies of scale are purposely avoided, as firms balance profitability with conscious attempts to remain small enough to not be noticed. Firms from home countries with laws forcing them to adhere to domestic norms, such as laws that prohibit them from offering graft, face a different set of consequences, as they may find themselves at a disadvantage vis-à-vis firms who operate under different moral codes and may, thus, decide to simply avoid especially corrupt countries. Indeed, Mauro's (1995) seminal study bears that assertion out, showing how corruption cripples investment, and lowered investment reduces growth.

Globerman and Shapiro (2002) suggest that good governance increases FDI inflows, while Kauffman et al. (1999) show that political instability and violence, government ineffectiveness, high regulatory burdens, weak rule of law, and graft each negatively affect FDI inflows. Using fuzzy-set analysis, Pajunen (2008) mentions many of the same institutional determinants, suggesting equifinality, with different attractive institutional mixes leading to improved FDI inflows. And Bennassy et al. (2005: 4) pointedly note that, 'good institutions almost always increase the amount of FDI received'. Overall, these literature streams suggest that institutions and MNEs affect development, and that institutions affect MNE decisions to enter specific foreign markets. Thus, we propose the following:

Proposition 1: The perceived quality of a nation's institutions affects the level of MNE investment.

Informal social norms also affect the conduct of firms. In his examination of institutional effects on managerial discretion in 24 countries, Crossland (2007) refers to Hambrick and Finkelstein (1987) and House, Hanges, Javidan, Dorfman, and Gupta's (2004) GLOBE dimension of institutional collectivism while suggesting that the normative constraints on unilateral managerial discretion are dependent upon the acceptance of powerful stakeholders and the society the MNE is embedded in. Elsewhere Crossland and Hambrick (2007) specifically examine Japan, noting that societal tendencies embracing consensus, inclusiveness, and risk-aversion help explain their finding that executive discretion is severely constrained there versus Germany and, especially, the US; they then refer to Abegglen and Stalk's (1985) observation of the frequent use of terms like *ringisho* (management by consensus) and *nemawashi* (prior consultation) among Japanese managers, and to Porter's suggestion that relatively homogeneous MNE strategies and performance in Japan are inertial (Porter et al., 2000). Thus, if a CEO feels as if his or her firm is operating in a competitive environment where they need to be able to quickly make unilateral decisions without having to build internal coalitions and lobby for the support of others before acting, he/she may feel limited by this informal institutional constraint and may, therefore, decide to avoid entering such countries altogether.

Another example of firms acting in accordance with prevailing social norms comes from Doh, Howton and Howton (2008) who find that institutional endorsement of socially responsible behavior may positively affect shareholder wealth, and note that Orlitzky, Schmidt, and Rynes' (2003) meta-analysis concludes that good corporate citizens are more likely to be rewarded than punished. If a firm, then, is about to undertake activities that go against the grain of socially acceptable behavior in certain countries, for example stem cell research or genetic engineering in a country opposed to such practices, then it would certainly wish to avoid moving related operations to those countries.

Witt and Lewin (2007), and Kedia, Clampit and Gaffney (2009), examine the fit between MNE goals and institutional mandates more directly, via the construct of institutional misalignment (that is misalignment between MNE goals and institutions), suggesting that firms do actively consider the degree to which institutional constraints affect their ability to optimally conduct the tasks needed to fulfill various stakeholder obligations. The previously discussed link between institutional characteristics as determinants of MNE investment has been an especially active area of research. It is our view that there are many facets of the relationship between institutions and MNEs that still offer rich avenues for further study, one of which is based upon this idea of fit between MNE goals and institutional mandates, whether formal or informal. We have touched upon some of the existing literature offering evidence related to the importance of alignment, or lack thereof, between these MNE goals and institutional constraints. Based on this evidence, we propose the following:

Proposition 2: The fit between industry goals and a nation's institutions is directly related to the level of investment by MNEs within those industries.

Once an MNE has entered a market, how exactly does it affect development? We suggest two basic channels by which MNEs facilitate economic development, one path with endogenous mediation and another with exogenous mediation. An example of an endogenous effect is the salary paid to a worker in a job that previously did not exist, or a higher salary paid to a worker who made less at his or her previous job. Examples of exogenous effects include spillovers along the lines of linkages with external buyers, suppliers, or sources of capital, and technology externalities or productivity increases stemming from demonstration effects, movement of skilled employees, and competition effects (Dunning and Fourtanier, 2007; Chauffour, 2009). These spillovers help domestic firms become more productive and prosperous, which has the effect of raising the standard of living in the host country, and may even prompt more ambitious domestic firms to decide to internationalize themselves (Globerman and Shapiro, 1999; Kedia et al., 2005). Thus, we propose the following:

Proposition 3(a): The relationship between MNEs and economic development is mediated by endogenous development channels.

Proposition 3(b): The relationship between MNEs and economic development is mediated by exogenous development channels.

Figure 4.4 suggests that institutions moderate the relationships between MNEs and both endogenous and exogenous development channels. For example, local wage regulations may cause firms to pay higher salaries than they otherwise might. Regarding exogenous effects, the question of whether spillovers are usually more positive than not is unanswered in the minds of many. Globerman and Shapiro (1999) claim that it is the presence of high quality institutions that not only attract FDI, but create favorable conditions for domestic companies to emerge, learn from foreign firms, and subsequently venture abroad themselves. Others, however, sometimes

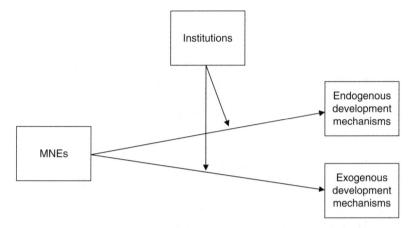

Figure 4.4   Institutions, MNEs and development mechanisms

point to spillovers not emerging or actually having negative effects, for example the crowding of domestic firms by fitter foreign entrants. A meta-analysis conducted by Görg and Strobl (2001) found 13 studies generally finding support for the existence of positive spillovers, four suggesting negative spillovers (such as the crowding out of local businesses), and four that found mixed results. The question, then, if positive spillovers do not automatically happen, is: what can host country institutions do to positively moderate the relationship between MNEs and their endogenous and exogenous effects?

Buckley et al. (2007), finding a curvilinear relationship for some spillovers in China with geographical proximity and the level of technology as moderators, suggest that China should not promote high inward FDI in low-technology industries. Tian (2007) studies 11 324 firms in China and concludes that positive technology spillovers occurred through tangible versus intangible assets (such as patents, copyrights), through domestically consumed products rather than exported products, through traditional rather than new products, and through MNEs employing unskilled rather than skilled workers. Negative spillovers, meanwhile, occurred through exports and through the employment of skilled workers.

Moran et al. (2005) find that openness is the main modifier, along with absorptive capacity, suggesting that when host countries impose restrictions on MNEs moving operations there (such as forcing MNEs to partner with local firms, or requiring the use of domestic content), MNEs may still find the country profitable enough to enter, but may avoid bringing their best technologies or linking to their best sourcing networks. This suggests that while wage regulations and partner requirements may seem, on the surface, to encourage high wages and linkages to domestic firms that spur technology spillovers, the opposite may in fact be true. In the end, if countries are too restrictive in their quest for spillovers, it seems that spillovers do not materialize. In our opinion, we still have much to learn about the exact nature of how, when, and to what degree institutions affect MNE conduct after entering a market, but the evidence does currently allow us to propose the following:

Proposition 4: The relationship between MNEs and endogenous development channels is moderated by the quality of a nation's institutions.

Proposition 5: The relationship between MNEs and exogenous development channels is moderated by the quality of a nation's institutions.

LINKING DEVELOPMENT AND THE ENVIRONMENT

Adaptation Concerns

The IPCC formally defines adaptation as an 'adjustment in natural or human systems in response to actual or expected climatic stimuli or their effects, to moderate harm or exploit beneficial opportunities' that includes 'anticipatory and reactive adaptation, private and public adaptation, and autonomous and planned adaptation'. Adaptation issues in the context of global poverty revolve around the disproportionate burden of the effects of climate change borne by poor countries, as they are less equipped to successfully cope with projected changes in the frequency, intensity, and/or duration of environmentally related shocks. Not only do many developing nations lack the funds and proper institutional framework to adequately manage the consequences of climate change, many are also located in especially vulnerable areas, such as tropical regions already prone to severe weather.

Hurricane Katrina's devastation of New Orleans in the US shows that even in rich nations, the effects of natural disaster can be large. If those predicting an increase in the frequency and intensity of natural disasters are correct, devastation of this magnitude may be repeated with unfortunate regularity in countries around the globe that are even less prepared to protect against such shocks in advance or rebuild in their aftermath. For example, Fisher (2009) notes that climate change may cause more earthquakes and volcano eruptions. A comparison of the 2010 earthquakes in Haiti, versus those in Taiwan, Japan, and Chile, vividly illustrates the difference between relatively wealthy countries, which are better prepared to protect against disaster, and poorer countries. The Chilean earthquake, for instance, was over 500 times as powerful as the Haitian quake, but over 200 times as many people died in Haiti (Bajack, 2010). Part of the reason was geographical proximity to population centers – Haiti's earthquake was centered near its capitol, Port-au-Prince, and was also closer to the surface. But it is no coincidence that when disaster strikes, more people die in poor countries than in richer ones. For example, San Francisco's 1989 Loma Prieta earthquake, a quake seismologists say was almost identical to Haiti's, killed less than 100 people (Eberhart-Phillips et al., 1994).

Furthermore, the vulnerability of many developing nations to gradual environmental changes that arise as a result of shifting climates (such as rising water levels displacing coastal populations or increased rainfall increasing malaria breeding grounds), as opposed to shocks, is also higher than that of developed nations. Some of the same institutions that promote poverty alleviation may help increase the adaptive capacity of these nations and, thus, decrease their vulnerability to the negative consequences of climate change.

Mitigation Concerns

Mitigation is defined by the IPCC as human intervention aimed at reducing the sources or enhancing the sinks of greenhouse gases. When discussed in conjunction with issues related to global poverty, debate seems to center around two primary issues related to equity: who should bear the monetary costs of mitigation and should developing nations have a right to emit. Lines are often drawn along rough geographical perspectives labeled *North* and *South*, with the Northern perspective viewing equity as 'meaningful participation' by all countries; in other words they wish to ensure that developed countries do not shoulder a disproportionate monetary or regulatory burden vis-à-vis the rest of the world. For example, with the global financial crisis in full bloom it is only natural that some in this camp are more concerned than ever that the migration of manufacturing jobs to developing countries may accelerate if those countries are not bound by a similar level of environmental constraint.

Meanwhile, the Southern perspective views equity as 'redistributive social justice' (Richards, 2003). According to this perspective, developed countries have not only been responsible for most of the greenhouse gas emissions up to this point in human history, the gap between emissions from developing and developed countries is actually widening. In short, they are saying, 'you caused the problem and should therefore be the ones who fix it'. Proponents also claim that developing countries have a right to

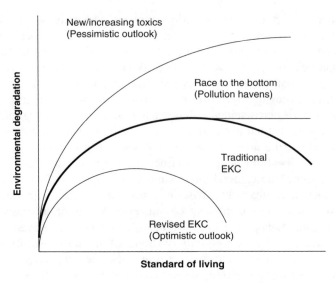

Source: adapted from Dasgupta (2002) and Stern (2004)

Figure 4.5   Alternate environmental Kuznets curves (EKC) outlooks

emit in order to develop to a point where the basic human needs of their population are satisfied, that is they should be given the same opportunity to develop as developed nations had. This perspective therefore tends to favor per capita, rather than per country, limits on emissions. Until those espousing both Northern and Southern views come to agreement, it is likely that the impact of environmental conferences such as those held in Kyoto or Copenhagen will be muted and, at times, merely symbolic rather than truly substantive.

EKCs – A Possible Solution?

The Environmental Kuznets Curve (EKC) hypothesis predicts a curvilinear relationship between a society's standard of living (often per capita levels of income or GDP) and environmental quality. The traditional EKC curve in Figure 4.5 suggests that while societies do pollute more as they begin to develop, at a certain point the curve turns downward and environmental degradation decreases.

   The first EKC study – though the term had yet to be coined – may have been conducted by Frederick Brodie who, in 1905, found a relationship between coal smoke emissions that grew until 1890 and then fell, as rising incomes brought about subsequent social, legal, and technological changes that helped reverse the rise (Clay and Troesken, 2010). The first modern empirical study of the EKC was conducted by Grossman and Kreueger (1991). Shortly thereafter, Panayotou (1993) coined the term Environmental Kuznets Curve, due to its resemblance in shape to Kuznet's (1955) original inverted-U shaped curve that was used to describe the relationship between a society's level of economic development and income inequality. Bhagawati (1993) and Shafik and Bandyopadhyay (1992) suggested that development was a precondition for environmental improvement, and since then a host of EKC-related studies have been conducted in an attempt to confirm its existence, determine under what conditions it occurs, and discover the various inflection points for different types of environmental phenomena (Dinda, 2004).

The general thinking is that during the early stages of development societies lack the resources, knowledge, and desire to bring about positive environmental change, and are apt to move away from cleaner agrarian economies to polluting industrial economies. Quite simply, they tend to feel that they have more pressing needs, as per Maslow's Hierarchy, than those related to sustainability (Arrow et al., 1995; Dasgupta et al., 2002). Environmental initiatives are, so to speak, a luxury good, and development, at this stage, is directly related to environmental degradation. Eventually, however, degradation stops and reverses. Figure 4.6 summarizes three key theoretical mechanisms which are often used to explain why this may be the case: increased environmental concern, increased environmental capacity, and more environmentally friendly consumption.

Bimonte (2009) confirms the hypothesized linear relationship between rising levels of prosperity and environmental concern within OECD countries, while Dasgupta (2002) confirms the relationship in 31 randomly selected countries (including countries that are poor and rich, large and small, and in every region of the world). Relative to undeveloped societies, concerned societies tend to favor doing business with firms that offer environmentally friendly products and services, while employing environmentally friendly processes. They also tend to favor laws and regulations that help promote positive environmental stewardship. Countries with well specified and enforced property rights also provide additional incentive to properly care for land, as vested interests replace tragedy-of-the-commons scenarios more frequently related to societies with lower levels of private property (Yandle, 2004).

More prosperous societies also tend to possess greater capacities for environmental mitigation. Not only do societies now have more resources, the cost of environmentally sound practices may decrease as well. For example, Managi (2006) finds the presence of increasing returns in the form of abatement efficiency rising faster than scale, rendering it less costly

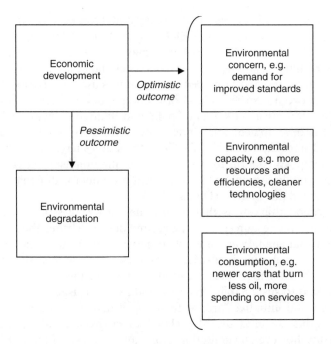

Figure 4.6   Environmental outcomes associated with development

and, subsequently, prompting increased levels of abatement. Andreoni and Levinson (2001), similarly, combine basic supply and demand theory to explain economies of scale in pollution control, increasing the efficiency levels, and lowering the costs, associated with environmental quality recovery efforts. Liberalization efforts, meanwhile, may lead to increased levels of operating efficiency, with less environmental resources required per unit of output, in addition to FDI-related spillovers in clean technologies (Dinda, 2004).

Finally, consumption in developed societies tends to be cleaner. For example, the ratio of new to old cars is higher, with new cars emitting less greenhouse gases. Moreover, at this stage of development societies tend to naturally transition from industrial to more service oriented economies (Panayotou et al., 1995). In summary, if the optimistic outcome occurs, then at later stages of development societies move away from less environmentally friendly manufacturing industries into cleaner service industries, care more about environmental issues, and are more likely to have the resources to fund environmental initiatives (Pezzey, 1989; Selden and Song, 1994; Baldwin, 1995, Dasgupta et al., 2001). In short, the term 'sustainable development' will not be a misnomer built upon the tendency of people to readily accept attractive improbabilities over unattractive probabilities, but an important and realistic goal.

There is a problem with the EKC, however: the empirical record is, quite simply, mixed. While studies of local water or air quality indicators that negatively impact human health generally support the EKC hypothesis, studies of pollutants that affect climate change (such as carbon dioxide) offer mixed results (Cavlovic, 2000; Li, Grijalva and Berrens, 2007), with some scholars, notably Stern (2004), definitively calling its validity into question on methodological grounds. Furthermore, when the EKC relationship is found, the variation among the exact shape and income turning points is often quite large. For example, while Dasgupta et al. (2002) and Dinda (2004) suggest that for most pollution indicators, the income turning point lies within US$5000–8000 and US$3000–10 000 respectively, others suggest income turning points for some pollutants approaching upwards of US$200 000 (Cavlovic, 2000), a figure that, for all intents and purposes, might as well be infinity, as it is hardly reasonable to expect developing nations to achieve per capita incomes that high anytime soon, if ever.

A number of more recent studies, however, several of which attempt to adress Stern's (2004) issues of methodology, seem more hopeful. Employing standard reduced form modeling with panel data, controlling for country specific unobserved heterogeneity, Tamazian et al. (2009) found EKC evidence in BRIC countries (Brazil, Russia, India and China), noting that liberalization and openness are essential to reduce carbon dioxide. Robustness checks in the US and Japan did not alter findings. Lee, Chiu, and Sun (2009), meanwhile, find evidence of the EKC hypothesis for carbon dioxide emissions in a global data set, middle-income, and American and European countries (but not in other income levels and regions).

Employing Bayesian econometric analysis of 47 countries, 34 explanatory variables, and three pollution proxies over a period of 20 years, Lamla (2009) confirms the EKC hypothesis and notes that while the inflection point for carbon dioxide is high (US$50 000 per capita GDP), it is markedly less than figures found by others employing older methodological techniques. Noting that conditional mean estimation is sensitive to outliers and can mask heterogeneities present at high and low emission levels, Flores, Flores-Lagunes, and Kapetanakis (2009) employ conditional-quantile panel fixed effects model analysis, finding that conditional mean methods provide outcomes that are, at times, both too optimistic and too pessimistic, depending on the specific type of pollutant in question.

Galeotti, Lanza, and Pauli (2006) find that when alternative functional forms are employed to the same data analyzed by others who did not find an EKC for carbon dioxide, EKCs appear with reasonable turning points for both OECD countries (regardless of the data set examined) and non-OECD countries (with some data sets). Galeotti, Manera, and Lanza (2009) note that while some object to EKC findings based on methods that use cointegrated unit roots among time series data, tests of system fractional integration and cointegration show that some carbon dioxide EKCs that were previously dismissed come back to life.

Overall, then, it seems that: (1) EKCs probably exist for non-greenhouse gas pollutants, (2) the evidence for greenhouse gas-based EKCs is mixed, but more hopeful than it was just a few years ago, and (3) the underlying mechanisms of inflection do seem to be fairly well defined, whether the inflection materializes at a reasonably low point or not. Therefore, we propose the following:

Proposition 6 (a): There is a direct relationship between a country's level of economic development and the amount of concern for the environment its citizens have.

Proposition 6 (b): There is a direct relationship between a country's level of economic development and its capacity to mitigate environmental degradation.

Proposition 6 (c): There is a direct relationship between a country's level of economic development and the amount of consumption that is not harmful to the environment.

Figure 4.5 (see earlier) illustrates several competing scenarios regarding the true relationship between environmental degradation and a society's standard of living. The 'race to the bottom' hypothesis (also referred to as displacement or pollution haven hypotheses) claims that firms from developed countries simply export their pollution producing activities to countries that gladly welcome them in hopes of improving living standards, regardless of downstream environmental consequences. In other words, even when EKC relationships are found, the reduction of environmental degradation in one country does not translate into global reduction but, instead, merely reflects a transfer of dirty industries to the developing world, where weaker environmental regulations may be viewed locally as a source of comparative advantage (Copeland and Taylor, 1995; Cole et al., 2000; Dinda, 2004). Dasgupta (2002), however, notes that available empirical evidence strongly suggests that this view is, on the whole, unwarranted, with studies often showing that the opposite is actually happening, that is exceptions aside, MNEs generally tend to improve environmental operating procedures inside host countries. Similarly, Kearsley and Riddel's (2010) study of seven common pollutants also failed to support the pollution haven hypothesis.

The 'new toxics' scenario envisions the creation of new pollutants added to the mix. Thornton (2000), for example, suggests that less well-known pollutant levels, such as toxic organochlorines introduced into the air and water, may rise with incomes in developing countries. At the other end of the spectrum lies the revised EKC, which represents more optimistic empirical work suggesting that the curve is actually dropping and shifting to the left as developing nations pollute less than was originally hypothesized, due to shifting away from manufacturing towards cleaner service industries sooner rather than later and adopting cleaner technologies, for example (Dasgupta et al., 2002).

One belief that does seem to be shared by both more optimistic and more pessimistic scholars is that economic development does not inherently guarantee improved environmental performance. Arrow et al. (1995), Lamla (2009), and Yandle, Bhattarai, and Vijayaraghavan (2004) suggest that when EKCs are found, we also often find institutions that: (1) enhance property rights and help avoid tragedy-of-the-commons situations, (2) increase the ability of resource users to properly interpret market signals, increase efficiency, and reduce waste, and (3) compel private users to account for the social costs of their activities when negative externalities arise.

Dasgupta (2002) specifically notes the role of eliminating government subsidies, resulting in improved levels of efficiency in terms of resource allocation and reduced roles for many of the heaviest polluters that are often privy to subsidies, such as steel and chemical companies. He also notes that liberalization tends to bring in cleaner, labor heavy business such as garment production, spillovers of cleaner (and often more profitable) technologies, and scale increases resulting in more operating efficiency.

As overall evidence regarding EKCs is still somewhat mixed, we believe that it will be fruitful to search for undiscovered interactions and further explore moderators we already suspect may be important. As the literature seems to point towards the importance of institutions as moderators, we propose the following:

Proposition 7 (a): There is a direct relationship between the degree to which a country's institutions adequately specify and enforce of property rights and the amount of environmental concern in that country.

Proposition 7 (b): There is a direct relationship between the degree to which a country's institutions regulate environmental activity and the level of environmental performance in that country.

Proposition 7 (c): Institutions moderate the relationship between economic development and environmental performance.

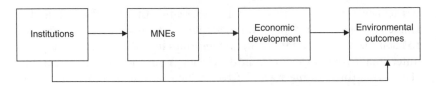

Figure 4.7   Institutions, MNEs, development and environmental outcomes

INTEGRATED FRAMEWORK

Figure 4.7 merges the constructs discussed throughout this chapter into an integrated model, with growth oriented institutions tending to attract MNE investment, which tends to uplift standards of living via direct mechanisms such as monetary compensation for the performance of jobs that did not previously exist, and also via indirect channels such as positive spillover effects. This resultant development, however, has environmental consequences which may be positive or negative. Various institutions and MNE activity may also affect environmental outcomes, such as laws which increase environmental standards or encourage more efficient resource use, and spillovers of clean technology.

While ultimate findings may not yet be definitive, some empirical evidence does tend to support the notion that there is, in the long run at least, a direct relationship between development and environmental performance. Unfortunately, the area where findings exhibit the greatest lack of consensus happens to be an area that is quite important. We are referring, of course, to the effect of development on climate change. Still, there is hope, and based on the evidence we have, we propose the following:

Proposition 8: There is a direct long run relationship between institutional quality, MNE entry, economic development, and environmental performance.

CONCLUSION

Prior to 1700, the world's richest countries were roughly two to three times wealthier than the world's poorest countries. Currently, the richest countries are roughly 60 times wealthier, with the income gap increasing by the day (Parente, 2008). The good news is that the rate at which countries can catch up those ahead of them is faster today than ever. With regard to possible solutions to global poverty, international business scholars have written extensively about the link between MNEs and the standard of living of the populations they invest in. Economists, meanwhile, have written extensively about the link between a nation state's institutional framework and the standard of living of its population. Together, we seem to have a rough idea as to what works – we know that certain institutional antecedents, such as rule of law, seem to be prerequisites for sustained economic growth. And we have numerous models to follow. The Asian Tigers, for example, doubled GDP in less than a decade. In both the developing and developed world, countries like Botswana, Chile, and Ireland have also shown how rapidly standards of living can rise when classically liberal institutional frameworks encourage MNEs to enter and pursue strategies that facilitate local growth.

Today, countries like Estonia seem to be on the right track, despite inevitable bumps on the road toward sustained prosperity. *FDI Magazine*'s annual European Cities and Regions of the Future Awards recently named Tallinn the city with the second most economic potential in Europe (*FDI Magazine*, 2008). As former Prime Minister of Estonia the Honorable Mart Laar (2008) recounts, substantive political reform (that is, genuinely open and transparent democracy, versus the veneer of reform seen in other countries), followed by economic reform (aimed at stabilizing and then liberalizing the economy, while exhibiting strong fiscal discipline), helped bring about both rising levels of prosperity and decreased levels of income inequality, with GDP per capita rising from roughly US$2000 in the late 1980s to over US$20000 in 2007. Regarding the recent economic setbacks that have affected much of the world – and Estonia is no exception – *FDI Magazine* (2009: 1) notes that 'Estonia's response to the economic crisis has been indicative of how extraordinarily flexible, efficient and nonrestrictive its economy is – traits that endear the small, nimble country to foreign investors'. While they are not where they want to be yet, Estonia is yet another country that has shown that it is possible for countries to greatly improve living standards in a relatively short amount of time.

Roughly knowing what works in a general sense, however, is not the same thing as knowing what will work in a specific context, nor is it the same thing as actually doing what works. Just because Estonia followed the lead of other nations that moved from poverty to relative prosperity, fostering an environment that attracted MNEs like Sony Ericsson and gave rise to innovative domestic firms like Skype, that does not mean other poor countries will do the same. The fact remains that many things are easier said than actually done, and the devil in the detail here is the fact that countries possess idiosyncratic histories, cultures, and levels of entrenched interests, each of which may demand the tailoring of institutions to local contexts, and each of which may either reinforce or undermine hopes of substantive reform.

Hopefully the rest of the world will be inspired enough by the plethora of success stories to follow the lead of countries who have escaped poverty. And as these countries develop, hopefully the same institutional frameworks that foster economic development will encourage further development that is sustainable and environmentally friendly, as the optimistic channels illustrated in Figure 4.6 (such as increasing levels of environmental concern among the populace) become stronger and more prevalent.

Cropper and Griffiths (1994), Panayoutou (1997) and Bhattarai and Hammig (2001) suggest that this is precisely what may happen, as they link institutions associated with poverty alleviation to eventual downturns in a nation's respective EKC (as opposed to the more pessimistic displacement and new toxics scenarios). Meanwhile, after accounting for methodological issues pointed out by various EKC critics, several scholars (Galeotti et al., 2009) provide newfound hope that EKCs are more robust than some had thought, and that EKCs for greenhouse gases, with relatively low inflection points, may materialize as well. Gwartney and Lawson (2008), and Holmes, Feulner, and O'Grady (2009) show direct, linear relationships between various measures of institutional quality and the 2008 Environmental Performance Index. So there is some evidence that institutions that foster growth may also facilitate genuine improvements in environmental performance.

In this paper we examined literature related to development, sustainability, MNEs, and institutions. We hoped to inform each stream of literature by developing an integrated framework that holistically explored the rich, interrelated nature of the relationship between these topics. In the end, whether one's view of the future is optimistic, or one believes the overall evidence is somewhat mixed and the future, thus, muddy, there is still hope that sustainability and development are not mutually exclusive. As scholars, hopefully we can collectively continue to uncover patterns and relationships that seem to move us toward both ends. Sustainable development is simply too important a goal to not strive for with the utmost vigor.

REFERENCES AND SELECT BIBLIOGRAPHY

Abegglen J. and G. Stalk (1985), *Kaisha: The Japanese Corporation*, New York: Basic Books, Inc.

Acemoglu, D., S. Johnson and J.A. Robinson (2001), 'The colonial origins of comparative development: an empirical investigation', *American Economic Review*, **91**:1369–401.

Albert, M. (1993), *Capitalism against capitalism*, London: Whurr.

Alston, L., T. Eggertsson and D. North (1996), *Empirical Studies in Institutional Change*, New York, USA: Cambridge University Press.

Andreoni, J. and A. Levinson (2001), 'The simple analytics of the environmental Kuznet's curve', *Journal of Public Economics*, **80**(2), 269–86

Arrow, K. et al. (1995), 'Economic growth, carrying capacity, and the environment', *Science*, **15**, 91–95 (reprinted in *Ecological Economics*).

A.T. Kearney (2003–07), FDI Confidence Index report.

Bajak, F. (2010), 'Chile earthquake 2010: why the Haiti earthquake wasn't as strong, but far more devastating', Huffington Post, 27 February 2010.

Baldwin, R. (1995), 'Does sustainability require growth?', in I. Goldin and L.A. Winters (eds), *The Economics of Sustainable Development*, Cambridge, UK: Cambridge University Press, pp. 19–47.

Barro, R. (1996), 'Democracy and growth,' *Journal of Economic Growth*, **1**(1).

Barro, R. (2007), 'Inequality and growth revisited', paper presented at ADB Distinguished Visitor Forum, September 2007.

Benassy Quere, Fontagne, and Lahreche-Revil (2005), 'How does FDI react to Corporate Taxation?', *International Tax and Public Finance*, **12**.

Bernanke, B. (2002), 'On Milton Friedman's nintieth birthday', presentation to Conference to Honor Milton Friedman, Chicago, IL, accessed from www.federalreserve.gov.

Bhagwati, J. (2007), 'Why multinationals help reduce poverty', *The World Economy (2007). Journal compilation*, Oxford, UK: Blackwell Publishing.

Bhattarai, M. and M. Hammig (2001), 'Institutions and the Environmental Kuznets Curve for deforestation: a cross-country analysis for Latin America, Africa, and Asia', *World Development*, **29** (6), 995–1010.

Bimonte, S. (2009), 'Growth and environmental quality: testing the double convergence hypothesis', *Ecological Economics*, **68**(8–9), 2406–11.

Borensztein, E., J. Gregorio and J-W. Lee (1998), 'How does foreign direct investment affect economic growth?', *Journal of International Economics*, **45**(1).

Brunetti, A. and B. Weder (2006), 'Political credibility and economic growth in less developed countries', *Constitutional Political Economy*, **5**(1).

Bruton, G.D., G. Dess and J. Janney (2007), 'Knowledge management in technology focused firms in emerging economies: caveats on capabilities, networks, and real options', *Asia Pacific Journal of Management*, **24**(2): 115–30.

Buckley, P., J. Clegg and C. Wang (2007), 'Is the relationship between inward FDI and spillover effects linear? An empirical examination of the case of China', *Journal of International Business Studies*, **38**: 447–69.

Bueno de Mesquita, B. and H. Root (2000), *Governing for Prosperity: When Bad Economics is Good Politics*, New Haven, CT: Yale University Press.

Cavlovic, T.A., K.H. Baker, R.P. Berrens and K. Gawande (2000), 'A meta-analysis of Environmental Kuznets Curve studies', *Agricultural and Resource Economics Review*, **29**(1): 32–42.

Chauffour, J-P. (2009), *The Power of Freedom: Uniting Development and Human Rights*, Washington DC: Cato Institution.

Chandler, A.D. (1990), *Scale and Scope*, Cambridge, MA: Harvard University Press.

Clay, K. and W. Troesken (2010), 'Did Frederick Brodie discover the world's first Environmental Kuznets Curve? Coal smoke and the rise and fall of the London fog', NBER working papers 15669, National Bureau of Economic Research.

Coase, R.H. (1937), 'The nature of the firm', *Economica*, (n.s), **4**(16): pp. 386–405.

Coatsworth, J. (2005), 'Structures, Endowments, and Institutions in the Economic History of Latin America', *Latin American Research Review*, **40**(3): 126–44.

Cole, M.A., R.J.R. Elliott and A.K. Azhar (2000), *The determinants of trade in pollution intensive industries: North–South* evidence, UK: University of Birmingham.

Copeland, B.R. and M.S. Taylor (1995), 'Trade and environment: a partial synthesis', *American Journal of Agricultural Economics*, **77**: 765–71.

Cropper, M. and C. Griffiths (1994), 'The interaction of populations, growth and environmental quality', *American Economic Review*, **84**: 250–54.

Crossland, C. (2007), 'National institutions and managerial discretion: a taxonomy of 24 countries', Academy of Management annual meeting, Philadelphia, PA, August 2007.

Crossland C. and D. Hambrick (2007), 'CEOs and national systems', *Strategic Management Journal*, **28**: 767–89.

Dasgupta, S., A. Mody, S. Roy and D. Wheeler (2001), 'Environmental regulation and development: a cross-country empirical analysis', *Oxford Development Studies*, **29**(2), 173–87.

Dasgupta, S., B. Laplante, H. Wang and D. Wheeler (2002), 'Confronting the Environmental Kuznets Curve', *Journal of Economic Perspectives*, **16**(1), 147–68.

Dinda, S. (2004), 'Environmental Kuznets Curve hypothesis: A survey', *Ecological Economics*, **49**: 431–55.

De Soto, H. (2000), *The Mystery of Capital*, NY: Bantam Press.

Doh, J. and S. Howton (forthcoming), 'Does the market respond to institutional endorsement of social responsibility?', *Journal of Management*.

Doucouliagos, H. and M. Paldam (2009) 'The aid effectiveness literature: the sad results of 40 years of research', *Journal of Economic Surveys*, **23**(3), 433–61.

Doucouliagos, C. and M. Ulubasoglu (2006), 'Economic freedom and economic growth: does specification make a difference?', *European Journal of Political Economy*, **22**.

Dunning, J.H. (1998), 'Location and the multinational enterprise: a neglected factor?', *Journal of International Business Studies*, **40**: 5–19.

Dunning, J.H. and F. Fourtanier (2007), 'Multinational enterprises and the new development paradigm: consequences for host country development', *Multinational Business Review*, **15**(1).

Eberhart-Phillips J.E., T.M. Saunders, A.L. Robinson, D.L. Hatch and R.G. Parrish (1994), 'Profile of mortality from the 1989 Loma Prieta earthquake using coroner and medical examiner reports', *Disasters*, **18**(2): 160–70.

EPA (2008), 'Recent climate change: atmosphere changes', *Climate Change Science Program*, USA: Environmental Protection Agency.

Fisher, R. (2009), 'Climate change may trigger earthquakes and volcanoes', *New Scientist*, Issue 2727.

FDI Magazine (2008), 'European cities and regions of the future'.

FDI Magazine (2009), 'Quick and nimble', 15 October.

Flores, C., A. Flores-Lagunes and D. Kapetanakis (2009), 'Lessons from quantile panel estimation of the Environmental Kuznets Curve', working paper 2010–4, University of Miami, Department of Economics.

Galeotti, M., A. Lanza and F. Pauli (2006), 'Reassessing the Environmental Kuznets Curve for CO_2 emissions: a robustness exercise', *Ecological Economics*, **57**(1).

Galeotti, M. (2007), 'Economic growth and the quality of the environment: taking stock. Environment, development and sustainability', **9**: 427–54.

Galeotti, M., M. Manera and A. Lanza (2009), 'On the robustness of robustness checks of the Environmental Kuznets Curve hypothesis', *Environmental & Resource Economics*, **42**(4): 551–74.

Globerman, S. and D. Shapiro (2002), 'Global foreign direct investment flows: the role of governance infrastructure', *World Development*, **30**(11): 1898–919.

Görg H. and E. Strobl (2001), 'Multinational companies and productivity spillovers: a meta-analysis', *Economic Journal*, **111**(475).

Government of India (2007), 'National Sample Survey', **61**.

Gwartney, J. and R. Lawson (2008), *Economic Freedom of the World: 2008 Annual Report*, Fraser Institute.

Grossman, G.M. and A.B. Krueger (1991), 'Environmental impacts of the North American Free Trade Agreement', NBER working paper 3914.

Hall, R.E. and C. Jones (1999), 'Why do some countries produce much more output per worker than others?', *Quarterly Journal of Economics*, **114**(1): 83–116.

Hall, P.A. and D. Soskice (2001), *An Introduction to Varieties of Capitalism*, Oxford University Press, 1–68.

Hambrick, D. and S. Finkelstein (1987), 'Managerial discretion: a bridge between polar views of organizational outcomes', in B. Staw and L.L. Cummings (eds), *Research in Organizational Behavior*, Greenwich, CT: JAI Press, pp. 369–406.

Henisz, WJ. (2000), 'The institutional environment for multinational investment', *The Journal of Law, Economics, and Organization*, **16**(2).

Hill, C.W. (2007), 'Digital piracy: causes, consequences, and strategic responses', *Asia Pacific Journal of Management*, **24**(1): 9–25.

Holmes, K., E. Feulner and M. O'Grady (2009), *2008 Index of Economic Freedom*, Washington DC and New York: The Heritage Foundation and Dow Jones & Co.

Hoskisson, R., L. Eden, C. Lau and M. Wright (2000), 'Strategy in emerging economies', *The Academy of Management Journal*, **43**(3): 249–67.

House, R., P. Hanges, M. Javidan, P. Dorfman and V. Gupta (2004), 'Leadership, culture, and organizations: the GLOBE study of 62 societies; 2004', Thousand Oaks, CA: Sage.

IPCC (2001), 'Climate Change 2001', IPCC Third Assessment Report.

IPCC (2007), 'Climate Change 2007', IPCC Fourth Assessment Report.

Kaufmann, D., A. Kraay and P. Zoido-Lobatón (1999), 'Governance matters', World Bank policy research working paper no. 2196.

Kearsley, A. and M. Riddel (2010), 'A further inquiry into the Pollution Haven Hypothesis and the Environmental Kuznets Curve', *Ecological Economics*, **69**(4): 905–19.

Kedia, B., J. Clampit and N. Gaffney (2009), 'Prospects for escape: institutional misalignment as a driver for OFDI', presented at the 2009 Academy of International Business.

Kedia, B., R. Mahto and L. Perez-Nordtvelt (2005), 'Role of multinational corporations in poverty reduction', in *Multinational Corporations and Global Poverty Reduction*, Edward Elgar Publishing Ltd.

Klein, M., C. Aaron and B. Hadjimichael (2008), 'Foreign direct investment and poverty reduction', presentation to the GEP Conference on Trade Costs, University of Nottingham, 19–20 June 2009.

Kolk, A. and J. Pinkse (2008), 'A perspective on multinational enterprises and climate change: learning from "an inconvenient truth"?', *Journal of International Business Studies*, **39**(8): 1359.

Konar, S. and M. Cohen (1997), 'Information as regulation: the effect of community right to know laws on toxic emissions', *Journal of Environmental Economics and Management*, **32**: 109–24.

Krugman, P. (1991), 'History versus expectation', *The Quarterly Journal of Economics*, **106**(2).

Krugman, P. (1996), 'Los ciclos en las ideas dominantes con relacion al desarrollo economic', *Desarrollo Economico*, **36**(143): 715–32.

Krugman, P. (2001), 'Reckonings; hearts and heads', *New York Times*, 22 April.

Kwok, C. and S. Tadesse (2006), 'The MNC as an agent of change for host-country institutions: FDI and corruption', *Journal of International Business Studies*, **37** (767–85).

Kuznets, P. and Simon, P. (1955), 'Economic growth and income inequality', *American Economic Review*, **45**: 1–28.

La Porta R., F. Lopez-De-Silanes, A. Schleifer and R.Vishny (1999), 'The quality of government', *The Journal of Law, Economics and Organization*, **15**: 222–79.

Laar, M. (2008), 'The Estonian Economic Miracle', backgrounder #2060, available at www.heritage.org.

Lamla, M.J. (2009), 'Long-run determinants of pollution: a robustness analysis', *Ecological Economics*, **69**(1), 135–44.

Lee, C., Y. Chiu and C. Sun (2009), 'Does one size fit all? A re-examination of the Environmental Kuznets Curve using the dynamic panel data approach', *Review of Agricultural Economics*, **31**(4): 751–78.

Lee, S., M. Peng and J. Barney (2007), 'Bankruptcy law and entrepreneurship development: a real options perspective', *Academy of Management Review*, **32**(1): 257–72.

Lewin, A. and J. Kim (2004), 'Organizational change and innovation', in M.S. Poole and A.H.Y. de Ven (eds), *Handbook of Organizational Change and Innovation*, New York: Oxford University Press, pp. 108–60,

Li, H., T. Grijalva and R. Berrens (2007), 'Economic growth and environmental quality: a meta-analysis of Environmental Kuznets Curve studies', *Economics Bulletin*, **17**(5).

Lodge, G. and C. Wilson (2006), 'Multinational corporations and global poverty reduction', *Challenge*, **49**(3).

Managi, S. (2006), 'Are there increasing returns to pollution abatement? Empirical analytics of the Environmental Kuznets Curve in pesticides', *Ecological Economics*, **58**(3): 617–36.

Meadows, D.H., D.L. Meadows, J. Randers and W. Behrens, (1972), 'The limits to growth: a report for the Club of Rome's project on the predicament of mankind', London: Earth Island.

Mauro, P. (1995), 'Corruption and Growth', *The Quarterly Journal of Economics*, **110**(3): 681–712.

Mooij, R.A.D. and S. Ederveen (2003), 'Taxation and foreign direct investment: a synthesis of empirical research', *International Tax and Public Finance*, **10** 673–93.

Moran, T., M. Graham and M. Blomstrom (2005), *Does Foreign Direct Investment Promote Development?*, Peterson Institute for Economics.

Nolan, B. and T. Smeeding (2005), 'Ireland's income distribution in coparative perspective', *Review of Income and Wealth*, **51**(4).

North, D. and B. Weingast (1989), 'Constitutions and commitment: the evolution of institutions governing public choice in seventeenth-century England', *Journal of Economic History*, **49**: 803–32.

North, D. (1990), *Institutions, Institutional Change, and Economic Performance*, New York: Press Syndicate of the University of Cambridge.

North, D. (2005). *Understanding the Process of Economic Change*, Princeton, NJ: Princeton University Press.

Notten, G. and C. Neubourg (2007), 'Relative or absolute poverty in the USA and EU? The battle of the rates', MGSoG working paper, 2007/001, Maastricht University, Maastricht.

Nove, A. (1969), *An Economic History of the USSR*, London: Allen Lane.

Oliver, C. (1991), 'Strategic responses to institutional processes', *Academy of Management Review*, **16**(1): 145–79

Orlitzky, M., F. Schmidt and S. Rynes (2003), 'Corporate social and financial performance: a meta-analysis', *Organization Studies*, **24**(3): 403–41.

Orru, M. (1997), 'The institutionalist analysis of capitalist economics', in M. Orru et al. (eds), *The Economic Organization of East Asian Capitalism*, Thousand Oaks, CA: Sage.

Pajunen, K. (2008), 'Institutions and inflows of foreign direct investment: a fuzzy-set analysis', *Journal of International Business Studies*, **39**(4).

Panayotou, T. (1993), 'Empirical tests and policy analysis of environmental degradation at different stages of economic development', ILO, Technology and Employment Programme, Geneva.

Panayatou, T., I. Ahmed and J.A. Doeleman (1995), 'Environmental degradation at different stages of economic development', *Technology Environment and Employment Geneva International Labour Office*, 13–36

Parente, S. (2008), 'Narrowing the economic gap in the 21st century', in *2008 Index of Economic Freedom*, Washington DC and New York: The Heritage Foundation and Dow Jones & Co, Inc.

Peng, Mike W., Denis Wang and Yi Jiang (2008), 'An institution-based view of international business strategy: a focus on emerging economies, *Journal of International Business Studies*, 39(5), 920–36.

Pezzey, J.C.V. (1989), 'Economic analysis of sustainable growth and sustainable development', Environment Department working paper 15, World Bank.

Poole, William (2007), 'Milton and money stock control', Milton Friedman Luncheon, co-sponsored by the University of Missouri-Columbia Department of Economics, the Economic and Policy Analysis Research Center, and the Show-Me Institute.

Porter, M.E., H. Takeuchi and M. Sakakibara (2000), *Can Japan Compete?*, Basic Books/Perseus Publications, p. 208.

Putnam, R., R. Leonardi and R. Nanetti (1993), *Making Democracy Work: Civic Traditions in Modern Italy*, Princeton, NJ: Princeton University Press.

Redding, G. (2005), 'The thick description and comparison of societal systems of capitalism', *Journal of International Business Studies*, **36**(2): 123–55.

Reuters (2006), 'Walmart eyes carbon bounty in its supply chain', 31 October available at http://www.climos.com/news/articles/walmarteyes.htm

Richards, M. (2003), 'Poverty reduction, equity and climate change: global governance synergies or contradictions?', Overseas Development Institute: Globalisation and Poverty Programme.

Rugman, A.M. and A. Verbeke (1998), 'Corporate strategies and environmental regulations: an organizing framework', *Strategic Management Journal*, **19**(4), 363–75

Sachs, J. and A. Warner (1999), 'The big push, natural resource booms and growth', *Journal of Development Economics*, **59**.

Selden, T. and D. Song (1994), 'Environmental quality and development: is there a Kuznets Curve for air pollution emissions?', *Journal of Environmental Economics and Management*, **27**, 147–62.

Shafik, N. and S. Bandyopadhyay (1992), 'Economic growth and environmental quality: time series and cross-country evidence', background paper for the World Development Report, Washington, DC: The World Bank.

Smeeding, T. (2006), 'Poor people in rich nations: the United States in comparative perspective', *Journal of Economic Perspectives*, **20**(1).

Smith, A. (1776), *An Inquiry into the Nature and Causes of the Wealth of Nations*, republished 1902, New York: Collier and Son.

Stern, D.I. (2004), 'The rise and fall of the Environmental Kuznets Curve', *World Development*, **32**: 1419–39.

Stone, A., B. Levy and R. Paredes (1996), 'Public institutions and private transactions', in *Empirical Studies in Institutional Change*, New York: Cambridge University Press.

Tamazian, A., J. Chousa and K. Vadlamannati (2009), 'Does higher economic and financial development lead to environmental degradation? Evidence from BRIC countries', *Energy Policy*, **37**(1), 246–53.

Thornton, J. (2000), *Pandora's Poison: Chlorine, Health, and a New Environmental Strategy*, Cambridge: MIT Press.

Tian, X. (2007), 'Accounting for sources of FDI technology spillovers: evidence from China', *Journal of International Business Studies*, **38**: 147–59.

Wade, R. (1990), *Governing the Market*, Princeton: Princeton University Press.

Wallace, J. and D. North (1986), 'Measuring the transaction sector in the American economy', in *Long Term Factors of Economic Growth*, Chicago: University of Chicago Press.

Wan, W., and R.E. Hoskisson (2003), 'Home country environments, corporate diversification strategies, and firm performance', *Academy of Management Journal*, **46**(1): 27–45.

Whitley, R. (1999), *Divergent capitalisms: the social structuring and change of business systems*, Oxford University Press.

Williamson, O. (1981), 'The economics of organization: the transaction cost approach', *The American Journal of Sociology*, **87**(3): 548–77.

Witt, M. and A. Lewin (2007), 'Outward foreign direct investment as escape response to home country institutional constraints', *Journal of International Business Studies*, **38**: 578–95.

World Bank (2006–2008), *World Development Indicators*, Washington DC: World Bank.

World Bank (2008), 'Rising food prices: policy options and World Bank response', available at http://siteresources.worldbank.org/NEWS/Resources/risingfood-prices_backgroundnote_apr08.pdf

World Bank (2009), 'E. Europe and C. Asia: crisis pushing people back into poverty', available at http://worldbank.or/html/extdr/financialcrisis

World Commission on Environment and Development (1987), *Our common future*, Oxford: Oxford University Press, p. 43.

Yandle, B., M. Bhattarai and M. Vijayaraghavan (2004), 'Environmental Kuznets Curves: a review of findings, methods, and policy implications', PERC research study No. 02-1.

5. The effect of technology type on the adoption and effectiveness of global environmental standards

Glen Dowell and Ben Lewis

INTRODUCTION

Fitting with the theme of this volume, we are interested in explaining firms' environmental performance, and factors affecting firms' abilities to improve that performance. We investigate the role of technology as a factor in influencing firms' environmental strategies. We also consider whether a firm's primary technology type is a moderating factor between its global environmental strategy and its financial performance.

Much of the prior literature on corporate environmental performance has considered the link between environmental performance and profit (see Orlitzky, Schmidt, and Rynes, 2003 for one of many reviews of this topic). If the broad message from the numerous studies of environmental and financial performance is that it can pay to be green (or perhaps, that it does not have to cost to be green), the bigger question that remains may be 'when *does* it pay to be green?' Embedded in that question, we believe, is the question of which organizations will have a greater ability to improve their environmental performance, and what role does a firm's industry and core technology play in its ability to improve its environmental performance (Schaltegger and Synnestvedt, 2002).

We argue that understanding environmental performance is, by itself, important for organizational scholars. That is, we need to understand the factors that affect environmental performance regardless of the link between financial performance and environmental factors. Margolis and Walsh (2003) argue forcefully for this perspective, as they suggest that the emphasis on understanding how social responsibility affects profit 'leaves unexplored questions about what it is firms are actually doing in response to social misery and what effects corporate actions have, not only on the bottom line but also on society'.

Below, we describe the role of technological change and technology type in affecting environmental performance. We argue that one of the key constraints on a firm's ability to improve its environmental performance is the technology in which it is embedded. We develop hypotheses regarding the influence of technology type on a firm's global environmental strategy, and test these hypotheses using a panel of MNEs. We find that technology type does influence a firm's global environmental strategy, and the financial return associated with using a global environmental standard.

TECHNOLOGY TYPE

In this chapter we follow the model proposed by Tushman and Rosenkopf (1992) and conceptualize technological complexity as a typology of products ranging from simple to complex. This typology includes four product types as shown in Table 5.1: (1) non-assembled products; (2) simple assembled products; (3) closed systems; and (4) open systems.

Non-assembled products consist of raw materials that are transformed through a series of sequentially linked steps or manufacturing subprocesses (such as chemical, thermal, or machining). Examples of non-assembled products include aluminum, steel, glass, and petroleum. Because of their simplistic nature, the performance of such products are evaluated on relatively simple unidimensional scales of efficiency and value (such as price/unit or price/performance). While technological progress can be made through process or product improvements, such decisions are largely made at the managerial level with minimal sociopolitical influence.

Simple assembled products are made up of distinct subsystems that fit together through a set of interlinked steps that are sequentially ordered. Examples include stoves, guns, skis, and books. Like non-assembled products, the performance criteria for simple assembled products are clear and easily measured (such as price/unit or price/performance). Technological progress occurs through process innovation or product substitution as technical considerations dominate organizational considerations in the quest for superior alternative processes or inputs.

Composed of various subsystems, assembled systems are much more complex than non-assembled or simple assembled products. Assembled systems can be conceptualized into two distinct classes: closed and open systems. Closed systems are bounded and often produced by a single organization whereas open systems are unbounded and produced by networks of organizations. Examples of closed systems include watches, automobiles, and airplanes. Because there are multiple subsystems, performance evaluation is much more complex as the overall

Table 5.1   Technology types

Technology type	Examples	Process	Performance Criteria	Influences on Change
Non-assembled	Aluminum, steel, glass, gears, paper, fibers, petroleum, springs	Chemical, thermal, machining – sequentially inter-linked steps	Unidimensional based upon price/ performance	Adoption as price/ performance of new process or product exceeds existing.
Simple assembled	Stoves, hoses, cans, skis, containers, guns	Assembly	Unidimensional based upon price/ performance	Adoption as price/ performance of new process or product exceeds existing.
Closed system	Watch, bicycle, car, airplane	Assembly at subsystem and system level	Multidimensional depending upon subsystem performance and linkages	Change at subsystem or system level; political processes important.
Open system	Computer, power generation, television	Assembly at subsystem and system level	Multidimensional depending upon subsystem performance, linkages and technological interdependencies	Inherently political – competition between systems and subsystems with multiple performance criteria available

system performance depends on the subsystem performance and interface technologies. Unlike non-assembled or simple assembled products, the subsystems of closed systems are not necessarily of equal importance – some subsystems are more central, others play a more peripheral role. For example, the engine is a core subsystem that plays a central role in the overall performance and technological progress of the automobile, whereas the wheels, brakes, and steering are peripheral subsystems that are highly dependent on the engine's characteristics. Because the closed system is composed of several subsystems, technical progress occurs at the subsystem level with each subsystem having its own unidimensional path of progress largely driven by process and/or product innovation at the non-assembled or simple product level. Like simple assembled products, a dominant design emerges through technical competition of alternative processes and subsystems.

Open systems are composed of a set of closed systems linked together through interface technologies. Examples of open systems include railroads, television, the Internet, and other telecommunication networks. While each closed subsystem evolves independently, the system as a whole is composed of a network of highly interdependent systems that is inherently complex and subject to a variety of sociopolitical forces. Technical progress generally occurs at the component and subsystem level until a dominant design can be achieved. Yet because of the high interdependency between the components and subsystems, technical progress of the overall system can be slowed as various organizations and other social and/or political institutions compete for the optimal design. In summary, the more complex the technological type, the greater the social and technical uncertainty and the influence of social and political processes on the nature and path of technical progress. In the following section, we develop hypotheses that address the role of technology type on environmental performance.

GLOBAL ENVIRONMENTAL STANDARDS AND ENVIRONMENTAL PERFORMANCE

Managing a firm's environmental performance is complicated by the plethora of regulatory regimes to which a firm has to attend. This process is difficult for firms that have operations distributed through a single country, but becomes even more complex for MNEs. Some corporations, with operations spread across very different jurisdictions, face not simply different regulations, but significantly differing levels of environmental requirements, with some jurisdictions requiring relatively stringent environmental performance, and other, so-called pollution havens allowing firms a wide latitude in their environmental impacts.

Meyer (2004) reviews the academic literature that addresses MNEs' effects on the environment. He discusses the arguments that MNEs have two potential environmental effects in their host-countries. First, firms may bring state-of-the-art environmental technology to jurisdictions that previously did not enjoy such technologies. Second, firms may take advantage of lax regulations and behave in ways that are not allowed in more stringent jurisdictions. Such behavior might include emitting more pollution or producing products that have been banned due to their environmental impact.

Anecdotal evidence of both chasing pollution havens and employing state-of-the-art technologies exists. More interesting, for the purposes of this chapter, is understanding when one strategy is more likely than the other, and how using one or the other strategy affects firm performance. Broadly speaking, firms have two choices. First, they can allow subsidiaries to meet local environmental standards, whether those standards are strict or lax. Second, the corporation can mandate that all subsidiaries follow the same standard, even if that standard exceeds what is required in the local jurisdiction.

Dowell, Hart, and Yeung (2000) review the arguments for and against employing a global environmental standard. The benefits, they suggest, fall into three categories. First, employing a single global standard facilitates knowledge sharing among the firm's subsidiaries. Second, firms can enjoy reputational benefits from adhering to strict standards even when the standards are not mandated. Third, if countries' standards tend to become stricter as they develop, going beyond currently-mandated requirements can preempt the need to improve performance to meet improving standards later.

The costs of employing a global standard arise because many solutions to environmental issues impose added production costs to companies (Walley and Whitehead; Newton and Harte, 1996). The degree to which stringency imposes added costs may depend upon how the stringency is achieved, however, as pollution prevention can involve efficiencies as firms find ways to avoid pollution altogether, rather than to involve costly treatment (Hart, 1995). Even so, there is evidence that not all forms of pollution prevention are profitable (King and Lenox, 2002), and that firms may need to develop complementary assets in order to profit from pollution prevention (Christmann, 2000). Thus, on average, going beyond environmental requirements may force firms to incur costs they would not otherwise experience.

Rather than argue whether, overall, global standards have net benefits for firms, it is more instructive to consider conditions that might affect the relative benefits of such standards. That is, we wish to outline contingencies in the global standard–profit relationship. While a number of internal and external contingencies are possible, we focus on the influence of technology type on both the probability that a firm will attempt to implement a global standard, and the profitability of doing so.

HYPOTHESES

We follow Dowell et al. (2000) and consider an MNE to have two broad choices in its global environmental practices. First, it can alter its environmental practices in its various international operations, so that in stringent jurisdictions it practices greater environmental stewardship than it practices in less stringent jurisdictions. Second, the firm can attempt to enact a single, global environmental standard in all jurisdictions in which it operates. While there are potential benefits to either of these strategies, Dowell et al. (2000) find that the market values of those firms that use a global environmental standard are significantly higher than the values of those firms using the host country standards.

In considering their results, we ask what we believe to be a fundamental question: why, if global environmental standards are associated with higher value, do all firms not pursue such standards? There are, of course, a number of internal and external factors that could affect a firm's ability to enact and derive value from a global environmental standard. Christmann (2000), for example, demonstrates that firms are better able to profit from environmental best practices if they also possess complementary assets such as capability for process innovation. While internal factors such as complementary assets are likely to be important for firms deriving value from global standards, we focus here on the role of a firm's technology type on its ability to (a) enact a global standard and (b) realize value from such a standard.

Global firms face a confusing array of regulations and standard practices in the varying jurisdictions in which they operate (Stiglitz, 2002, Hebb and Wójcik, 2005). While it may be tempting to consider global standards to be a ready solution to these differences, we argue that, in fact, global standards are difficult to enact, particularly in the presence of legacy investments (Lundan, 2004). The legacy investments place constraints on a firm's attempts to produce in the same way in all jurisdictions, which means that a firm that uses proactive pollution prevention technologies in more modern plants may be forced to use pollution control techniques in older facilities.

Taking the difficulty of enacting a global standard as given, the question remains whether and how technology type might affect a firm's ability to enact a standard. At first glance, it might seem that systems technologies are naturally more conducive to enacting global environmental standards, we argue that, in fact, they are the most difficult technologies in which to do so. As described above, systems technologies are particularly prone to political influence, and thus standards and practices can differ greatly between jurisdictions. The increased political influence on these standards means that deviance from a practice in a given jurisdiction is particularly circumscribed.

The case of television illustrates the difficulty of enacting a global standard in an open systems technology. In the mid-1980s the US began to consider adopting a standard for high definition television, and though Japan had already created high definition broadcast capabilities, political processes (fueled by anti-Japanese sentiment due to the loss of US competitiveness in electronics) led to the Federal Communications Commission (FCC) creating a standards competition, which eventually settled on a series of standards, none of which were compatible with the Japanese system (Brinkley, 1997). The standards in television broadcasting remain different across jurisdictions today.

The well-known Intel strategy of 'copy exactly', in which equipment and processes are duplicated precisely across its global factories, might seem to contradict our contention that open system technologies exacerbate the difficulty of creating global standards. Certainly, microprocessors are components of an open system technology in computing. We offer two observations of the situation for Intel that, we believe, reduce its power as a counter-example. First, it is notable that though Intel completed adoption of its 'copy exactly' strategy in 1996, it remains an iconic, perhaps unique, example of such a strategy, which to us underscores the difficulty of enacting this strategy. Second, Intel reports that implementing the strategy, even in its high capital-turnover industry, took over a decade, which suggests that for firms lacking Intel's resources and capital replacement cycle (meaning, of course, nearly all other firms in the world), it would take even longer and be even more difficult to create payback.

Our contention, then, is that firms that operate in less complex technological spaces will have an easier time enacting global environmental standards. We expect, therefore, that firms in non-assembled and simple assembled technology industries will be more likely to enact global environmental standards, and that the relationship between global standards and market value is stronger for such firms:

Hypothesis 1a: The probability that a firm will use a global environmental standard is lower if the firm primarily uses an open or closed system technology than if it uses a non-assembled or simple assembled technology.

Hypothesis 1b: The market value of firms using global environmental standards is lower for those firms that primarily use open or closed system technologies compared to those that use non-assembled or simple assembled technologies.

DATA AND METHODS

For hypotheses 1a and 1b, we assess a firm's global environmental standards using the Investor Responsibility Research Center (IRRC) survey data of S&P 500 firms. These data and the global standard measure specifically, were used in Dowell, Hart and Yeung's (2000) study of the relationship between environmental standards and market value. The data, gathered by IRRC surveys, are available from 1994–97, so they cover a limited time period, but one in which there was an ongoing managerial debate over the profitability of going beyond compliance in environmental efforts, thus making this an important period for analysis.

Each firm in the IRRC data set indicates whether it uses the host country standard in each country in which it operates, attempts to use US standards around the world, or has an internal global environmental standard that it attempts to apply throughout its operations. Dowell et al. (2000) find that firms that use global environmental standards had significantly higher market values, as measured by Tobin's Q, than firms that used either the US standards or the host country standards. From the IRRC survey, we create an indicator variable that takes on the value of 1 if the firm uses an internal global environmental standard, and 0 otherwise.

Our second key variable is the firm's technology type. To construct this variable, we begin by assigning each four-digit Standard Industrial Classification (SIC) code that is represented in our sample to one of the Tushman and Rosenkopf (1992) classifications. We performed this classification prior to examining the IRRC sample, so that the technology classifications would not be biased by knowing which firms in our sample were in which SIC. The IRRC data include the firm's main SIC, and we assign each firm to a technology category based upon that SIC designation. Many of these companies are diversified, but the data do not allow us to divide their operations among multiple SICs, so we use the SIC category that the firm considers its main industry classification.

The equations that we employ for hypotheses 1a and 1b are:

$$Global\ Standard_{it} = \beta_1 TechType_{it} + \beta X_{it} + e_{it} \tag{1}$$

$$Tobin_{it} = \beta_1 TechType_{it} + \beta_2 Global\ Standard + \beta_3 TechType_{it} X\ Standard_{it} + \beta X_{it} + e_{it} \tag{2}$$

In equation (1), *Global Standard* is the indicator variable described above. The *TechType* is a series of indicator variables, each taking on a '1' if the firm's industry is classified as a given type, and **X** is a vector of control variables. Hypothesis 1a is assessed by the coefficients on the indicator variables in *TechType*. In equation (2), *Tobin* is the firm's Tobin's Q value in year t.[1] *Global Standard* and *TechType* are as described above. Hypothesis 1b is assessed by the coefficient β_3, which is the coefficient for the interaction of *Global Standard* and *TechType*.

Control variables
For equations (1) and (2), we follow Dowell et al. (2000) in our choice of control variables. For equation (1), we include a firm's size, measured by its assets and the degree to which its operations are multinational (percent of foreign assets). Larger, more international firms may have to expend greater efforts to manage a global environmental standard, but the ensuing benefits may also be greater for such firms. For equation (2), we include size (assets), research and development intensity, advertising intensity, and degree of leverage, as these variables have been shown to affect the firm's Tobin's Q (Morck and Yeung, 1991; Dowell et al., 2000). We also include an indicator variable that takes on a value of 1 if the firm operates a production facility in a low-income country, as prior work suggests that low-income countries have lower environmental standards (Grossman and Krueger, 1995), and the benefits of using global environmental standards might differ for firms that operate in such jurisdictions.

Methods
For hypothesis 1a, we use a logistic regression with random effects at the facility level. The dependent variable, as described above, is 1 if the firm uses a global environmental standard in a given year, and 0 if it uses a host country standard or uses the US standard. For hypothesis 1b, we again use regression with random effects at the facility level, with the firm's Tobin's q as the dependent variable.

RESULTS AND DISCUSSION

Table 5.2 contains the descriptive statistics and correlation coefficients for the variables. The correlation results suggest that there are significant differences between firms, depending upon the technology type in which they operate. For example, firms in systems technologies (both open and closed) tend to be larger, and open system technology firms tend to spend more on research and development and less on advertising than other firms, but have a lower percentage of assets in foreign countries.

We now turn to the questions posed in hypotheses 1a and 1b. Does technology type affect the likelihood of a firm using a single, global environmental standard? Does it affect the return from doing so? We begin by

Table 5.2 Descriptive statistics and correlation coefficients

Variable	Mean (Std Dev)	(1)	(2)	(3)	(4)	(5)	(6)	(7)	(8)	(9)	(10)
(1) Tobin's q	2.98 (2.82)	1.00									
(2) Ln(assets) in millions	8.91 (1.21)	-0.023	1.00								
(3) R&D intensity	0.04 (0.04)	0.240	-0.224	1.00							
(4) Advertising intensity	0.02 (0.04)	0.375	-0.050	0.018	1.00						
(5) Leverage	0.18 (0.11)	-0.278	0.159	-0.486	-0.156	1.00					
(6) Percentage of foreign assets	0.28 (0.17)	0.206	-0.068	0.386	0.134	-0.323	1.00				
(7) Global environmental standard	0.37 (0.48)	0.325	0.246	0.108	0.092	-0.077	0.154	1.00			
(8) Non-assembled technology	0.39 (0.48)	0.103	0.034	-0.089	0.048	-0.082	0.158	0.181	1.00		
(9) Simple assembled technology	0.21 (0.41)	0.128	-0.208	-0.037	0.197	0.010	0.054	-0.042	-0.415	1.00	
(10) Closed systems technology	0.14 (0.35)	-0.113	0.133	0.030	-0.053	0.0660	-0.030	-0.015	-0.326	-0.209	1.00
(11) Open systems technology	0.18 (0.38)	-0.092	0.159	0.142	-0.140	0.008	0.188	-0.146	-0.376	-0.242	0.190

Table 5.3   Frequency of global environmental standards by technology type

Technology type	Internal global standard	Other	Total
Non-assembled	151 (48.4%)	161 (51.6%)	312
Assembled	111 (33.5%)	56 (66.5%)	167
Closed system	44 (39.3%)	68 (60.7%)	112
Open system	32 (22.4%)	111 (77.6%)	143
Total	283 (38.6%)	451 (61.4%)	734

exploring the data. Table 5.3 shows the frequency of global environmental standards by technology type. The results show support for the argument that technology type affects the likelihood of using a global environmental standard, though the pattern may be a little more complex than hypothesis 1 suggests. It appears that companies that primarily operate in industries characterized by non-assembled technologies are most likely to use global standards, as we predicted. Likewise, those companies that are in industries classified as open systems technologies have the lowest likelihood of using global standards. The t-test of the difference in the proportion of non-assembled and open systems firms using global standards is significant (t-value = 5.41, p = 0.000). Those firms that are in industries classified as closed system technologies, however, are equally likely to use global standards as the firms in non-assembled technology industries are, while those using assembled systems have a moderate probability of using global standards.

Overall, the results of Table 5.3 suggest that technology type may play an important role in affecting a firm's likelihood of using a single, global environmental standard. The analysis in Table 5.3, however, does not allow us to control for other factors that might affect the probability of employing a global standard. For example, if it is more complex to implement a global standard when the firm has a higher proportion of its assets outside the US, and more of the open systems firms have a higher proportion of international operations, the results in Table 5.3 could reflect this, rather than being driven by technology type. To attempt to control for possibilities such as this, we turn to regression analysis.

Table 5.4 contains the results of random-effects logistic regression

Table 5.4   *Effect of technology type on probability of using a global environmental standard*

Variable	Model 1	Model 2
Constant	−11.58***	−11.00***
	(2.247)	(2.128)
Size (ln assets)	1.015***	1.059***
	(0.227)	(0.218)
R&D intensity	4.177	9.860*
	(5.841)	(5.863)
Advertising intensity	1.049	−0.091
	(5.435)	(5.204)
Leverage	−1.526	−1.259
	(1.979)	(1.933)
Percentage of foreign operations	0.050***	0.035**
	(0.016)	(0.016)
Assembled technology		−0.613
		(0.615)
Closed system technology		−0.873
		(0.687)
Open system technology		−2.549***
		(0.736)

Notes:
All models have 734 observations.
***, **, *: significant at 0.01, 0.05, and 0.10 respectively.

analysis where the dependent variable takes on a 1 for firms that use a global environmental standard. Model 1 contains the control variables. The results indicate that larger firms and those with a greater proportion of international operations are more likely to use a global standard.

Model 2 adds the indicator variables for technology type. The omitted category is non-assembled technology, so the coefficients on the technology type variables represent the increase or decrease in probability that a firm in an industry characterized by a given technology uses a global standard, relative to a firm in a non-assembled technology industry. The results indicate that firms in open systems technology industries are significantly less likely to use global standards than are those firms in non-assembled industries. In fact, testing the equality of coefficients shows that the firms in open systems technologies are significantly less likely to use global standards than firms in closed systems or simple assembled technologies as well.

The results thus far provide strong evidence that a firm's core technology

Table 5.5   Effect of technology type on relation between global environmental standard and Tobin's Q

Variable	Model 1	Model 2
Constant	−0.458	−0.848
	(1.224)	(1.244)
Size (ln assets)	0.256*	0.326**
	(0.133)	(0.136)
R&D intensity	9.159***	10.47***
	(3.439)	(3.513)
Advertising intensity	19.610***	18.64***
	(3.45)	(3.455)
Leverage	−2.401 **	−2.528**
	(1.110)	(1.107)
Percentage of foreign operations	0.018**	0.013
	(0.009)	(0.009)
Assembled technology		0.473
		(0.459)
Closed system technology		−0.623
		(0.537)
Open system technology		−0.569
		(0.500)
Global environmental standard	0.977***	0.985***
	(0.158)	(0.222)
Global standard X assembled		0.127
		(0.400)
Global standard X closed system		−0.696
		(0.453)
Global standard X open system		0.407
		(0.477)

Notes:
All models have 734 observations.
***, **, *: significant at 0.01, 0.05, and 0.10 respectively.

type does affect its likelihood of using a global environmental standard. We now turn our attention to whether the return to employing a global standard differs depending upon the technology type, as predicted in hypothesis 2. In Table 5.5, we present the results of random-effects regression of a firm's Tobin's Q on the control and independent variables described above. Model 1 contains the control variables. This model replicates the findings of Dowell et al. (2000), and demonstrates that firms with more intangible assets, as represented by research and development and advertising intensity, have higher Tobin's Q ratios. The key finding from

Dowell et al. (2000) is also demonstrated, as firms that use internal global environmental standards have significantly higher Tobin's Q ratios.

In Model 2 we add the indicator variables for technology type (non-assembled technology is again the omitted category). We also add the interaction between technology type and global environmental standards. Hypothesis 2 suggests that the coefficient on Global Standard X Open System should be negative and significant, reflecting the difficulty of enacting a global environmental standard in an open system technological environment. The results do not support hypothesis 2, as the coefficient on the interaction between global standards and open systems is positive but insignificant.

DISCUSSION AND CONCLUSION

By their very size and pervasiveness, MNEs have a massive impact on not only the global economy, but also on the natural environment. Understanding the factors that affect these corporations' impact on the environment, therefore, is an important research question. In this paper, we have taken a small step forward in advancing our understanding of these factors, by exploring the relationship between technology type and global environmental strategy.

We find that technology type, as measured by the Tushman and Rosenkopf (1992) typology, is related to the likelihood that a firm undertakes an internal global environmental standard. Those firms that operate in industries characterized by open systems technologies are significantly less likely to use an internal global standard, compared to firms that are in non-assembled technology sectors. For firms in the open systems sectors, coordinating the practices across multiple jurisdictions is a complex undertaking, as an open systems technology is characterized by the presence of multiple, interacting subsystems. In such an environment, a firm cannot make a decision to modify its practices independent of the other parties involved in the open system, which makes global coordination difficult for a firm. This difficulty is amplified by the MNC's operations that may span vastly different political and technical environments.

We find no evidence that the return on employing a global standard differs depending upon the technology type. Though this contradicts our prediction that open systems technology firms would have a lower return on employing a global standard, it suggests that the managers are acting rationally. That is, firms are not employing global standards in situations in which such standards reduce their financial returns. Within the sectors characterized by open systems technologies, therefore, it is likely that there are some firms for which it is easier to manage globally coordinated processes, and these firms are the ones that are doing so. With our data, we are not able to determine what might affect the firms' abilities to manage global standards, but one candidate is experience with global operations, as experience has been shown to increase firms' abilities to deal with complexity (Dowell and Killaly, 2009).

Taking our key findings together, we believe that our results provide evidence that firms' abilities to proactively manage their interactions with the physical environment are positively related to their overall quality of management. This relationship has been discussed at least since Cairncross (1991), who argued that 'Companies that take the environment seriously change not only their processes and products but also the way they run themselves (p. 279)'. Dowell et al.'s (2000) results are consistent with this argument as they suggest that companies that use a global standard rather than ratcheting down to a host country standard were better-run companies. Our results further this 'green management is good management' hypothesis, as we find that some companies are better able to overcome technical restrictions and profit by doing so.

Overall, our results have several implications. First, they point to the importance of understanding the external context in targeting firms and industries for environmental improvement. Christmann (2000) and others have shown the importance of understanding context in assessing environmental performance. Our findings suggest that the external context, which we represent here by the technology in a firm's core industry, is also important.

Our results also speak to research that seeks to understand the leap from pollution prevention to sustainability. If we take as given that the leap to sustainability is even more complicated than the greening attempts we have observed, then we need to have a strong understanding of the barriers to companies becoming more sustainable. This link is important not only for academics studying environmental performance, but also for managers seeking to understand the task of organizational change involved in enacting better environmental performance.

Finally, the results have implications for public policy. As policy experts look to find the right combination of carrots and sticks to enable firms to move to more sustainable positions, it is important to understand how to fit the policy to the technology. The results of our global sample indicate that firms in complex technologies, for example, may react differently to legislation than firms that are in less complex situations.

This research should be seen as exploratory. Many other issues to consider and control variables could be important, but could not be incorporated in this initial attempt to understand the relationships. We believe that this is the first attempt to understand how technology type affects environmental performance, and indeed is one of the few attempts to date to really try to assess the role of technology type in organizational change in any setting. Our results are likely to create more questions than answers in our quest to understand how to move to a more sustainable world.

ENDNOTE

1. Tobin's Q is a measure of the market value per dollar of replacement cost of tangible assets. We use the market value of a firm's common stock at year end and the replacement costs are calculated using values from *Compustat*.

REFERENCES

Brinkley, J. (1997), *Defining Vision: The Battle for the Future of Television*, New York: Harcourt Brace.

Cairncross, F. (1991), *Costing the Earth*, Cambridge, MA: Harvard Business School Press.

Christmann, P. (2000), 'Effects of "best practices" of environmental management on cost advantage: the role of complementary assets', *Academy of Management Journal*, **43**(4): 663–80.

Dowell, G., S. Hart and B. Yeung (2000), 'Do corporate global environmental standards create or destroy market value?', *Management Science*, **46**(8): 1059.

Dowell, G. and B. Killaly (2009), 'The impact of market volatility on firm entry decisions: evidence from US telecom firms' international expansion', *Organization Science*, **20**: 69–84.

Grossman, G.M. and A.B. Krueger (1995), 'Economic growth and the environment', *The Quarterly Journal of Economics*, **110**(2): 353–77.

Hart, S.L. (1995), 'A natural-resource-based view of the firm', *Academy of Management Review*, **20**(4): 986–1014.

Hebb, T. and D. Wójcik (2005), 'Global standards and emerging markets: the institutional investment value chain and CalPERS' investment strategy', *Environment and Planning*, **37**: 1955–74.

King, A. and M. Lenox (2002), 'Exploring the locus of profitable pollution reduction', *Management Science*, **48**(2): 289–99.

Lundan, S. (2004), 'Multinationals, environment and global competition: a conceptual framework', in S. Lundan (ed.), *Multinationals, environment, and Global Competition*, Oxford: Elsevier, pp. 1–22.

Margolis, J.D. and J.P. Walsh (2003), 'Misery loves companies: rethinking social initiatives by business', *Administrative Science Quarterly*, **48**(2): 268–305.

Meyer, K.E. (2004), 'Perspectives on multinational enterprises in emerging economies', *Journal of International Business Studies*, **35**: 259–76.

Morck, R. and B. Yeung (1991), 'Why investors value multinationality', *The Journal of Business*, **64**(2): 165–87.

Newton, T. and G. Harte (1996), 'Green business: technicist kitsch?', *Journal of Management Studies*, **34**: 75–98.

Orlitzky, M., F.L. Schmidt and S.L. Rynes (2003), 'Corporate social and financial performance: a meta-analysis', *Organization Studies*, **24**(3): 403–41.

Schaltegger, S. and T. Synnestvedt (2002), 'The link between [']green' and economic success: environmental management as the crucial trigger between environmental and economic performance', *Journal of Environmental Management*, **65**(4): 339–46.

Stiglitz, G. (2002), *Globalization and Its Discontents*, New York: W.W. Norton.

Tushman, M. and L. Rosenkopf (1992), 'Organizational determinants of technological change: toward a sociology of technological evolution', *Research in Organizational Behavior*, **14**: 311–40.

Walley, N. and B. Whitehead (1994), 'It's not easy being green', *Harvard Business Review*, **72**: 46–52.

PART III

Strategic approaches to sustainability

6. The Global Reporting Initiative: collaboration and conflict in the development of non-financial reporting

David L. Levy and Halina Szejnwald Brown

INTRODUCTION

The founders of the Global Reporting Initiative (GRI), Bob Massie and Allen White, faced a daunting task: how would two individuals, located in two small Boston-area NGOs and without access to formal authority or substantial resources, create a framework for social and environmental reporting that would come to be embraced by more than half of the S&P 100 companies, and be recognized as the leading global framework for non-financial reporting? We argue that the entrepreneurs Massie and White served as a contemporary Modern Prince, a political agent who transforms systems through effective leadership, skillful analysis and strategy, and developing organizational capacity (Levy and Scully, 2007). The Modern Prince exercises a form of strategic power to navigate the contested terrain, to project moral and intellectual leadership, and ultimately to reconfigure the field.

The GRI is widely seen as the leading standard for voluntary corporate reporting of environmental and social performance worldwide. It has been very successful since its modest inception in 1999, adopted by large numbers of companies in multiple countries, and garnering widespread legitimacy (Brown, de Jong, and Lessidrenska, 2009; Brown, de Jong, and Levy, 2009; Etzion and Ferraro, 2010). It has attained official recognition by governmental agencies and multilateral organizations such as the UN in its Global Compact (Bair, 2007; Dingwerth, 2007).

The founders of GRI, acting as 'institutional entrepreneurs', promoted a vision of a multi-stakeholder process with broad and shared benefits. The founders expected that GRI would shift the balance of power in corporate governance toward NGOs as representatives of civil society. GRI's premise was that standardized information could be used for benchmarking and ranking companies, providing a valuable supplement to financial reporting for investors and empowering civil society organizations to demand greater corporate accountability (Fiorino, 2006; Florini, 2003). GRI has, however, proven to be much more successful in securing corporate acceptance than in gaining traction with NGOs or investors. GRI has clearly contributed to the legitimacy and routinization of corporate social reporting as a practice, and has conferred a common language and set of procedures on the field. However, GRI is still one of several competing standards and has not resulted in the generation of comparable data sets that enable analysis across companies and sectors. Neither has it stimulated the emergence of a community of financial or NGO consumers of these reports. On these counts, GRI has fallen short of the intent of establishing social reporting standards with the same status as that held by financial reporting standards. Indeed, in the US and UK, there are signs that the diffusion of GRI is stagnating. More fundamentally, GRI has disappointed the founders' expectations that the balance of power in corporate governance could be shifted toward civil society.

We analyze the success and limitations of GRI by considering it as an emerging institutional field, a dynamic system structured in the discursive, economic, and organizational domains. Institutional fields can achieve a degree of contingent stability when the three elements are aligned, but they are also somewhat unstable and unpredictable in the face of exogenous shocks, actors' strategies, and endogenous forces. The GRI institutional entrepreneurs are political actors who seek to transform the field of corporate governance through skillful analysis and combining discursive, organizational, and economic strategies. Their agency constitutes a form of strategic power that provides a counterweight to the structural inertia of fields in an attempt to overcome the resistance of 'field dominants' with superior access to resources (Levy and Scully, 2007; McAdam and Scott, 2005: 17).

The GRI's founders saw a core tension in the social reporting field between two competing institutional logics, discursive frames for understanding the field. The logic of civil regulation views social reporting as a mechanism to empower civil society groups to play a more active and assertive role in corporate governance. The logic of corporate social performance, by contrast, emphasizes the instrumental value of social reporting to corporate management, the investor community, as well as auditing and consulting firms. The founders sought to create an alliance of NGOs and business by advocating a win-win frame in which these logics are portrayed as complementary rather than incompatible (Levy, 1997). The win-win proposition, which is closely related to the concept of triple bottom-line, asserts that companies can address environmental and social concerns in ways that improve profitability (Elkington, 1994; Russo and Fouts, 1997), thus reducing conflicts of interest among stakeholders.

At the core of GRI's strategy is the institutionalization of non-financial reporting (NFR) as a routine practice, and as legitimate and taken-for-granted as financial reporting. The win-win discourse of CSR has certainly helped move GRI toward this goal. A key contribution of this chapter, however, is the argument that a new institution requires a supportive economic framework to flourish in the longer term. The evidence in the paper suggests that GRI is losing momentum, at least in the US, primarily because of a failure to deliver value to various stakeholders. Investors remain unconvinced that NFR is valuable in pricing financial assets, companies are expressing doubts about the payoffs from reporting social performance, and NGOs are not finding GRI data to be particularly useful in their campaigns.

A second contribution of this paper is the insight that institutional emergence is a dynamic process, whose trajectory reflects the outcome of strategic interactions between NGOs and firms, in a particular economic, social, and political context; it does not always reflect the intentions of its founders (Selznick, 1980). The GRI entrepreneurs correctly understood the centrality of support from the corporate sector to the success of the initiative, and they recognized the constraints imposed by capital markets and corporate resistance to radical shifts in structures of governance. Considerable attention was thus paid to the business case for social reporting and ensuring collaboration from major MNEs, while the support of activists and labor was, to some degree, taken for granted. As a result, the corporate sector plays an increasingly prominent role, while activists find themselves somewhat marginalized, eclipsing the 'civil regulation' vision of transforming corporate governance.

GRI's trajectory was shaped not just by the intentions of its founders, but by the strategic interplay among the various actors, the power relations among them, and their strategic skills and capabilities. The potential for a more fundamental shift in governance was also constrained by the broader institutions of financial and capital markets in which the CSR field is nested. The evolution and limitations of GRI can thus be understood in terms of the possibilities and limitations of strategic power. Indeed, we suggest more generally that the strategic compromises and fragile coalitions necessary to undertake institutional entrepreneurship and initiate field-level change inherently generate tensions that inhibit and circumscribe more systematic field transformation.

The chapter proceeds by describing the research methodology, developing the theoretical framework in more detail, then providing an in-depth examination of the GRI case. Data for this project were collected from an extensive documentary analysis of the GRI archives and secondary sources, observations at annual GRI conferences, and semi-structured interviews with approximately 50 individuals who participated in the development, operation, and use of the GRI. These included: two GRI co-founders; three former members of GRI's first steering committee; two former members of Ceres' board of directors; and representatives of 14 companies, 14 civil society organizations and international NGOs, one US organized labor organization, eight investment organizations and investment research organizations, three international consultancies, and one from the US Environmental Protection Agency. These individuals were located in the US, UK and the Netherlands. We coded these materials in order to map the structure of the GRI organizational field, the strategies of the actors, a timeline of events and major developments. As the key themes of this paper emerged, we returned to the data to code and filter them, in order to examine them in further detail. We also sought feedback from interviewees in order to probe and sharpen our analysis.

THEORETICAL FRAMEWORK

Within the framework of institutional theory, institutional entrepreneurs (Clemens and Cook, 1999; Greenwood and Suddaby, 2006) are 'actors who have an interest in particular institutional arrangements and who leverage resources to create new institutions or to transform existing ones' (Maguire, Hardy, and Lawrence, 2004: 657). Where neo-institutional theory has traditionally emphasized isomorphic forces that tend to lead to static, harmonious conformity, institutional entrepreneurship is viewed as a more 'political process that reflects the power and interests of organized actors' (Maguire, Hardy, and Lawrence, 2004: 658). The focus has shifted from the structural power of an institution to constrain agents and stabilize a field, toward an appreciation of the power of agents to generate institutional conflict and change (McAdam and Scott, 2005). These efforts to transform fields can resemble social movements, whereby 'entrenched, field-wide authority is collectively challenged and restructured' (Rao, Morrill, and Zald, 2000: 276). In this process, 'field constituents are often armed with opposing perspectives rather than with common rhetorics. The process may more resemble institutional war than isomorphic dialogue' (Hoffman, 1999: 352).

Institutional theory has traditionally pointed to the social embeddedness of market practices and structures. Institutional theorists have been intrigued, for example, by the conformity of professional legal and accounting firms to sets of practices that do not hold obvious economic advantages (Greenwood and Suddaby, 2006; Lawrence, 1999). Resisting predominant economic accounts, institutionalists have examined how 'the persistence of institutionalized practices and structures cannot be fully explained by their technical virtuosity or unparalleled efficiency' (Colomy, 1998: 266). Instead, institutions are viewed as 'socially constructed, routine-reproduced programs or rule systems' (Jepperson, 1991: 149), which become stabilized around a particular institutional logic, defined as the 'belief systems and associated practices that predominate in an organizational field' (Scott, Ruef, Mendel, and Caronna, 2000: 170). The social forces shaping institutions are increasingly understood as discursive formations, where discourse refers to the structures of meaning that attach to texts and practices (Phillips, Lawrence, and Hardy, 2004). As Munir and Philips (2005: 1669) express it, 'institutions are social constructions produced by discourses'.

Levy and Scully have argued that the emphasis on the discursive structure of fields has come at the expense of attention to their economic and political dimensions, resulting in an inadequate theorization of power, strategy and dynamics in processes of institutional change. Levy and Scully (2007) draw from the Gramscian concept of hegemony to depict fields as complex systems that achieved a degree of stability when their discursive, economic, and political dimensions are aligned and mutually reinforcing. Fields need to reproduce themselves not just as social, symbolic structures but also on a material level; they require a viable business model that generates sufficient resources to enable the reproduction of the field and gain the cooperation of the relevant network of actors. The concept of hegemony points to a dialectical process in which economic processes are embedded within social structures, but the economic context in turn shapes practices and norms; the political economy of institutional logics thus demands greater attention. The notion of hegemony also enriches our understanding of the political and organizational structure of a field. It suggests a process of bargaining and compromise that results in a negotiated arrangement, or 'institutional settlement' (Zysman, 1994), which primarily serves the interests of a dominant coalition, or historical bloc, but is portrayed as representing the general interest. It achieves this hegemonic status with a degree of material accommodation for other actors, a supportive discursive framework, and an appropriate structure of field governance and authority.

In parallel to its focus on discursive structures, existing literature emphasizes discursive strategies, involving activities such as reframing the cultural meaning of practices (Munir and Phillips, 2005), theorizing and legitimizing new practices (Maguire, Hardy, and Lawrence, 2004; Rao,

Morrill, and Zald, 2000), importing and adapting discourses from other arenas (Boxenbaum and Battilana, 2005; Lawrence and Phillips, 2004; Phillips, Lawrence, and Hardy, 2004), and articulating, or linking, discursive elements (Etzion and Ferraro, 2006; Laclau and Mouffe, 1985). Our multi-dimensional conception of fields, one that includes economic and organizational elements, yields a much richer palette of strategies. The tensions between the elements of field structure not only help account for the dynamics of field evolution but also can provide leverage for actors seeking change.

Fundamentally, it is the complex dynamic character of fields that gives meaning to the concept of strategy as a form of power and enables the Modern Prince to analyze, organize, and intervene. Actors can gain only a partial understanding of the structures and processes within a field, but some are better analysts and strategists than others. Complexity leads to errors and unintended outcomes, potentially frustrating the efforts of field dominants to resist change, and enabling weaker actors, with less access to material resources or formal authority, to outmaneuver field dominants. Yet strategic power is also constrained by the same forces of indeterminacy and complexity, as well as by the resistance of 'institutional defenders' who benefit from the structural inertia of fields (Levy and Scully, 2007).

THE GLOBAL REPORTING INITIATIVE

The GRI was conceived as a deliberate intervention in the field of social and environmental reporting. The explicit goal of GRI was to clarify and harmonize the practice of NFR, and thereby to empower various societal actors. The 1997 draft paper stated that '. . .[the GRI] vision is to improve corporate accountability by ensuring that all stakeholders – communities, environmentalists, labour, religious groups, shareholders, investment managers – have access to standardized, comparable, and consistent environmental information akin to corporate financial reporting. Only in this fashion will we be able to (1) use the capital markets to promote and ensure sustainable business practices; (2) measure companies' adherence to standards set from Ceres principles; and (3) empower NGOs around the globe with the information they need to hold corporations accountable' (Ceres, 1997).

CSR is a contested arena, with tendencies toward more democratic and accountable forms of governance, as well as toward privatized corporate power and a diminished regulatory state (Shamir, 2004a). NGOs and businesses deploy the language and practices of CSR as strategic tools in political struggles over corporate governance (Levy and Kaplan, 2008;

Ougaard, 2006). NGOs, as the 'organizational manifestations of civil society interests', (Teegen, Doh, and Vachani, 2004: 466), have deployed the discourse of CSR to try to shift the locus of corporate governance toward civil society stakeholders, creating a mode of 'civil regulation' (Murphy and Bendell, 1997) promising expanded democracy, account-ability, and problem-solving capacity. Companies, on the other hand, frequently employ CSR strategically as a form of self-regulation that serves to construct the corporation as a moral agent (DeWinter, 2001; Marchand, 1998), deflect the threat of regulation, and marginalize more radical activists (Shamir, 2004b).

GRI's proponents assumed that information serves as an instrument of civil–private regulation by mobilizing its recipients to demand certain performance levels and providing a channel for transparency and account-ability. In particular, standardized information could be used for bench-marking, ranking and cross-comparisons, enabling activists and NGOs to reward practices considered socially responsible and exert pressure on poor performers (Fiorino, 2006; Florini, 2003). The early success of the 1987 Toxic Release Inventory in reducing toxic emissions from industrial plants in the US (Graham, 2002) provided some support for this strat-egy. There was also growing interest in the late 1990s among academ-ics, policymakers and environmental activists in private, voluntary, and market-oriented modes of governance that would reside in new forms of engagement among governments, civil society and business (Cashore, Auld, and Newsom, 2004; Prakash and Hart, 1999; Utting, 2002).

The process of creating and evolving the guidelines was intended to insti-tutionalize a dialogue among a wide range of actors, generate new norms and practices, and facilitate the emergence of new understandings of cor-porate and collective responsibility and accountability. It was conceived as a nuanced, non-confrontational strategy that could draw NGOs and corporations into a collaborative partnership to serve mutual interests, while gently cajoling companies to change their attitudes and practices. In Massie's words:[1] '. . .[we wanted] to ensure that future leaders within the society will pick up the role of stewards of the future. . . .the process of giving a name to something and turning it into a base for a dialogue. . .'.

Four permanent bodies comprise the GRI organization: The board of directors, the secretariat, the stakeholder council, and the technical advisor council. The board of directors sets broad strategic direction and exerts ultimate authority over organizational policies. It has been chaired by heads of major business organizations or NGOs, such as Judy Henderson, Commissioner of the World Commission on Dams. The stakeholder council is designed to provide a multi-stakeholder process through broad consultation and representation of a wide range of perspectives in the development and revision of GRI guidelines. It meets annually to monitor progress, discuss key strategic issues, and to advise and elect the board of directors. Its 60 members are selected in a way intended to provide balance between geographical regions and stakeholder groups, with 22 seats for business, 16 seats for NGOs and six for labor. The secretariat, located in Amsterdam employs about 25 professionals from various backgrounds and national origins. The secretariat is the operational staff but also develops new ideas and initiatives. Finally, the technical advisor council is charged with technically overseeing the development of the GRI family of documents.

The GRI's members form the organizational stakeholders group, numbering over 380 organizations and individuals in 2007 who pay a modest annual membership fee. This group has the formal duty of electing 60 percent of the members of the stakeholder council, but also serves an important informal function influencing the broader mission of the GRI through service on various working groups and participation in numerous meetings. The organizational stakeholders group is dominated by large companies, banks, other financial institutions, international accountancies and business consultancies, with relatively few NGOs or organized labor organizations

The United Nations Environment Programme (UNEP) formally joined the GRI in 1998 as a partnering institution, which enhanced the GRI's legitimacy, access to funding and administrative and intellectual support. Between 1999 and 2002 the GRI's founders succeeded in obtaining over US$7 million from several foundations and from the World Bank as well as additional support from various participating organizations. During a six year period since its formal inauguration in 2000, the GRI produced three generations of guidelines, several sector supplements and a host of technical papers and user guides. Several thousand individuals and organizations worldwide contributed to the development of the GRI, through the stakeholder council and various working groups. Elements of the GRI guidelines have been adopted by the GRI's competitors, which reflects its pervasive influence, but also hinders the GRI's mission to standardize reporting.

The GRI emerged by the early 2000s as the best developed international framework for sustainability reporting. The GRI's annual meeting in 2008 in Amsterdam was an impressive demonstration of success. Attended by over a thousand representatives of global business, investment capital, civil society organizations, and professionals, the conference's plenary sessions featured royalty, well-known politicians, corporate CEOs and high-level members of multilateral institutions. A 2002 survey of 107 MNCs showed that the GRI took second position after the well-established ISO 14 001 standard in having the greatest influence on their social responsibility practices (Berman et al., 2003). Outside the US, the uptake of the GRI has been particularly extensive in Spain, the Netherlands, Brazil, and South Africa, though patterns of institutionalization differ according to local circumstances. At present, the OECD Committee on International Investment and Multinational Enterprises promotes the use of the GRI. The ISO 26 000 Sustainability Management Standard under development also draws on the GRI.

The operational reality of the GRI on the behaviour of corporate reporters and other stakeholders has been more modest, however. Most of the GRI's participants focus on the development of the guidelines, particularly the revision and development of sectoral supplements (Brown, de Jong and Levy, 2009). The uptake of the GRI guidelines by companies who issue sustainability reports reached approximately 1000 in 2007.[2] While growth continues in developing countries, reporting has begun to stagnate in the US and some European countries. While the diffusion of reporting has been substantial, particularly among large brand-name companies, the GRI's founders were somewhat disappointed in relation to their initial aspirations. A large service industry comprised mainly of sustainability consultancies and auditing firms has emerged around the revision of the guidelines, preparation of reports, their verification, stakeholder outreach, and various efforts to standardise and institutionalize the above activities. But the readership and usage of the reports by NGOs, organized labor and financial analysts are very modest.

To examine these trends, we analyze the GRI as an institution comprising discursive, economic, and organizational dimensions. The case illustrates how institutions grow around these intertwined and mutually constitutive elements, but also how field development is constrained when elements are misaligned. We consider each dimension in turn, probing the structure of the field, the underlying tensions, and the strategies adopted by actors as they attempt to restructure the field in particular ways. The framework suggests that the evolving GRI institution represents a classic Gramscian accommodation between business and social pressures for change, in which a new institution is assimilated and transformed to conform with broader power structures. The case thus illustrates well the potential and limitations of strategic power.

DISCURSIVE TENSIONS AND STRATEGIES

A key task facing the GRI's founders was to address a core tension in the field over the meaning and purpose of NFR, if they were to build a diverse coalition of NGOs and businesses to support it. NGOs are primarily motivated by the logic of 'civil regulation' (Murphy and Bendell, 1999), in which NFR increases the transparency and accountability of corporations to external stakeholders, leading not just to changes in corporate practice, but ultimately to a shift in the locus of governance toward civil society. The logic of corporate social performance, by contrast, signifies the instrumental value of NFR to the corporate community through building brand value and rationalizing the reporting process. NFR could also constitute an instrumental source of economic value to consultants, auditors, and financial analysts concerned with the financial implications of social performance.

The GRI entrepreneurs used several strategies to negotiate the tensions between these twin logics. First, they drew from the win-win logic of corporate environmentalism and CSR to frame the GRI as mutually beneficial to NGOs and the corporate community. If social performance enhances financial performance, then interests are congruent rather than conflictual, and the GRI becomes a vehicle for partnerships and collaboration. Second, the GRI entrepreneurs influenced the agenda at various meetings to deliberately avoid conflictual discussions of fundamental goals and values, and focus instead on the common ground of changing corporate practice. As Massie noted, 'You do not need to agree on first principles. In fact, it is better to avoid having an explicit discussion of core values and the fundamental views on the social order. Instead, you focus on more instrumental ideas'. Third, while avoiding this source of conflict in public meetings, in private the GRI's founders tailored their message framing in ways that stressed its potential advantages for particular constituencies. These strategies succeeded in temporarily managing, though not eliminating, the tensions between the twin logics of NFR.

Framing the GRI as analogous to the well-known system of Financial Accounting Standards Board Interpretations (FASBI) in the US was an important legitimation strategy pursued by the GRI. It has been widely observed that even as institutional entrepreneurs attempt to create change, they need to secure legitimacy and 'emphasize how those innovations comply with the established institutional frames' in the wider society (Déjean, Gond, and Leca, 2004: 745). The GRI consistently stressed the similarity between social and financial reporting. Four GRI principles (relevance, timeliness, neutrality, and comparability) are identical to four FASBI principles, while several other principles are closely related (Etzion and Ferraro, 2006). The GRI could thus gain acceptance from its discursive lineage from an authoritative and well established system of reporting (Levy and Kaplan, 2008), and present itself as merely an effort to expand the scope of this reporting to social and environmental indicators. Accounting principles, however, are intended to generate reliable financial data reducible to performance statistics that can be compared across sectors and firms. The GRI's emphasis, like other managerial standards for quality or environmental management, remains at the managerial process level, and does not attempt to set or measure social performance in an absolute sense.

Rather than pursue a direct confrontation with well-entrenched institutions of corporate governance, encompassing powerful actors and firmly held belief systems, the GRI's strategy can be understood as a 'war of position', in Gramsci's terms, a dynamic long-term strategy to gain legitimacy, secure resources, develop organizational capacity, and win new allies. Etzion and Ferraro (2006) suggest that the GRI attempted to use a two-stage strategy, initially gaining legitimacy through analogies with existing practices, then later emphasizing differences to develop the social and environmental mission. Massie expressed the hope that the GRI process would achieve a 'ratchet effect', as the best performers would drive norms, disseminate best practices, and lead to tightening of standards in the guidelines. This hope has been borne out, at least in part; a large survey of companies undertaken by UNEP found that pressure to follow competitors was the second most important reason for adopting NFR (Palenberg, Reinicke, and Witte, 2006: 20). Yet the momentum of the GRI ratchet appears to be stalling.

Economic and organizational dimensions of actors' strategies and field governance are often overlooked; attending to these dimensions provides a fuller account of the rise of the GRI as well as the constraints it now faces. The competing logics of civil regulation and social performance management, for example, represent sets of beliefs and values concerning NFR. Yet it is important to note that these are also competing ideas about the organizational structures of corporate governance and their economic consequences. As such, they are not arbitrary, free-floating discourses unmoored from economic and political processes. Indeed, there is a central tension between the discursive promise of the GRI and the emerging economic and political experience of the GRI.

ECONOMIC STRUCTURES AND STRATEGIES

For managers who have traditionally considered environmental and social concerns to be costly burdens and unwelcome constraints on their strategic autonomy, the notion that improving social performance can lead to better financial results represents a substantial shift in managerial logic. Promoting the business case for the GRI is thus, in one sense, a discursive strategy. The successful diffusion of win-win discourse, however, does not rely solely on the skillful rhetoric or legitimacy of its advocates. The institutionalization of CSR and social reporting requires the alignment of discursive, economic, and organizational elements within an organic, self-sustaining and mutually reinforcing totality. For win-win discourse to gain initial traction, it needed to make credible claims regarding specific mechanisms by which financial and social performance could be linked. These claims are reinforced if subsequent economic results substantiate the claims, but will be weakened if these results fail to materialize.

The GRI has been presented as a managerial tool useful for driving material benefits such as product differentiation, reputational value, lower legal risks, and employee motivation. Justifying win-win discourse by theorizing these causal mechanisms is, in itself, a discursive strategy, but the strategy would gain little traction unless the claims were sufficiently credible and eventually borne out. Framing the GRI as analogous to FASBI, for example, is more than a legitimation strategy (Etzion and Ferraro, 2006); it relies on GRI data having a material impact on financial performance to enroll investors and corporate managers in the GRI alliance.

The prospect of material benefits seems to be the primary motivation for business adoption of the GRI. The GRI secretariat has claimed that the reporting system 'provides tools for: management, increased comparability and reduced costs of sustainability, brand and reputation enhancement, differentiation in the marketplace, protection from brand erosion resulting from the actions of suppliers or competitors, networking and communications . . . provides the private sector with a vehicle to better inform capital-market decision makers and analysts to ensure stakeholder value (GRI 2007a)'. The UNEP survey found that the strategic management of brand reputation was by far the most significant driver behind NFR, with 94 percent rating it as very important or important (Palenberg, Reinicke, and Witte, 2006: 20). Our own interviews suggested that the GRI is most important as a tool for managing corporate sustainability efforts, assessing and protecting corporate reputation, and enhancing brand values. One manager in a large office products retailer commented: 'Reporting is expensive . . . we do it to get recognition as a sustainability conscious business and to be listed on the DJ Sustainability Index.'

The business case for CSR is not well supported by empirical research. The relationship between social and financial performance has received intense academic scrutiny in recent years, but no firm conclusions emerge from this body of work. At best, a weak positive correlation can be discerned, though it is always a challenge to infer the direction of causation; well-managed, financially successful companies are likely to devote more resources to social performance (Guerard, 1997; Margolis, Elfenbein, and Walsh, 2007; Simpson and Kohers, 2002; Waddock and Graves, 2000). Vogel (2005) has argued that CSR only holds potential for premium product pricing within narrow niche segments comprising affluent, socially aware consumers. Modest but well-publicized investments in CSR might play a broader role in a defensive marketing strategy that protects brand reputation. Part of the methodological and analytical problem is that CSR is a complex and multifaceted phenomenon, taking different forms in different companies, countries and industries. We therefore need finer-grained research to understand which forms of social performance under which conditions might indeed affect financial outcomes.

The indeterminacy and ambiguity regarding the financial-social performance relationship has important implications. On the one hand, it opens more discretionary space for managers and for discursive strategies by CSR advocates. Oliver (1991) has argued that the institutional forces of normative influence and imitation are stronger under conditions of uncertainty because the economic consequences of actions are unclear. On the other hand, in the absence of demonstrable financial benefits, there is not a strong positive feedback loop between discursive advocacy for CSR, the adoption of practices, and financial performance.

The initial enthusiasm surrounding NFR, and the GRI in particular, appears to be eroding as economic benefits fail to materialize. According to the UNEP survey, annual growth in NFR reporting fluctuated between 20 percent and 40 percent in the period 1996 to 2003. Since 2004, however, annual growth has fallen to near zero, and in some countries, including the US and Scandinavia, reporting rates have actually declined (KPMG, 2005). Some managers explicitly connected this decline to the absence of benefits from NFR, and one interviewee in the UNEP study stated: 'the benefits [of NFR] that so many people have been talking about simply have not been realized. There is a supposed business case but many companies have not yet found it' (Palenberg, Reinicke, and Witte, 2006: 14). Companies also expressed concern at the growing costs of increasingly sophisticated and complex NFR, particularly the expense of external auditing and assurance services. In our interviews, a sustainability manager at a large beverage company noted: 'considering the cost of preparing the report – 1 million Euros [US$ 1.25 million] – I cannot show that I earned money from it'. A manager at a European bank remarked that cost concerns were driving a decision to reduce the corporate social report from 100 to seven pages and incorporate it into the annual financial report.

To develop a successful institution, the GRI entrepreneurs understood that they needed to secure the collaboration not only of reporting companies but also of other stakeholder organizations including labor, NGOs, consultants, auditors and financial analysts. Yet the material value of NFR has not lived up to its promise for most of these groups either, weakening the coalition underpinning the emerging institution. A key reason is the difficulty in realizing value from 'supplying CSR' to stakeholders other than consumers (Vogel, 2005). Participating in the GRI development process is a significant resource burden for smaller labor organizations and NGOs, and these groups have expressed disappointment with the value of the reports. There is widespread agreement that NFR reports are rarely studied in any detail. The director of sustainability of a large chemicals company noted that: 'Reporting is important because we need to show that we are transparent . . . but there are not too many readers of the reports actually'. One interviewee stated that: 'recently a journalist told us to keep on writing, but do not expect us to read it'.

NGOs are generally looking for detailed, critical, and issue-specific data that help them pursue their campaigns. The GRI lacks this level of detail and critical orientation, due to its focus on management processes. As a consequence, participation by labor and NGOs in the GRI process has declined markedly. An interviewee at a major US environmental NGO commented that: 'We don't really use GRI reports. The information is not detailed enough; a single number is not enough; we are interested in strategies and plans behind the numbers'. On the other hand, much of the information is qualitative and thus hard to quantify and standardize across companies and industries, making it difficult to use to rank and compare performance. NGOs appear to be losing faith that investing in the development of NFR represents a good use of their resources, and tend not to trust the external assurance provided by commercial auditors.

Financial analysts have also been reluctant partners in the GRI. The GRI entrepreneurs had anticipated that their reports would have instrumental value to financial analysts, whose primary task is to assess corporate market value and the risks facing various companies. The goal was not just to build legitimacy for social reporting in parallel to financial reporting, by way of analogy as argued by Etzion and Ferraro (2006), but rather to locate social reporting as integral to financial reporting. The GRI, it was claimed, would highlight sources of potential value as well as risks that would not be captured in conventional financial data. The UNEP report, however, (Palenberg, Einicke, and Witte, 2006: 24) concluded that although one or two large players were beginning to engage with NFR to some degree, overall 'interest in non-financial issues is currently negligible, if it exists at all. Non-financial risks have little if any visibility among mainstream investment analysts'. Moreover, the instrumental value of the GRI for financial analysts depends on the existence of a correlation between social and financial performance; financial analysts remain unconvinced on this point.

Initiatives such as the Investor Network on Climate Risk and the Carbon Disclosure Project (CDP) have recently tried to use a similar strategy to the GRI. The CDP, representing investors with more than US$31 trillion in assets, has begun collecting annual data from large MNEs about their carbon emissions and climate-related risks (Lash and Wellington, 2007; The Climate Group, 2007). The GRI, however is a much more generic reporting tool than the CDP and, according to our interviewees, does not provide financial analysts with the detailed company and sector-specific information they need. An executive with a social investment firm with a website that compares and ranks companies' sustainability performance stated: 'The value of information derives from it coming from a very large number of companies, preferably quantitative. The GRI does not provide us with such information because too few companies report'. Another interviewee remarked that: 'The GRI information is not specific enough on non-environmental topics . . . it is not sufficiently specific for shareholders' engagement'.

GRI advocates had anticipated the expansion of Socially Responsible Investment (SRI) funds and the application of the GRI as an assessment tool within the SRI segment. The SRI segment of the financial industry has, of course, been engaged in NFR and the development of the GRI in particular. Joan Bavaria, president of Trillium investments, was a founder of Ceres and an early participant in the GRI's development. SRI funds, however, are looking for rationalized, quantifiable social performance measures that can be entered on a spreadsheet and used to guide portfolio allocations. Déjean et al. (2004) have demonstrated how the French SRI industry evolved using simple indices from a specialized company, ARESE, providing the legitimacy of reliable and objective measures derived from a complex process and professional expertise. In the US, moreover, intense market pressures have pushed SRI funds to develop their own proprietary data collection mechanisms rather than rely on a standard reporting system such as the GRI. A long-time observer of the reporting field and a former investment analyst remarked:

> These days, private research in-house by SRI funds has replaced the work done in the past by non-profits. This raises the overhead costs of these funds. Since information is free (on the web) the market value comes from processing the information using proprietary algorithms and ranking schemes and from the experience, good judgment and client relationships of the people who process the information, who raise proprietary claims on the methods and the results. GRI did not reduce these costs by consolidating and harmonizing the information. To the contrary, GRI set its main goal as outcompeting other reporting systems.

In other words, the GRI faces not just a problem of legitimacy, but also of practical and market value in the context of the economic dynamics of market competition within the SRI segment. SRI funds, under conditions of intense competition, are striving to charge higher fees for differentiated, proprietary services. The GRI, however, as a generic, standardized and publicly-available system, offers a commodity product. Moreover, SRI funds remain a very small component of total financial investments, estimated between 1 percent and 2 percent globally (Vogel, 2005: 60). This stagnation of SRI funds is unsurprising given the lack of any perceptible financial performance advantage (Vogel, 2005: 37). One interviewee in the UNEP study said: 'We expected this market to grow fast and not to linger around 1 percent of all investments as is the case today. Our prognosis of higher returns has not materialized' (Palenberg, Reinicke, and Witte, 2006: 24). The win-win claims for SRI, like those for NFR, are not reinforced by material experience.

The auditors, consultants and certifiers of corporate social performance reports have derived the most tangible economic benefits from NFR, and remain among its strongest supporters. Traditional accountancy firms, who lost substantial chunks of their consulting business in the wake of the Enron and WorldCom scandals and ensuing financial regulation, have been eager to develop the sustainability reporting market. PwC and KPMG have been the main competitors in this market segment, which emphasizes the verification of reports but does not generally attempt to assess sustainability performance. Non-profit consultancies, such as AccountAbility and Forum for the Future, provide a broader range of services to companies related to improving, measuring, and assessing their social and environmental performance. The president of a global standard-setting organization commented that: 'The accounting firms got a big piece of GRI from the very beginning – the focus on other users and their needs was not very well developed'.

ORGANIZATIONAL STRUCTURES AND STRATEGIES

The constituent organizations of a field are a key element in field-level governance. They participate in more formal activities such as negotiating the structure and rules of the institution, and they exercise governance more informally by promoting certain practices and norms. They form alliances with some organizations and engage in struggles against others. In their everyday activities, organizations actively contribute to the structuring of a field: the NFR field is shaped and constituted by the social and environmental activities of companies, their reporting practices, the strategies pursued by NGOs, and the nature of work done by consultants and auditors associated with the field. The organizational structure of a field represents, in a profound sense, its political structure.

The GRI entrepreneurs clearly appreciated that the establishment of a new institution required the mobilization of a broad coalition of diverse actors. This mobilization rested, in part, on the discursive and economic strategies discussed earlier. But it also required more overtly organizational strategies that were developed out of a sophisticated appreciation of organizational processes and structures. For example, the GRI was not launched as a finished product; rather, the entrepreneurs established a multi-stakeholder process for developing a set of rules and practices and building a sense of shared ownership. They created an organization, the GRI secretariat, to serve as steward and guide it through an evolutionary process of growth and adaptation. They also understood the importance of establishing the GRI as a new organizational form independent of its roots in Ceres. These organizational sensitivities are reflected in Bob Massie's message to potential GRI partners:

> We want you to be part of the Steering Committee so that you can have some control over it. But if you choose not to, we shall keep you fully informed anyway. If at one point you decide to join, you will be welcomed. And, most importantly, if it proves to be successful, we will spin it off as an independent organization, so you can be sure that GRI is not a plot to grow the power of Ceres, which, of course, is an advocacy organization with an agenda.

The GRI's founders had strong personal and organizational networks with influential people and better resourced organizations, which helped overcome their own location in Ceres and Tellus, small organizations without substantial resources or any formal authority. It was these networks that provided them with the access and legitimacy to construct the necessary coalition, securing the early participation of some large corporations and financial institutions. The GRI entrepreneurs understood the dynamics by which the participation of some organizations would provide leverage to bring others in. They deliberately avoided association with government agencies such as the Securities and Exchange Commission (SEC) that might deter corporate participation by signaling a mandatory regulatory approach. Instead, they secured the support of the Association of Public Accountants in the US, the Federation of European Accountants, and UNEP – signaling the seriousness and legitimacy of the initiative.

The dynamic evolution of the GRI is not just a function of the entrepreneurial efforts of its founders, but also of the interactions, negotiations and struggles among its constituent organizations. A key reason for companies to engage in social reporting is in response to pressure from activist NGOs and other stakeholders; the UNEP survey ranked this as the third most important driver (Palenberg, Reinicke, and Witte, 2006: 20). NGO pressure appears to be waning, as they shift their strategies away from demands for more reporting. This decline in NGO interest has shifted the center of gravity of field level governance toward MNEs, consultants and auditors. At the 2008 GRI annual meeting only 60 participants represented NGOs and four represented labor out of a total of more than 1000 attendees.

A number of states and the EU considered making social reporting mandatory, and pressure from state authorities could potentially have sustained growth in NFR. In the US, most GRI participants, corporate and NGO alike, have opposed mandatory reporting, however, as contrary to the spirit of the initiative and likely to lead to a legalistic compliance approach rather than a multi-stakeholder collaboration. A few companies, including the Dutch banking group ABN Amro, have supported mandatory reporting in order to level the playing field with competitors. In 2001, France became the first country to mandate social and environmental reporting, though not in a form derived from the GRI, while other governments appear to be losing interest. The EU has enacted a Transparency Directive, which was implemented beginning 2007, but efforts to include social and environmental reporting requirements have stalled. According to the UNEP report, the EU's CSR agenda has been effectively 'torpedoed by business associations' that lobbied against the program (Palenberg, Reinicke, and Witte, 2006: 26–7).

DISCUSSION

By many measures, the GRI entrepreneurs were phenomenally successful in launching the initiative and achieved a high rate of uptake among large companies across many countries. The success of the GRI presents an example of strategic power; the founders of the GRI came from small organizations lacking substantial resources or formal authority, yet were able to propagate an institution that has shifted the practices of large MNEs and gained recognition, if not formal backing, from states and international organizations. The GRI founders used skillful strategy in analyzing the existing field and implementing a combination of interventions in an attempt to realize their vision. Acting as the Modern Prince, they simultaneously tended to internal strategy, the development of the GRI itself as an organization, and external strategy. They built a network of allies, promoting a business model that would provide resources not just for the GRI but also rewards for network participants, and adopting a discursive strategy centered on the win-win claims of CSR and similarities to FASBI.

The GRI now appears to be losing momentum, however. The complex dynamic nature of fields suggests that strategy is fallible, however skillful institutional entrepreneurs might be. It is impossible to develop a perfect strategy with predictable outcomes; incomplete and inaccurate understandings of field structures and processes result in unforeseen consequences, and other actors possess the agency to react in unexpected ways. Indeed, it is this very fallibility and complexity that both enables and constrains strategic power. In a fully predictable world, there would be no room for indeterminacy and contestation; outcomes would be structurally determined and those with superior access to resources, usually with a vested interest in the status quo, would always triumph.

One limitation on the strategic power of institutional entrepreneurs is that institutions cannot be created out of thin air. The institutional elements need to form a functioning, self-sustaining system, one which operates as a subsystem within a broader social and economic formation. New institutions are built by weaving together existing economic, discursive, and organizational threads; they represent transformations and reconfigurations rather than creation *ex nihilo*. The process of change is therefore one of steering the system trajectory, of 'transition management' (Meadowcroft, 2005) and 'mindful deviation' from the original path (Garud and Karnoe, 2001). The point of departure is, of necessity, the current situation. Any change effort needs to account for the current reality in its material, organizational and ideational dimensions, and to exploit the existing dynamic forces at play.

The very strategies that enabled the successful launch of the GRI contained tensions that later emerged as significant constraints. The GRI entrepreneurs framed the initiative in somewhat different terms for different audiences. NGOs were promised a greater role in corporate governance, firms were promised higher profits, while consultants and auditors expected a new source of business. The win-win discourse of CSR provided did not eliminate the tensions when the promised benefits failed to materialize. The compromises involved in shaping the GRI also limited its value; it lacked the detailed information needed by some stakeholders and the quantifiable measures sought by others.

Did the GRI's founders make strategic errors? Perhaps a different strategy, based on NGO mobilization, might have met more initial resistance, but laid the groundwork for a more fundamental shift in corporate governance. The nature of institutional entrepreneurship in complex fields, however, suggests that it is impossible to identify an optimum strategy guaranteed to achieve a particular result. The need to align the new institutional form with the 'master rules of society' (Haveman and Rao, 1997) inevitably creates tensions and inhibits change. Strategy is thus inherently 'satisficing' rather than optimizing, with a more pragmatic goal to keep the process moving, navigate around obstacles, and manage the ongoing tensions.

Indeed, the GRI has displayed a degree of resilience and adaptability. Since 2006, the GRI has made a significant effort to engage small and medium sized enterprises (SMEs), which constitute the vast majority of all companies worldwide. In a partnership with the World Resources Institute, the GRI is reaching out to SMEs in Brazil, China, India, Indonesia, and Mexico. The GRI has also partnered with several Europe-based MNEs to engage small companies in their global supply chains to become GRI reporters. In early 2008, the GRI launched an initiative to develop guidelines for sustainability reporting by the non-profit sector, organizations which had previously been conceived as consumers rather than producers of reports.

The GRI case highlights the importance of economic structures, processes and strategies in shaping emerging institutions. Etzion and Ferraro's (2006) account of the GRI, by focusing narrowly on discursive structures and strategies, risks overplaying the agency of institutional entrepreneurs and underestimating the structural inertia of hegemonic fields. As benefits of the GRI have failed to materialize, support for NFR from NGOs, investors, and companies has waned. It was not sufficient to create a discursive linkage between NFR and FASBI; NFR needed to prove its economic value for financial analysts. This contradiction between the economic and discursive dimensions of win-win has prevented the GRI from constructing and stabilizing a new hegemonic bloc in which NGOs would play a stronger governance role. Even SRI funds have embraced a more overtly capitalist logic, looking to differentiate their ratings mechanisms and increasingly prioritizing economic over social performance (Palenberg, Reinicke, and Witte, 2006: 24). Over time, the institutional logic of NFR has shifted toward corporate marketing and enhancing corporate reputation rather than a more profound shift of governance toward a more diverse array of stakeholders. Indeed, the center of gravity of NFR governance has shifted from NGOs toward corporate consultants and auditors.

NFR is nested within the broader institutions of capitalism, particularly financial markets and legal structures of corporate governance, which are resilient and well entrenched. The case illustrates how NGO initiatives are constrained by these larger structures of power, particularly the economic and political power of corporate elites and consumerist popular culture. The GRI would never have made any progress had it directly challenged the primacy of profit maximization, the legal rights of shareholders, the autonomy of corporate management, or the conventional US corporate board structure that excludes representatives of the community, the environment, or labor. It is easier to create change within nested subsystems than the more stable and hegemonic wider system.

These considerations led the GRI entrepreneurs to shape the reporting guidelines as complementary to corporate and financial market needs. The strategic risk, of course, is that the GRI would be co-opted and assimilated within these structures rather than transforming them. This does appear to be the emerging outcome. Companies are frequently willing to embrace NFR as a demonstration of their social concern, but have proven unwilling to tolerate a system that provides clear measures and rankings of their social and environmental performance. Moreover, NFR does not appear to be affecting core product or market strategies. The corporate sector has expressed its opposition to a mandatory reporting system or the extension of formal governance mechanisms. Successfully navigating these tensions in the social reporting field, however, might simply be impossible without a broader mobilization of civil society groups that would engage across a range of issues and institutions.

ENDNOTES

1. This and other quotations from Robert Massie are from personal interviews, 2005 and 2006.
2. This includes a small number of 'in accordance' reports that are modelled closely on the GRI guidelines, but not reports based on competing reporting guidelines, though these often contain GRI components.

REFERENCES

Bair, J. (2007), 'From the politics of development to the challenges of globalization', *Globalizations*, 4(4): 486–99.

Berman, J.E. et al. (2003), *Race to the top: Attracting and enabling global sustainable business, Business Survey Report*, World Bank Group.

Boxenbaum, E. and J. Battilana (2005), 'Importation as innovation: transposing managerial practices across fields', *Strategic Organization*, 3(4): 355–83.

Brown, H.S., M. de Jong and T. Lessidrenska (2009), 'The rise of the Global Reporting Initiative as a case of institutional entrepreneurship', *Environmental Politics*, 18(2): 182–200.

Brown, H.S., M. de Jong and D. Levy (2009), 'Building institutions based on information disclosure: lessons from GRI's sustainability reporting', *Journal of Cleaner Production*, 17(6): 571–80.

Callon, M. (1998), *The laws of the markets*, Oxford: Blackwell.

Cashore, B., G. Auld and D. Newsom (2004), *Governing through markets*, New Haven, CT: Yale University Press.

Ceres, (1997), 'Global Reporting Initiative concept paper', unpublished working-paper, Boston, MA: Coalition of Environmentally Responsible Economies.

Clemens, E.S. and J.M. Cook (1999), 'Politics and institutionalism: explaining durability and change', *Annual Review of Sociology*, **25**(1): 441–66.

Colomy, P. (1998), 'Neofunctionalism and neoinstitutionalism: human agency and interest in institutional change', *Sociological Forum*, **13**(2): 265–300.

Déjean, F., J.-P. Gond and B. Leca (2004), 'Measuring the unmeasured: an institutional entrepreneur strategy in an emerging industry', *Human Relations*, **57**(6): 741–64.

DeWinter, R. (2001), 'The anti-sweatshop movement: constructing corporate moral agency in the global apparel industry', *Ethics & International Affairs*, **15**(2): 99–115.

Dingwerth, K. (2007), *The new transnationalism: transnational governance and democratic legitimacy*, Basingstoke: Palgrave Macmillan.

Elkington, J. (1994), 'Towards the sustainable corporation: win-win-win business strategies for sustainable development', *California Management Review*, **36**(2): 90–100.

Etzion, D. and F. Ferraro (2010), 'The role of analogy in the institutionalization of sustainability reporting', *Organization Science*, **21**(5): 1092–107.

Fiorino, D.J. (2006), *The new environmental regulation*, Cambridge, MA: MIT Press.

Florini, A. (2003), *The coming democracy: New rules for running a new world*, Washington DC: Island Press.

Garud, R. and P. Karnoe (2001), 'Path creation as a process of mindful deviation', in R. Garud and P. Karnoe (eds), *Path dependence and creation*, Mahwah, NJ: Lawrence Erlbaum Associates.

Graham, M. (2002), *Democracy by disclosure: The rise of technopopulism*, Washington, DC: Brookings Institute.

Gramsci, A. (1971), *Selections from the prison notebooks*, trans. Q. Hoare and G. Nowell-Smith, New York: International Publishers.

Greenwood, R. and R. Suddaby (2006), 'Institutional entrepreneurship in mature fields: the Big Five accounting firms', *Academy of Management Journal*, **49**(1): 27–48.

Griffen, J.J. and J.F. Mahon (1997), 'The corporate social performance and corporate financial performance debate: twenty-five years of incomparable research', *Business and Society*, **36**(1): 5–31.

Guerard, J.B. (1997), 'Is there a cost to being socially responsible in investing?', *The Journal of Investing*, **6**: 11–18.

Hart, S.L. (1995), 'A natural-resource-based view of the firm', *Academy of Management Review*, **20**(4): 986–1015.

Haveman, H.A. and H. Rao (1997), 'Structuring a theory of moral sentiments: institutional and organizational coevolution in the early thrift industry', *American Journal of Sociology*, **102**: 1606–51.

Hoffman, A.J. (1999), 'Institutional evolution and change: environmentalism and the US chemical industry', *Academy of Management Journal*, **42**(4): 351–71.

Jepperson, R.L. (1991), 'Institutions, institutional effects, and institutionalism', in W.W. Powell and P.J. DiMaggio (eds), *The new institutionalism in organizational analysis*, Chicago: University of Chicago Press, pp. 143–63.

KPMG (2005), *KPMG International Survey of Corporate Responsibility Reporting*, Amsterdam: KPMG Global Sustainability Services.

Laclau, E. and C. Mouffe (1985), *Hegemony and socialist strategy; towards a radical democratic politics*, New York: Verso.

Lash, J. and F. Wellington (2007), 'Competitive advantage on a warming planet', *Harvard Business Review*, **85**(3): 95–102.

Lawrence, T.B. (1999), 'Institutional strategy', *Journal of Management*, **25**: 161–87.

Lawrence, T.B. and N. Phillips (2004), 'From Moby Dick to Free Willy: macro-cultural discourse and institutional entrepreneurship in emerging institutional fields', *Organization*, **11**(5): 689–711.

Levy, D.L. (1997), 'Environmental management as political sustainability', *Organization and Environment*, **10**(2): 126–47.

Levy, D.L. and R. Kaplan (2008), 'Corporate social responsibility and theories of global governance: strategic contestation in global issue arenas', in A. Crane, A. McWilliams, D. Matten, J. Moon and D. Siegel (eds), *Oxford Handbook of Corporate Social Responsibility*, Oxford: Oxford University Press.

Levy, D.L. and M. Scully (2007), 'The institutional entrepreneur as modern prince: the strategic face of power in contested fields', *Organization Studies*, **28**(7): 971–91.

Maguire, S., C. Hardy and T.B. Lawrence (2004), 'Institutional entrepreneurship in emerging fields: HIV/AIDS treatment advocacy in Canada', *Academy of Management Journal*, **47**(5): 657–79.

Marchand, R. (1998), *Creating the corporate soul: the rise of public relations and corporate imagery in American big business*, Berkeley, CA: University of California Press.

Margolis, J.D., H.A. Elfenbein and J.P. Walsh (2007), 'Does it pay to be good? A meta-analysis and redirection of research on the relationship between corporate social and financial performance', working paper, Harvard Business School.

McAdam, D. and R.W. Scott (2005), 'Organizations and movements', in G.F. Davis, D. McAdam, R.W. Scott and M. Zald (eds), *Social movements and organization theory*, Cambridge, UK: Cambridge University Press, pp. 4–40.

Meadowcroft, J. (2005), 'Environmental political economy, technological transitions, and the state', *New Political Economy*, **10**(4): 479–98.

Munir, K.A. and N. Phillips (2005), 'The birth of the "Kodak Moment": institutional entrepreneurship and the adoption of new technologies', *Organization Studies*, **26**(11): 1665–87.

Murphy, D.F. and J. Bendell (1997), *In the company of partners: business, environmental groups and sustainable development*, Bristol: The Policy Press.

Murphy, D.F. and J. Bendell (1999), *Partners in time? Business, NGOs, and sustainable development*, Geneva: United Nations Reserach Institute for Social Development.

Oliver, C. (1991), Strategic responses to institutional processes, *Academy of Management Review*, **16**: 145–79.

Ougaard, M. (2006), 'Instituting the power to do good?', in C. May (ed.), *Global corporate power*, Boulder, CO: Lynne Rienner.

Palenberg, M., W. Reinicke and J.M. Witte (2006), *Trends in non-financial reporting*, Berlin, Germany: GPPI/UNEP, Division of Technology, Industry and Economics.

Phillips, N., T.B. Lawrence and C. Hardy (2004), 'Discourse and institutions', *Academy of Management Review*, **29**(4): 635–52.

Prakash, A. and J. Hart (eds) (1999), *Globalization and governance*, London: Routledge.

Rao, H., C. Morrill and M.N. Zald (2000), 'Power plays: how social movements and collective action create new organizational forms', *Research in Organizational Behaviour*, **22**: 239–82.

Russo, M.V. and P.A. Fouts (1997), 'A resource-based perspective on corporate environmental performance and profitability', *Academy of Management Journal*, **40**(3): 534–59.

Scott, W.R., M. Ruef, P.J.Mendel and C.A. Caronna (2000), *Institutional change and healthcare organizations*, Chicago: University of Chicago Press.

Selznick, P. (1980), *Tennessee Valley Authority and the grass roots: A study in the sociology of formal organization*, Berkeley, CA: University of California Press.

Shamir, R. (2004a), 'Between self-regulation and the Alien Tort Claims Act: on the contested concept of corporate social responsibility', *Law & Society Review*, **38**(4): 635–53.

Shamir, R. (2004b). 'The de-radicalization of corporate social responsibility'. *Critical Sociology*, **30**(3): 669–89.

Simpson, W.G. and T. Kohers (2002), 'The link between corporate social and financial performance: evidence from the banking industry', *Journal of Business Ethics*, **35**(2): 97–109.

Teegen, H., J.P. Doh and S. Vachani (2004), 'The importance of nongovernmental organizations in global governance and value creation: an international business research agenda', *Journal of International Business Studies*, **35**(6): 463–83.

The Climate Group (2007), *Carbon down, profits up (3rd edition)*, Weybridge, Surrey, UK: The Climate Group.

Utting, P. (2002), 'Regulating business via multistakeholder initiatives: a preliminary assessment', in P. Utting (ed.), *Voluntary Approaches to Corporate Responsibility*, Geneva: United Nations Non-Governmental Liaison Service, pp. 61–130.

Vogel, D.J. (2005), *The market for virtue: the potential and limits of corporate social responsibility*, Washington, DC: Brookings Institution Press.

Waddock, S. and S. Graves (2000), 'Performance characteristics of social and traditional investments', *Journal of Investing*, **9**(2): 27–38.

Zysman, J. (1994), 'How institutions create historically rooted trajectories of growth', *Industrial and Corporate Change*, **3**: 243–83.

7. Driving to distraction or disclosure? Shareholder activism, institutional investors and firms' environmental transparency

R. Scott Marshall, Darrell Brown and Marlene Plumlee

Recent actions by a variety of constituencies suggest an increased interest in the voluntary disclosure of environmental information by publicly traded firms. In the US a congressional hearing addressed issues of corporate disclosure of environmental information (CSWG, 2004), while the SEC assigned the Government Accounting Office to report on environmental disclosures within corporate reports (GAO, 2004). The Netherlands, Finland, Spain and Japan currently require corporate reporting of environmental data by certain publicly listed companies (KPMG, 2005; Llena, Moneva and Hernandez, 2006); other countries are contemplating following suit (Kolk, 2008). These developments are consistent with an increased role for environmental information about corporate operations to investment and managerial decision-makers. However, aside from required disclosures related to contingent environmental liabilities and toxic waste emissions, disclosure of environmental-related information remains largely unregulated in the US. Ultimately the decision to disclose environmental information and the quality of those disclosures is managerial-based as influenced by the board of directors and shareholders (Millstein, 1991).

While many suggest that corporate governance defined as the rules and practices that govern the relationship between managers, boards and shareholders (Jensen and Meckling, 1976), guides the extent and method of information disclosures made by companies, evidence of this relation is limited. In this study we build from the increased emphasis on environmental disclosures and the expressed importance of good corporate governance in determining the extent of information disclosure in general to explore this relation. Specifically, we examine the association between specific aspects of corporate governance and the quality of environmental information disclosed by firms. Our findings contribute to the literature documenting the relation between governance and transparency and, to some extent, exploring the question of whether sustainability reporting is being driven top-down or by stakeholders (Schaltegger and Burritt, 2006).

We also extend existing research in the corporate governance area by isolating a unique set of characteristics related to three specific governance related factors – institutional investor type, shareholder proposal outcomes and board composition. We discuss how these characteristics affect a comprehensive measure of the quality of voluntary environmental disclosure. Our development and discussion provides a context for examining the empirical relation between corporate governance and voluntary environmental disclosure. We examine the relation between the corporate governance characteristics and voluntary environmental disclosures for a sample of 183 firms over a three-year period (2000, 2001 and 2002). This paper lends some insights into the question of whether external and internal stakeholders are motivating firms to, or distracting firms from, higher quality environmental disclosures.

Finally, we extend existing research in the CSR disclosure area. In this study we employ a measure of the quality of voluntary environmental disclosure based on progressive levels of environmental strategy and management. This instrument captures variance over a broad range of voluntary environmental disclosures made by firms – data often unmeasured by less comprehensive instruments – ultimately providing a more precise measure of differences in voluntary environmental reporting quality across firms.

We organize the remainder of the chapter as follows. First we discuss the two concepts of primary interest – voluntary disclosure and corporate governance. We then define our disclosure measure, including a description of how we determine the quality of voluntary environmental disclosure, and discuss prior research focusing on the drivers of such disclosures. Next we discuss the characteristics of corporate governance employed in our study and develop a set of hypotheses linking these with voluntary environmental disclosures. After describing our data collection and hypothesis testing we conclude with a discussion of the implications for scholars and practitioners.

BACKGROUND AND HYPOTHESIS DEVELOPMENT

In this section we provide an understanding of the two primary concepts examined in this study and develop hypotheses that link them.

Voluntary Environmental Disclosure

Berthelot, Cormier and Magnan (2003: 1) define corporate environmental disclosure as 'the set of information items that relate to a firm's past, current and future environmental management activities and performance ... and the past, current and future financial implications resulting from a firm's environmental management decisions or actions'. We examine voluntary environmental disclosures (VEDs), the quantitative and qualitative measures related to firm-specific environmental issues that provide a wide variety of stakeholders with information beyond that required by law. In this chapter we capture the quality of VEDs using both the substance and form of environmental indicators reported by a firm. We argue that while disclosing information about specific environmental issues informs stakeholders, presenting the information relative to production enhances corporate transparency; presenting the information along with the firm's past performance enhances transparency even more.[1] Capturing the variance in the related disclosures enhances the ability of our measure to capture disclosure quality instead of relying simply on the quantity of the disclosed items.

Corporate Governance

Corporate governance encompasses a variety of mechanisms by which corporate stakeholders exercise control over management in order to protect their interests (Ingley and van der Walt, 2004). In our study we examine the relationship between three specific aspects of corporate governance: (1) type of institutional investors, (2) shareholders' proposal outcomes, and (3) board composition. Prior research suggests institutional investors and boards of directors have the ability to influence management, ensuring that a firm's assets are used in the interests of all financial stakeholders (Bradley, 2004). Examining variance in the specific attributes included in this study provides a better understanding of how corporate governance might affect firms' VED decisions.

Institutional investors, including pension funds, mutual funds and insurance companies, collectively account for more than half of all registered shares in publicly held firms (Ingley and van der Walt, 2004). As such, they represent significant stakeholders with strong incentives to monitor firms in which they own stock (Demsetz and Lehn, 1985). For example, the California Public Employees' Retirement System (CalPERS) recently announced that it would track companies in environmentally sensitive industries that failed to adequately disclose environmental data (Taub, 2006).

Prior research suggests institutional investors have distinct preferences for some firm attributes and that different types of institutional investors provide differential levels of firm monitoring or influence. For example, Hoskisson et al. (2002) and Tihanyi et al. (2003) provide evidence that institutional investors vary in their preferences for internal versus external innovation and international diversification, while Bushee (1998) finds institutional investors vary in their preferences for firms that invest in research and development. Prior research examining institutional investor preferences related to CSR (Johnson and Greening, 1999) found a significant relationship between higher pension fund equity and socially based and product quality characteristics of firms.

Findings from some of this research suggest that differences in institutional time horizons and liquidity issues drive differences in institutional investors influence. On the one hand, pension plans generally have a longer term perspective regarding their investments; they are also more likely to engage in activities focused on longer term investments by management (Bushee, 1998; Ryan and Schneider, 2002). On the other hand, investment funds have a shorter term perspective and rely on market forces for obtaining performance. These funds are less likely to engage in activities that influence managerial decision-making (Ryan and Schneider, 2002).

Hypothesis Development

Our study builds on the prior research in both environmental disclosure and corporate governance in two ways. First, based on prior theoretical and empirical work (such as Haniffa and Cooke, 2002; Hoskisson, et al., 2002), we examine the influence of three specific aspects of corporate governance on VED quality. Second, we provide a comprehensive method of measuring VED quality by analyzing the means by which firms choose to frame their disclosures. We believe that incorporating how firms systematically disclose information provides a finer measure of VED quality than quantity alone.

Prior studies (Haniffa and Cooke, 2002; Ho and Wong, 2001) describe the conceptual link between firm disclosure decisions and corporate governance. Figure 7.1 illustrates the aspects of corporate governance related to institutional investor type, shareholder proposal outcomes and board composition examined in this study. The discussion below details the hypotheses drawn from this literature.

Emerson et al. (2005) document that long-horizon investors consider such factors as environmental growth potential, climate change, environmental liabilities and environmental license to operate in their assessment of investments In the absence of standardized reporting about

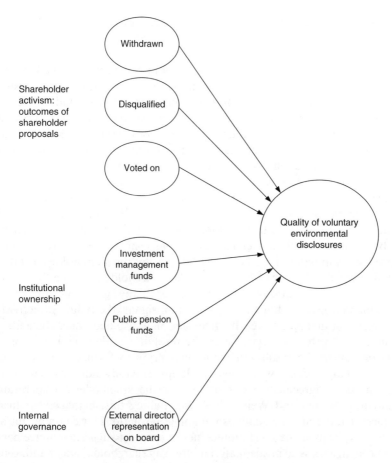

Figure 7.1   Shareholder activism, institutional ownership and internal governance as drivers of the quality of firm's voluntary environmental disclosures

environmental attributes, long-horizon investors rely on voluntary corporate environmental disclosures. High quality environmental disclosures, focusing on leading indicators, environmental performance and explicit goals or commitments are most likely to provide information related to long-term organizational results (Marshall and Brown, 2003; EEA, 1999). Based on this and related research, we offer the following hypotheses related to the quality of VEDs and investor type.

Hypothesis 1a: Pension fund equity in a firm is positively related to the firm's quality of voluntary environmental disclosures.

Hypothesis 1b: Investment fund equity in a firm is negatively related to the firm's quality of voluntary environmental disclosures.

Shareholder proposals.   A means of corporate governance available to investors, given they have chosen to invest in a firm, is investor activism.[2] Activism can take a variety of forms, from cooperative (including behind the scenes dialogue and meetings with top management) to adversarial (including shareholder resolutions and proxy voting) (Graves, Rehbein and Waddock, 2001). To capture this form of corporate governance, we explore the link between shareholder resolution outcomes and VED quality.

Within certain limits, shareholders who own at least US$2000 or 1 percent (whichever is less) of a company's stock may file resolutions regarding issues they want brought to a shareholder vote. The number of shareholder resolutions filed has increased over the recent past, particularly social responsibility-related resolutions (Smith, 2005). Resolutions, once filed, ultimately may be (1) withdrawn by the shareholder, (2) disqualified by the SEC or (3) voted on at the shareholder meeting.

Shareholder resolutions may be filed prior to any significant interaction with management, although the filing often signals the failure of activist-management dialogue to reach agreement on a disputed issue. Once filed, management often negotiates with the resolution's filers with the objective of having the resolution withdrawn prior to formal consideration (Graves et al., 2001). A withdrawn resolution generally indicates that negotiations led to agreement or compromise on the issue under consideration (Carelton, Nelson and Weisbach, 1998). Failing this, management may request that the SEC disqualify shareholder resolutions based on technical issues. Typically if the resolution comes to a vote it suggests management has been unsuccessful in adequately addressing shareholder issues and, generally, the sponsor is permitted to speak to the resolution at annual meetings. Thus, proxy contests allow the sponsor to gain greater attention for the issue among shareholders, generate broader publicity and place heightened pressure on the firm to attend to the resolution issue (Waddock, 2000).

Based on the above discussion we posit the following hypotheses relating to various resolution outcomes and the quality of VED.

Hypothesis 2a: The number of withdrawn shareholder resolutions dealing with environmental information disclosure is positively related to a firm's quality of voluntary environmental disclosures.

Hypothesis 2b: The number of disqualified shareholder resolutions dealing with environmental information disclosure is negatively related to a firm's quality of voluntary environmental disclosure.

Hypothesis 2c: The number of shareholder resolutions dealing with environmental information disclosure voted on at shareholder meetings is positively related to a firm's quality of voluntary environmental disclosures.

Board composition. Boards of directors oversee the actions and decisions of corporate management. Kostant (1999) suggests that directors act as stewards of communication among corporate stakeholders; a role essential to improving efficiency and increasing cooperation. We argue that board composition, defined as the proportion of external directors to the total number of directors (Goodstein, Gautam and Boeker, 1994; Pfeffer, 1972), affects how boards fulfill that role. Advocates for external board representation suggest that external members are needed to monitor and control the actions of internal directors and offset inside members' opportunistic behaviors (Jensen and Meckling, 1976). Further, external directors generally have stronger stakeholder orientations and expand corporate engagement beyond shareholders to various corporate constituencies (Wang and Dewhirst, 1992). As such, external directors are often included on a board to assist in managing external constituencies (Pfeffer, 1972). Because external directors bring a broader awareness of and concern for stakeholder issues, we posit that their presence leads to increased quality of VED.

Hypothesis 3: External director representation on a firm's board is positively related to the firm's quality of voluntary environmental disclosures.

METHODS

Sample

To test our hypotheses, we employ a sample of firms drawn from five industries: (1) chemical, (2) oil and gas, (3) utilities (electrical), (4) pharmaceutical and biotech, and (5) food and beverage. We restrict our sample to firms within a limited set of industries to improve the quality of our data collection; we select these specific industries to provide a contrast of higher to lower polluters based on the Toxic Release Inventory database (Christmann, 2000; Bansal and Clelland, 2004; Kassinis and Vafeas, 2006).[3] Including industries considered high to low polluters provides a comparison of firms that might be differentially driven to voluntarily disclose environmental information (Brammer and Pavelin, 2008), enhancing the power of our empirical tests.

Our initial sample included 416 firms across the five industries from the Dow Jones Global Index. From that set we identified 183 firms with available data to obtain information to complete our disclosure index, although these data were not available for all firms across all three years of our sample period. Next we identified the set of firms for which we could obtain the required control variables. The final data set included 479 firm-years observations. The reduction in our sample from the original group of firms is due to various reasons, including firm mergers and the lack of required data for foreign companies.

Measures

Quality of voluntary environmental disclosure. We employ four related measures of environmental disclosure quality for our dependent variables of interest – compliance, pollution prevention, product stewardship and ecological sustainability. These measures are constructed using data hand-collected from firms' environmental disclosures. Environmental disclosures may be released within a separate Corporate Environmental Report (CER), as an integral component of a firm's overall sustainability report or its environmental, health, and safety report, or as disclosures included in the annual report or 10K annual financial report to the US Securities and Exchange Commission. Prior research to date has looked at the quality of these disclosures in a general manner (Noci, 2000), although research using detailed data that captures variation in the quality of environmental disclosures has been limited to a few recent studies (Brammer and Pavelin, 2008).

To form our measures of VED quality, we use a disclosure index (shown in Appendix 1) developed as follows. Based on a review of the environmental management literature, four levels of environmental strategy were identified.[4] Using these strategy levels and an understanding of disclosure quality assessments obtained through a review of academic and practitioner sources, a coding scheme was developed and tested. Through several iterations we developed a detailed environmental disclosure index (62 specific issues with up to eight different forms of disclosure relating to the four levels of environmental strategy).[5]

For each of our sample firms we collected three years of environmental data (2000, 2001, 2002). If a firm issued a CER for a given year, information contained within the CER was used to complete the index. If no CER was issued for a given firm year, we collected information contained within the firm's annual report or, if no annual report was issued, within the 10K. The dependent variables for quality of VED represent the total number of indicators at each level of disclosure quality for each firm-year.

Institutional investor type. To capture the type of institutional investor we employ two measures: the percentage of equity owned by long-horizon institutional investors such as pension and mutual funds (%Pension) and the percentage of equity owned by institutional short-horizon investors such as banks (%Investment) (Johnson and Greening, 1999). These data are drawn from corporate proxy statements over the study time period.

Shareholder proposals.   The three shareholder resolution outcomes described earlier serve as proxies for the results of negotiations between the sponsor and firm management. The variables are *Withdrawn*, the number of resolutions withdrawn; *Disqualified*, the number of resolutions disqualified; and, *Voted*, the number of resolutions brought to a proxy vote. These data are pooled for each firm-year and represented in our analyses as continuous variables as well as percentages of total environmental disclosure shareholder proposals filed. The data were collected from the Interfaith Center for Corporate Responsibility, which records information regarding all shareholder resolutions related to social and environmental issues filed each year in the US, including the target company, sponsor(s), description of the resolution issue, date of filing and final status of the resolution.

Board composition.   We capture board composition (%External) by the number of directors with no personal or professional relationship to a firm other than board membership, divided by board size (Pfeffer, 1972; Hoskisson et al., 2002). These data were collected for the years 2000, 2001 and 2002 from corporate proxy statements.

Control variables.   Based on previous literature (Bansal and Clelland, 2000; Brammer and Pavelin, 2008), we control for firm size and profitability in our analysis.[6] We employ the natural log of total sales and assets to capture size; return on assets and sales to measure profitability. These data were obtained from Compustat for the years 2000, 2001 and 2002. We also include indicator variables in our regressions for industry at the three levels of pollution: high (chemical and electric utilities), moderate (oil and gas and food and beverage) and low (pharmaceutical and biotech).

RESULTS

Table 7.1 presents a Spearman correlation matrix and descriptive statistics for the variables included in our analyses. Because of the high correlations of the size variables (total sales, total assets) of 0.88 and the profitability variables (logs of return on assets, sales) of 0.49, we include only one size (total sales) and one profitability (return on assets) variable in our regression analyses.

Table 7.1   Descriptive statistics and Spearman correlations for all variables (N = 479)

Variable	Mean	s.d.	1	2	3	4	5	6	7	8	9	10	11	12	13	14	15	16	17
1. %Pension	.01	.03																	
2. %Investment	.08	.11	-.02																
3. Withdrawn	.02	.14	-.05	.08															
4. Disqualified	.02	.12	.01	.01	-.02														
5. Voted	.09	.35	-.01	-.02	.02	.10													
6. %External	.68	4.2	.16	.45	.01	.05	.16												
7. Total sales	8.3	1.3	.06	.12	.11	.11	.27	.27											
8. Total assets	8.7	1.2	.05	.10	.13	.10	.30	.28	.88										
9. ROA	.16	.09	-.13	-.17	.05	.05	.03	-.25	-.02	-.19									
10. ROS	.25	.20	-.17	-.15	.07	.01	.01	-.22	.28	-.02	.49								
11. High_poll	.46	.50	.29	.31	-.02	-.02	.07	.43	.07	.23	-.55	-.17							
12. Mod_poll	.33	.47	-.16	.05	.02	.08	.05	.07	.18	-.01	.42	-.05	-.66						
13. Low_poll	.20	.40	-.16	-.43	-.01	-.07	-.14	-.61	-.29	-.27	.19	.26	-.47	-.36					
14. Compliance	2.6	5.0	.12	.05	.15	.05	.15	.18	.34	.39	-.16	-.06	.36	-.18	-.22				
15. Poll. prev.	3.5	6.2	.10	.11	.16	.08	.14	.24	.39	.44	-.16	-.05	.37	-.15	-.29	.83			
16. Prod. stew.	3.4	6.3	.02	.05	.15	.10	.19	.10	.41	.42	-.13	-.08	.27	-.12	-.20	.63	.68		
17. Ecol. sust.	.11	.49	.08	-.12	.14	.03	.06	-.10	.21	.19	.13	.07	-.03	-.06	.10	.37	.40	.38	
18. All disc.	9.7	16.3	.09	.13	.15	.11	.18	.23	.45	.50	-.22	-.09	.42	-.19	-.30	.85	.91	.85	.40

Notes: Correlations greater than .09 are significant at p < .05; those greater than .13 are significant at p < .01; all two-tailed tests.

We use standard linear regression analysis to test our hypotheses. Table 7.2 presents the regression models for the four types of VED quality – compliance, pollution prevention, product stewardship, and ecological sustainability – along with a measure of total VED.

Hypotheses 1a and 1b posit that pension equity in a firm is positively related and investment fund equity is negatively related to firms' quality of VED. We find no evidence of a relation between pension fund equity percentage and any of our measures of VED. However we do find that investment fund equity is negatively related to all four levels of disclosure, providing support for hypothesis 1b. As the level of ownership by investment funds – short-horizon investors – increases, VED quality decreases.

Hypotheses 2a-c examine the relationships between the outcomes of shareholder activism and VED quality. We find that the number of withdrawn resolutions is significantly and positively related to increased quality of environmental disclosures in terms of compliance, pollution prevention and product stewardship. Overall these results suggest that withdrawal of a resolution prior to proxy voting is consistent with higher VED quality and our hypothesis 2a. For hypothesis 2b, resolution disqualification was found to be marginally significant ($p < .10$) and, counter to expectations, positively related to VED quality in terms of product stewardship, although it is unrelated to any of the other measures of environmental disclosure quality. Hypothesis 2c proposes that the number of resolutions that are ultimately voted on is positively related to VED quality. Again, we fail to find support for this hypothesis. In summary, the only outcome of environmental shareholder resolutions significantly related to higher quality VEDs is the number of resolutions withdrawn.

Hypothesis 3 suggests that external director representation on a firm's board is positively related to the firm's quality of VED. We find no empirical support for hypothesis 3; board composition is unrelated to all four measures of VED quality.

Return on Assets and total sales, two control variables, are significantly and positively related to all four measures of VED quality, consistent with previous research showing that larger and more profitable firms tend to disclose more non-financial information (Brammer and Pavelin, 2008). Firms in high polluting industries have significantly higher quality VEDs in terms of compliance, pollution prevention and product stewardship. Firms that are considered moderate polluters tend to have lower quality VEDs in all areas. Firms classified as low polluters are inconsistently related to the various measures of VED. They are marginally significant and negative in relation to product stewardship VEDs, and positive and significant in relation to ecological sustainability VEDs. Generally, these results complement the pattern revealed in previous research (Brammer

Table 7.2 Regressions on quality of voluntary environmental disclosure (N = 479)

Ind. variables	Compliance	%	Pollution prevention	%	Product stewardship	%	Ecological sustainability	%	All disclosure	%
%Pension	-.03	-.03	-.05	-.05	-.06	-.06	-.01	-.01	-.05	-.05
%Investment	-.07	-.07	-.09†	-.09*	-.12*	-.12*	-.09†	-.08†	-.10*	-.10*
Withdrawn	.19***	.20***	.20***	.21***	.21***	.22***	.06	.07	.21***	.23***
Disqualified	-.02	.00	-.01	.01	.07†	.10*	.02	.03	.02	.05
Voted	.08†	.08†	.01	.03	.05	.10*	-.03	-.01	.05	.07†
%External	-.01	-.01	-.02	-.02	-.02	-.02	-.00	-.00	-.02	-.02
Total sales	.23***	.23***	.30***	.29***	.23***	.22***	.25***	.24***	.27***	.27***
ROA	.06	.06	.08†	.08†	.09†	.09†	.12*	.12*	.09†	.08†
High_poll	.21**	.21**	.22**	.22**	.26**	.26***	.01	.02	.25***	.24***
Mod_poll	-.25**	-.25**	-.25**	-.25**	-.25**	-.25**	-.18*	-.18*	-.27***	-.27***
Low_poll	-.07	-.07	-.09	-.08	-.19†	-.18†	.25*	.26*	-.12	-.11
Model summary										
R²	.15	.15	.17	.18	.18	.19	.09	.09	.19	.20
Adjusted R²	.13	.13	.15	.16	.16	.18	.07	.07	.17	.18
F	7.26***	7.46***	8.85***	8.86***	9.33***	10.26***	4.27***	4.32***	9.73***	10.31***

Notes:
†   p < .10
*   p < .05
** p < .01
*** p < .001

164

and Pavelin, 2008; Patten, 1990, 1992) – firms in environmentally sensitive industries are more likely to disclose more environmental information and, as suggested by our results, in the form of higher quality VEDs. Our findings suggest that these higher quality disclosures are not limited to a single type of VED.

DISCUSSION

Interest in corporate disclosure of environmental information has grown in recent years (Perrini, 2006). Research in this area has considered corporate size and industry as well as exposure to media and lobbying pressures as drivers of disclosure; the majority of this research focuses on the quantity of information disclosed. This study looks at governance-related drivers of disclosure, specifically board composition and institutional investors, and considers the impact of these factors on the quality of VED. Further, by capturing the relation amongst various VEDs in addition to simply the disclosure of the items, we provide a more comprehensive measure of disclosure quality.

Institutional Ownership

Our results support the contention of previous research that investment equity ownership may limit the extent of corporate voluntary disclosure (Ryan and Schneider, 2002). Voluntary disclosure of environmental information, particularly beyond the compliance-related indicators, is likely to be perceived as long term in orientation and higher risk. Some research considers the short term orientation and risk aversion of investment funds as the reasons why higher equity ownership by fund managers leads to limited disclosure by firms (Ryan and Schneider, 2002). Our results are consistent with this. However, we find no support for the relationship between pension fund equity and the quality of VED.

In the emerging environment of 'investor capitalism' (Useem, 1996), pension fund managers act collaboratively to address social and environmental issues with companies (Graves et al., 2001). Further, although pension funds in general have become increasingly interested in social and environmental issues as it pertains to corporate performance, the funds do not necessarily focus on the same specific issues. Thus, a measure of overall pension fund ownership may not capture the idiosyncratic interests, and thus, influence, of each particular fund. For these reasons it is not entirely surprising to find that the overall pension fund ownership does not appear to influence the quality of VED.

Shareholder Activism

It is in the organized efforts of investors that we find an influence on VED quality (Geltman and Skroback, 1997). Our results suggest that negotiations between the shareholder activists and target companies that lead to the withdrawal of resolutions are related to higher quality VED. Shareholder activists, in the role of external monitors of corporate behavior, are increasingly able to wield the resolution as a threat to reputation but also as a prod to engage in dialogue around disclosure (Graves et al., 2001; Waddock, 2000). Counter to our expectations, proxy voting does not lead to higher quality disclosure; these results actually make sense in the context of the collaborative–conflictual tension between shareholder activists and corporate management. If a resolution reaches proxy vote, the resolution sponsors and corporate management failed to reach an agreed solution and it is likely that management will work against the sponsor and the resolution (Millstein, 1991).

Our study's results support Useem's (1996) conclusion of investor capitalism with a larger role for institutional investors in monitoring and control. These results highlight how investor capitalism is playing out – shareholder activism is a means to persuade managers to focus on a firm's long term prospects and it is the collaborative–conflictual tension that pushes both the activists and managers to engage in dialogue prior to the proxy contest (Carleton et al., 1998). Management may not negotiate in the absence of the threat of a resolution, and waging a war of words against the resolution before and during a proxy vote with shareholders is costly and better avoided (Millstein, 1991). One of the key conclusions of this study is that, in the current structure of corporate governance in the US, the threat of bringing a resolution to proxy vote and the possibility of sponsor-target negotiations prior to the vote seem to be influential factors in driving increased VEDs.

Board Composition

A number of scholars argue that internal governance structure, including independent board representation, provides for enhanced monitoring of management and greater external stakeholder engagement and is related to disclosure of pertinent information, financial and non-financial (Emmot, 2003; Kassinis and Vafeas, 2006). However, based on our findings, higher external representation on boards does not appear to impact the quality of VEDs, even at the most basic level of compliance type indicators. These results match those of Ho and Wong's (2001) study of the relationship between corporate governance structure and voluntary disclosure in Hong

Kong. This raises the question of what, if any, internal governance mechanisms may be effective in improving the quality of environmental and other non-financial information disclosure. Board size, member reputation and board cross-affiliations have been found to impact environmental performance and therefore may be related to disclosure quality (Kassinis and Vafeas, 2002). Efforts by socially responsible investor groups, such as CERES, have focused on designating a board member with explicit responsibility for environmental issues (Geltman and Skroback, 1997); and some corporations, such as Cadbury Schweppes (now Cadbury) and BP, have created board-level committees with corporate responsibility or environmental oversight. These governance characteristics remain empirically unexplored, raising the question as to whether they lead to higher quality non-financial disclosure.

Industry and Firm Characteristics

Similar to the findings of Brammer and Pavelin (2008), our results show firms in higher polluting industries are voluntarily presenting higher quality VEDs. These findings are consistent with the belief that legacies associated with high external pressure to improve environmental performance, and perhaps more sophisticated means for managing legitimacy through information disclosure, leads higher polluting firms to higher quality disclosure (SustainAbility, 2002). We emphasize that it is not simply that these firms are reporting more information. The form that this information takes is more sophisticated in terms of pollution prevention and product stewardship VED, suggesting that long term exposure to external pressure may have provided the firms the time to learn how to measure, collect and report complex environmental performance information (Brown, Dillard and Marshall, 2005). Conversely, firms in lower-polluting industries have had less need to develop sophisticated measures of environmental performance and means for managing legitimacy through information disclosure.

Firm size and profitability continue to be related to the quality of VED. Coinciding with previous studies that measure disclosure quantity (Brammer and Pavelin, 2008; Gao, Heravi and Xiao, 2005; Ho and Wong, 2001), larger and more profitable firms provide higher quality disclosure than smaller and less profitable firms. This relation is consistent across the four dimensions of quality included in this study. It is likely that larger and more profitable firms are able to commit greater resources to measuring, collecting and disseminating information. Further, as leading firms they are more often targets of external pressures and therefore more likely to develop the means to report higher quality and greater amounts of information.

Future Research and Limitations

This study provides empirical evidence of the relation between increased transparency, as measured by the quality of VED, and corporate governance factors. We document a consistently positive relationship between withdrawn resolutions and the quality of four types of VED, suggesting opportunities for future research that examines the relationships between shareholder activists and management. This research could be of particular value as it focuses at the micro-level, considering the method and content of the dialogue between activists and management. Using interviews and content analyses of archival documents, such research may provide insights into how negotiations on non-financial disclosure issues are conducted and agreement is or is not reached.

There is also ample prospect to examine internal governance structures as they relate to disclosure. Our study only considers board composition in terms of external representation. As suggested by other scholars, the existence of board committees and members' reputation and affiliations may impact corporate decisions regarding non-financial disclosures (Kassinis and Vafeas, 2005). Using detailed analyses of SEC filings these data can be collected and analyzed in respect to the levels of disclosure quality.

Beyond examining drivers of the quality of environmental (and social) disclosure, it is also important for future research to look at the outcomes of varied levels of voluntary environmental and social disclosure. Does the quality of VEDs influence corporate legitimacy, cost of equity capital, stock returns and other performance related variables? The management and accounting literatures have developed a number of measures that may be incorporated into future research, such as that of legitimacy based on media reports by Bansal and Clelland (2004) and cost of equity capital offered by Botosan and Plumlee (2002).

Some limitations of this study should be noted. Because of the cross-sectional and pooled nature of the data we were not able to examine time series effects in the variable relationships. Further, the sample only included US firms. A substantial amount of environmental disclosure is occurring in other regions and countries, in particular Europe, Australia and Japan. Because each of these regions/countries is characterized by unique governance structures and disclosure regulatory regimes our results can not be generalized beyond the US context. Finally, our categorization of the industries into three levels based on pollution levels may be overly simplistic. There remain industry effects, such as pending litigation or industry-specific programs (for example, Responsible Care in the chemical industry), which may impact the quality of VEDs and is not captured by this categorization.

ENDNOTES

1. For example, a firm may present its (1) overall waste discharged to water, (2) overall waste discharged to water as a percent of total production, and/or (3) overall waste discharged to water as a percent of total production with a comparison to the previous year. These three indicators are of differing quality, from lower to higher, respectively.
2. Investor activism is defined as 'the use of power by an investor either to influence the processes or outcomes of a given portfolio firm or to evoke large-scale change in processes or outcomes across multiple firms through symbolic targeting of one or more portfolio firms' (Ryan and Schneider, 2002; 555).
3. Using Toxic Release Inventory data related to reported chemical releases and waste produced average over the years 2000–2002, chemical and utilities industries are high polluters, oil and gas and food and beverage industries are middle range polluters, and the pharmaceutical and biotech industry is a low polluter.
4. The environmental management literature, (especially Aragón-Correa (1998), Bansal and Roth (2000), Hart (1995), Starik and Rands (1995), and Roome (1992)) identifies four increasingly complex levels of environmental strategy reflected in disclosures: (1) compliance, (2) pollution prevention, (3) product stewardship and (4) ecological sustainability. Progression from one level to the next requires building socially complex competencies, taking an increasingly holistic approach to product design, production and marketing, incorporating stakeholders into strategic decision-making, and creating and relying on a vision based in environmental stewardship. Disclosures of environmental information through indicators representative of these four levels represent increasing levels of sophistication in understanding, measuring and communicating environmental strategy (see Al-Tuwaijri et al., 2004; Kolk, 2004a, 2004b).
5. The authors conducted a comprehensive search in the academic literature and among practitioner organizations for disclosure quality assessments methods. Using information obtained, a matrix that contained the predominant commonalities and discrepancies among the different methods was developed and used, along with the four disclosure quality categories to draft a preliminary coding scheme. This coding scheme was pretested with two coders; identified discrepancies in the coding scheme were resolved to obtain the final index.
6. Prior research finds that firms' VEDs increase with: (1) firm size (Bewtey and Li, 2000; Brammer and Pavelin, 2006), (2) firm membership in environment-sensitive industries (Patten, 1990, 1992), (3) the extent a firm is widely-owned (Patten, 1992; Cormier and Magnan, 1999, 2003), (4) firms' exposure to environment-related legal proceedings (Deegan and Rankin, 1996), and (5) firms' media exposure to environmental activities (Neu et al., 1998; Li et al., 1997), (6) environmental lobby groups' concern about a firm's environmental performance (Deegan and Gordon, 1996).

REFERENCES

Al-Tuwaijri, S.A., T.E. Christensen, K.E. Hughes (2004), 'The relations among environmental disclosure, environmental performance, and economic performance: a simultaneous equations approach', *Accounting, Organizations and Society*, **29**: 447–71.

Aragón-Correa, J.A. and S. Sharma (2003), 'A contingent resource-based view of proactive corporate environmental strategy', *Academy of Management Review*, **28** (1): 71–78.

Atkinson, G. (2000), 'Measuring corporate sustainability', *Journal of Environmental Planning & Management*, **43**(2): 235–52.

Bansal, P. and I. Clelland (2004), 'Talking "trash": legitimacy, impression management, and unsystematic risk in the context of the natural environment', *Academy of Management Journal*, **47**(1): 93–103.

Bansal, P. and K. Roth (2000), 'Why companies go green: a model of ecological responsiveness', *Academy of Management Journal*, **13**(4): 717–36.

Beets, S.D. and C.C. Souther (1999), 'Corporate environmental reports: the need for standards and an environmental assurance service', *Accounting Horizons*, **13**(2): 129–45.

Berthelot, S., D. Cormier and M. Magnan (2003), 'Environmental disclosure research: review and synthesis', *Journal of Accounting Literature*, **22**: 1–44.

Bewtey, K. and Y. Li (2000), 'Disclosure of environmental information by Canadian manufacturing companies: a voluntary disclosure perspective', *Advances in Environmental Accounting & Management*, **1**: 201–26.

Black, B. (1992), 'Agents watching agents: the promise of institutional investor voice', *UCLA Law Review*, **39**: 811–93.

Botosan, C. and M. Plumlee (2002), 'A re-examination of disclosure level and the expected cost of equity capital', *Journal of Accounting Research*, **March**: 21–40.

Bradley, N. (2004), 'How to measure and analyze corporate governance', *International Financial Law Review*, (September), 40–47.

Brammer, S. and S. Pavelin (2008), 'Factors influencing the quality of corporate environmental disclosure', *Business Strategy and Environment*, **17**(2): 120–36.

Brown, D., J.F. Dillard and R.S. Marshall (2005), 'Strategically informed, environmentally conscious information requirements for accounting information systems', *Journal of Information Systems*, **19**(2): 79–103.

Bushee, B. (1998), 'The influence of institutional investors on myopic R&D investment behavior', *The Accounting Review*, **73**(3): 305–33.

Carleton, W.T., J.M. Nelson and M.S. Weisbach (1998), 'The influence of institutions on corporate governance through private negotiations: evidence from TIAA-CREF', *The Journal of Finance*, **53**(4): 1335–62.

Christmann, P. (2000), 'Effects of "best practices" of environmental management on cost advantages: the role of complementary assets', *Academy of Management Journal*, **43**(4): 663–80.

CERES (2005), 'US companies face record number of global warming shareholder resolutions on wider range of business sectors', 17 February.

Cormier, D. and M. Magnan (1997), 'Investors' assessment of implicit environmental liabilities: an empirical investigation', *Journal of Accounting and Public Policy*, **16**: 215–41.

Cormier, D. and M. Magnan (2003), 'Environmental reporting management: a continental European perspective', *Journal of Accounting and Public Policy*, **22**: 43–62.

CSWG (Corporate Sunshine Working Group) (2004), 'Corporate Sunshine Working Group bulletin', SEC and Social/Environmental Accounting, September.

David, P., M. Hitt and J. Gimeno (2001), 'The influence of activism by institutional investors on R&D', *Academy of Management Journal*, **44**(1): 144–57.

Deegan, C. and B. Gordon (1996), 'A study of environmental disclosure practices of Australian corporations', *Accounting and Business Research*, **26**(3): 187–99.

Deegan, C. and M. Rankin (1996), 'Do Australian companies report environmental news objectively? An analysis of environmental disclosures by firms prosecuted successfully by the Environmental Protection Authority', *Accounting, Auditing & Accountability Journal*, **9**(2): 50–67.

Deegan, C., M. Rankin and J. Tobin (2002), 'An examination of corporate social and environmental disclosures of BHP from 1983–1997: a test of legitimacy theory', *Accounting, Auditing and Accountability Journal*, **15**(3): 312–43.

Demsetz, H. and K. Lehn (1985), 'The structure of corporate ownership: causes and consequences', *Journal of Political Economy*, **93**: 1155–77.

EEA (1999), 'Environmental indicators: typology and overview', European Environment Agency, Copenhagen, Denmark: p. 19.

Emerson, J., T. Little and J. Kron (2005), 'The prudent trustee: the evolution of the long-term investor', The Rose Foundation for Committees and the Environment, p. 16.

Emmott, B. (2003), 'Beyond shareholder value', in *A Survey of Capitalism and Democracy, The Economist*, 28 June, pp. 9–12.

Fombrun, C.J. (2006), 'Corporate governance', *Corporate Reputation Review*, **8**(4): 267–71.

GAO (Government Accounting Office) (2004), 'Environmental disclosure – SEC should explore ways to improve tracking and transparency of information', Report to Congressional Requestors, US Government Accountability Office.

Gao, S.S., S. Heravi and J.Z. Xiao (2005), 'Determinants of corporate social and environmental reporting in Hong Kong: a research note', *Accounting Forum*, **19**: 233–42.

Geltman, E.G. and A.E. Skrobach (1997), 'Environmental activism and the ethical investor', *Journal of Corporate Law*, **22**: 465–70.

Goodstein, J., K. Gautam and W. Boeker (1994), 'The effects of board size and diversity on strategic change', *Strategic Management Journal*, **15**(3): 241–50.

Graves, S.B., K. Rehbein and S. Waddock (2001), 'Fad and fashion in shareholder activism: the landscape of shareholder resolutions, 1988–1998', *Business & Society Review*, **106**(4): 293–315.

Haniffa, R.M. and T.E. Cooke (2002), 'Culture, corporate governance and disclosure in Malaysian corporations', *ABACUS*, **38**(3): 317–49.

Hart, S.L. (1995), 'A natural-resource based view of the firm', *Academy of Management Journal*, **37**: 986–1014.

Ho, S.S.M. and K.S. Wong (2001), 'A study of the relationship between corporate governance structures and the extent of voluntary disclosure', *Journal of International Accounting, Auditing & Taxation*, **10**: 139–56.

Hoskisson, R.E., M.A. Hitt, R.A. Johnson and W. Gossman (2002), 'Conflicting voices: the effects of institutional ownership heterogeneity and internal governance on corporate innovation strategies', *Academy of Management Journal*, **43**(4): 697–716.

Ingley, C.B and N.T. van der Walt (2004), 'Corporate governance, institutional investors and conflicts of interest', *Corporate Governance*, **12**(4): 534–51.

Jensen, M.C. and W. Meckling (1976), 'Theory of the firm: managerial behavior, agency costs and capital structure', *Journal of Financial Economics*, **3**: 305–80.

Johnson, R.A. and D.W. Greening (1999), 'The effects of corporate governance and institutional ownership types on corporate social performance', *Academy of Management Journal*, **42**(5): 564–76.

Kassinis, G. and N. Vafeas (2002), 'Corporate boards and outside stakeholders as determinants of environmental litigation', *Strategic Management Journal*, **23**(5): 399–415.

Kassinis, G. and N. Vafeas (2006), 'Stakeholder pressures and environmental pressures', *Academy of Management Journal*, **49**(1): 145–59.

Kolk, A. (2008), 'Sustainability, accountability and corporate governance: exploring multinationals' reporting practices', *Business Strategy and the Environment*, **17**(1): 1–15.

Kostant, P.C. (1999), 'Exit, voice and loyalty in the course of corporate governance and counsel's changing role', *Journal of Socio-Economics*, **28**: 203–47.

KPMG (2005), *KPMG International Survey of Corporate Sustainability Reporting 2005*, Amsterdam, Netherlands: KPMG.

Leung, S. and B. Horwitz (2004), 'Director ownership and voluntary segment disclosure: Hong Kong evidence', *Journal of International Financial Management & Accounting*, **15**(3): 235–60.

Li, Y., G. Richardson and D. Thornton (1997), 'Corporate disclosure of environmental liability information: theory and evidence', *Contemporary Accounting Research*, **14**(3): 435–74.

Llena, F, J.M. Moneva and B. Hernandez (2007), 'Environmental disclosures and compulsory accounting standards: the case of Spanish annual reports', *Business Strategy and the Environment*, **16**(1): 50–63.

Lober, D.K., D. Bynum, E. Campbell and M. Jacques (1997), 'The 100 plus corporate environmental report study: a survey of an evolving environmental management tool', *Business Strategy and the Environment*, **6**: 57–73.

Marshall, R.S., and D. Brown (2003), 'Corporate environmental reporting: what's in a metric?', *Business Strategy and the Environment*, **12**(2): 87–106.

Miles, M.P., and J.G. Covin (2000), 'Environmental marketing: a source of reputational, competitive, and financial advantage', *Journal of Business Ethics*, **23**: 299–311.

Millstein, I.A. (1991), 'The responsibility of the institutional investor in corporate management', in A.W. Sametz (ed.), *The battle for corporate control: Shareholder rights, stakeholder interests, and managerial responsibilities*, Homewood, IL: Business One Irwin, pp. 67–76.

Neu, D., H. Warsame, and K. Pedwell (1998), 'Managing public impressions: environmental disclosures in annual reports', *Accounting, Organizations and Society*, **23**(3): 265–282.

Noci, G. (2000), 'Environmental reporting in Italy: current practices and future developments', *Business Strategy and the Environment*, **9**: 211–23.

OECD (Organisation for Economic Co-operation and Development) (2004), 'The OECD principles of corporate governance', OECD Observer Policy Brief, August.

Passoff, M. (2005), 'Hot issues: global warming, HIV/AIDS, sexual bias', Proxy Season Preview, As You Sow Foundation, Spring.

Patten, D.M. (1990), 'The market reaction to social responsibility disclosures: the case of the Sullivan principles signings', *Accounting, Organizations and Society*, **15**(6): 575–87.

Patten, D.M. (1992), 'Intra-industry environmental disclosures in response to the Alaskan oil spill: a note on legitimacy theory', *Accounting, Organizations and Society*, **17**(5): 471–75.

Perrini, F. (2006), 'The practitioner's perspective on non-financial reporting', *California Management Review*, **48**(2): 73–103.

Pfeffer, J. (1972), 'Size and composition of corporate boards of directors: the organization and its environment', *Administrative Science Quarterly*, **17**: 218–28.

Roome, N. (1992), 'Developing environmental management systems', *Business Strategy and the Environment*, **1**: 11–24.

Ryan, L.V., and M. Schneider (2002), 'The antecedents of institutional activism', *Academy of Management Review*, **27**(4): 554–73.

Schaltegger, S., and R.L. Burritt (2006), 'Corporate sustainability accounting: a nightmare or a dream coming true?', *Business Strategy and the Environment*, **15**(5): 293–95.

Schneider, G. (2005), 'GE determined to show more "ecomagination"', *Washington Post*, 10 May.

Smith, T. (2005), 'Institutional and social investors find common ground', *Journal of Investing*, **14**(3): 57–65.

Stapledon, G.P. (1996), *Institutional shareholders and corporate governance*, Oxford: Oxford University Press.

Starik, M., and G.P. Rands (1995), 'Weaving an integrated web: multilevel and multisystem perspectives of ecologically sustainable organizations', *Academy of Management Review*, **20**: 908–35.

SustainAbility (2002), 'The global reporters', SustainAbility.

Taub, S. (2006), 'Institutions, activist investors bring climate change to a simmer', *Compliance Week*, **July**: 52–53.

Tihanyi, L., R.A. Johnson, R.E. Hoskisson, and M.A. Hitt (2003), 'Institutional ownership differences and international diversification: the effects of boards of directors and technological opportunity', *Academy of Management Journal*, **46**(2): 195–211.

Useem, M. (1996), *Investor capitalism: How money managers are changing the face of corporate America*, New York: Basic Books.

Waddock, S. (2000), 'The multiple bottom lines of corporate citizenship: social investing, reputation, and responsibility audits', *Business & Society Review*, **105**(3): 323–46.

Walden, D., and B.N. Schwartz (1997), 'Environmental disclosures and public policy pressures', *Journal of Accounting and Public Policy*, **16**(Summer): 125–54.

Wang, J. and H.D. Dewhirst (1992), 'Boards of directors and stakeholder orientation', *Journal of Business Ethics*, **11**(2): 115–23.

Williams, C.A. (1999), 'The Securities and Exchange Commission and corporate social transparency', *Harvard Law Review*, **112**(6): 1197–212.

APPENDIX 1: VOLUNTARY ENVIRONMENTAL DISCLOSURE INDEX SCORECARD

Categories of quality of disclosure

Based on Roome (1992), Henriques and Sadorsky (1995)

1. Compliance/end of pipe:

Driving force: meet regulatory requirements; Key resource: regulatory knowledge; Competitive advantage: minimize compliance costs

Based on Hart (1995)

2. Pollution prevention:

Driving force: minimize emissions, effluents, and waste; Key resource: continuous improvement; Competitive advantage: lower costs

3. Product stewardship:

Driving force: minimize life-cycle cost of products; Key resource: stakeholder integration; Competitive advantage: preempt competitors

4. Sustainable development:

Driving force: minimize environmental burden of firm growth: Key resource: shared vision; Competitive advantage: future position

#	Measure	Current period absolute amount	Relative to/or co-disclosure with production/sales	Historical		Targets		Comparisons to prior targets
				Single year	Multiple years	Single year	Multiple years	
		A	B	C	D	F	G	H
	Materials							
1	Materials input into the production process.	C	PP	C	PP	PP	PP	PP
2	Materials input into the production process from internally or externally supplied recycled materials	PS	PS	PS	PS	PS	PS	PS
3	Sales of materials formerly discarded	PS	PS	PS	PS	PS	PS	PS
	Energy							
4	Consumption of energy (joules, BTUs, or similar measure)	C	PP	C	PP	PP	PP	PP
5	Consumption of energy from renewable resources	PS	PS	PS	PS	PS	PS	PS
6	Consumption of energy from renewable resources, specifically excluding hydropower.	PS	PS	PS	PS	PS	PS	PS
	Water							
7	Use of water	C	PP	C	PP	PP	PP	PP
8	Rehabilitation of water, put back into watershed	PP	PP	PP	PP	PP	PP	PP
9	Reused water, for additional processes	PP	PP	PP	PP	PP	PP	PP

175

#	Measure	Current period absolute amount	Relative to/or co-disclosure with production/sales	Historical		Targets		Comparisons to prior targets
				Single year	Multiple years	Single year	Multiple years	
		A	B	C	D	F	G	H
Atmospheric emissions								
10	• Emission of greenhouse gases	C	PP	C	PP	PP	PP	PP
11	• Emission of ozone-depleting substances	C	PP	C	PP	PP	PP	PP
12	• Emission of other significant gasses	C	PP	C	PP	PP	PP	PP
13	• Carbon offsets	PS	PS	PS	PS	PS	PS	PS
Total waste								
14	• Total waste created and/or disposed, disposal sink not specified or all sinks aggregated	C	PP	C	PP	PP	PP	PP
15	• Total waste disposed of, one sink specified	C	PP	C	PP	PP	PP	PP
16	• Total waste disposed of, two sinks specified	C	PP	C	PP	PP	PP	PP
17	• Total waste disposed of, three sinks specified	C	PP	C	PP	PP	PP	PP
18	• Total waste treated, recycled, and/or reused	PS	PS	PS	PS	PS	PS	PS

Hazardous/toxic waste

19	• Hazardous/toxic waste created and/ or disposed, disposal sink not specified or all sinks aggregated	C	PP	C	PP	PP	PP	PP
20	• Hazardous/toxic waste disposed of, one sink specified	C	PP	C	PP	PP	PP	PP
21	• Hazardous/toxic waste disposed of, two sinks specified	C	PP	C	PP	PP	PP	PP
22	• Hazardous/toxic waste disposed of, three sinks specified	C	PP	C	PP	PP	PP	PP
23	• Hazardous/toxic waste treated, recycled, and/or reused	PS	PS	PS	PS	PS	PS	PS

Radioactive waste

24	• Radioactive waste created and/or disposed, disposal sink not specified or all sinks aggregated	C	PP	C	PP	PP	PP	PP
25	• Radioactive waste disposed of, one sink specified	C	PP	C	PP	PP	PP	PP
26	• Radioactive waste disposed of, two sinks specified	C	PP	C	PP	PP	PP	PP
27	• Radioactive waste disposed of, three sinks specified	C	PP	C	PP	PP	PP	PP

Spills of possible pollutants

28	• Number of spills – chemical, oil or fuel	C	PP	C	PP	PP	PP	PP
29	• Volume of spills – chemical, oil or fuel	C	PP	C	PP	PP	PP	PP

#	Measure	Specific identification of impact	Quantification of impact
		A	B

Biodiversity

#	Measure	A	B
30	• Sensitive lands impacted by activities and operations	PP	PP
31	• Impacts on endangered species due to activities and operations	PP	PP

#	Measure	Specific identification of product	Current period absolute amount	Relative to/or co-disclosure with production/ sales	Historical		Targets		Comparisons to prior targets
					Single year	Multiple years	Single year	Multiple years	
		A	B	C	D	E	G	H	I

Products

#	Measure	A	B	C	D	E	G	H	I
32	• Take back or reclaimed products or components	PS	PS	PS	PS	PS	PS	PS	PS
33	• 'Green' products	PS	PS	PS	PS	PS	PS	PS	PS
34	• Environmental impacts due to use of green products made by company	PS	PS						

#	Measure	Identified as a corporate tool	Detailed description of the concept	Example
		A	B	C
	Process			
35	• Life Cycle Analysis (LCA)	SD	SD	SD
36	• Design for Environment (DfE)	SD	SD	SD
37	• Environmental Management System (EMS)	PP	PP	PP

#	Measure	Absolute amount	Relative to/or co-disclosure with production	Historical Single year	Historical Multiple years	Targets Single year	Targets Multiple years	Comparisons to prior targets
		A	B	C	D	F	G	H
	Compliance							
38	• Incidents	C	PP	C	PP	PP	PP	PP
39	• Fines	C	PP	C	PP	PP	PP	PP
	Environmental expenditures							
40	• Environmental expenditures, total	C	PP	C	PP	PP	PP	PP
41	• Environmental expenditures, by type	C	PP	C	PP	PP	PP	PP

#	Measure	Provided	Detailed description
		A	B
	Other accounting/scoring systems		
42	• Environmental accounting	SD	SD
43	• Green balanced score card	SD	SD

#	Measure	Absolute amount	Relative to/or co-disclosure with production/ sales	Historical		Targets		Comparisons to prior targets
				Single year	Multiple years	Single year	Multiple years	
		A	B	C	D	F	G	H
	Employee training							
44	• Environmental training, hours	C	PP	C	PP	PP	PP	PP
45	• Environmental training, monetary value ($)	C	PP	C	PP	PP	PP	PP
46	• Percentage of employees receiving environmental training	C	PP	C	PP	PP	PP	PP

#	Measure	Received	Absolute amount and/or percentage	Historical		Targets		Comparisons to prior targets
				Single year	Multiple years	Single year	Multiple years	
		A	B	C	D	F	G	H
	Certifications							
47	• Environmental process certifications	PS	PS	PS	PS	PS	PS	PS
48	• Environmental product certifications	PS	PS	PS	PS	PS	PS	PS

181

	Specifically identified stakeholders	Detailed description		
		Engagement process discussed	Example with process focus	Example with product focus
	A	B	C	D
Stakeholder engagement				
49 • Stakeholder engagement – communities	PS	PS	PS	PS
50 • Stakeholder engagement – NGOs	PS	PS	PS	PS
51 • Stakeholder engagement – government	PS	PS	PS	PS
52 • Stakeholder engagement – consumers	PS	PS	PS	PS
53 • Stakeholder engagement – employees	PS	PS	PS	PS
54 • Stakeholder engagement – supplier	PS	PS	PS	PS
55 • Stakeholder engagement – shareholders	PS	PS	PS	PS

Environmental policy / Reporting — disclosure index

		A	B
		Environmental policy statement, with specifics, included	**Numeric targets and/or timeline included in environmental policy statement**
Environmental policy			
56	• Environmental policy	PP	PP
57	• Environmental policy or program audit	**Internal** — PP	**3rd Party** — PP
58	• Structure of environmental responsibility	**Specific individual identified** — PP	**Governance structure identified** — PP
Reporting			
59	• Published CER according to established standards	**Standards body identified** — PS	**Description of standards provided** — PS
60	• Report verification	**Internal** — PS	**3rd party** — PS

8. Dynamic networks and successful social action: a theoretical framework to examine the Coca-Cola controversy in Kerala, India

Sridevi Shivarajan

In July 2010, in the wake of the recommendations of a high-powered investigation committee, the government of Kerala (a southern state of India), decided to constitute a tribunal to obtain compensation of approximately $50 million from the Hindustan Coca-Cola Beverages Company for the ecological damage it caused in and around Plachimada village in the state. This appears to be the last chapter in the long and fractured history of the Coca-Cola plant which was set up amidst much fanfare in 2001, only to be unceremoniously shut down in 2004, following widespread allegations of ecological and social wrongdoing, never to reopen again.

TIMELINE OF THE COCA-COLA CONTROVERSY

The plant, known as the Hindustan Coca-Cola Beverages Private Ltd (HCCBPL), was commissioned on March 2000 in Plachimada, Kerala. Earlier, during a global investors meeting in 1999, the state government of Kerala had extended an invitation to Coca-Cola to invest in the state. The location was chosen by the company based on a satellite survey, which indicated the presence of abundant groundwater in the area.

The picturesque village of Plachimada is located in Palakkad district in Kerala, one of the southernmost states of India. Plachimada figures in the list of areas listed as economically disadvantaged by the state government. In fact, the Coca-Cola plant was one of only two industrial units registered with the local government, the *Panchayat*. Agriculture is the predominant occupation here, with coconuts, vegetables, groundnuts and pulses being the major crops (Shivarajan and Halbert, 2005).

This region falls in the Palakkad gap of the Western Ghats and is a 'rain shadow' region, with average rainfall less than half of the state average. The water needs of this region, both domestic and agricultural, are met by groundwater resources. The population living in the vicinity of the Coca-Cola plant mainly comprises economically undeveloped indigenous people known as Adivasis, who migrated from the neighboring state of Tamil Nadu several decades ago.

The plant had 400 employees, both temporary and permanent, and also indirectly provided employment to 5000 families in Kerala. HCCBPL produced soft drinks, juice and bottled water, and was the sole supplier to Kerala and parts of the neighboring state of Tamil Nadu. Its three production lines produced an average of 700 bottles per minute. Shortly after it began operations, as a goodwill gesture, the plant also began distributing the sludge created by its operations as fertilizer to the local farmers.

The plant appeared to have all the requisite clearances and licences for its operation, namely a license to operate from the local governing body, the *Panchayat*, and the required clearances from the Kerala State Pollution Control Board (KSPCB) and the Kerala State Ground Water Board (KSGWB). The plant consumed 400 kiloliters of water per day, which is far below the maximum of 800 kl/day prescribed by KSGWB. This water was drawn from six bore wells and two open wells in the plant. In order to make one liter of beverage, around three to four liters of water are required, the excess being used to wash bottles and tanks. The plant also had a state-of-the-art rain harvesting system and effluent treatment plant.

Initial signs of trouble
Around 2001, some of the Adivasis living in the plant's vicinity began experiencing water shortages in their wells. Water in some of the wells also began to turn acidic, rendering it unfit to drink (Shivarajan and Halbert, 2005). As these problems hadn't been experienced before, the Adivasis (who had been living in the plant's vicinity for several decades) attributed their water woes to the operations of HCCBPL. In the meantime, some local activists had joined the Adivasis and organized a protest, requesting that HCCBPL distribute fresh water to local people. HCCBPL did not comply with this request, stating that the bore well in the plant that could have been used for this purpose had dried up. As the water shortages and pollution intensified, talks of an anti-Coca-Cola agitation began to gain strength. The Adivasis first sent letters of complaint to the legislative bodies of the state of Kerala and to Coca-Cola, and also marched to the plant gates as a warning strike.

Formal agitation begins

On Earth Day, 2002 April 22, the Adivasis launched a formal anti-Coca-Cola agitation by setting up a platform across the plant gates from where they began an indefinite day and night vigil. They did not get much support or media attention for the first few months. In the meantime, HCCBPL, in a goodwill gesture, began distributing water to the locals. This was welcomed with open arms by everyone except those involved in the strike. HCCBPL also began buying water from private sources to bring down its consumption of groundwater.

Over the course of the next two years, the anti-Coca-Cola agitation managed to influence several hitherto unfavorable stakeholders, culminating in the temporary closure of the plant in 2004. Attempts to reopen the plant since then have been unsuccessful due to the continuing legal and political deadlock.

Research Questions

So how was it that this Coca-Cola plant – the largest in southern India, commissioned amidst widespread optimism that it would bring much needed economic development to the area – became subject to widespread antagonism and was forced to shut down? The facts suggest that the Adivasis' success lay not in their superior marshalling, but rather in transforming their narrow interests in alleviating a water shortage that affected only a small group of community residents into a nationwide debate on the ownership of water. The changing nature of the protest evolved in parallel with the changing landscape of groups that mobilized in support of the Adivasis. The research questions in this case centre on two issues: successful stakeholder influence strategies and the transformation of the stakeholder issue into a social issue.

As discussed earlier, the Coca-Cola plant was commissioned amidst widespread expectations that it would catalyze much needed economic growth in the region. The tax revenues generated by the company, particularly for the cash strapped *Panchayat* was not insignificant either. Coca-Cola also had the complete support of the state government on whose invitation it had set up its plant. However, over time several powerful regulatory stakeholders starting with the *Panchayat*, and including the state government and the Indian government, began sharing the anti-Coca-Cola view, and decided to act against the firm. *How do marginalized stakeholders, unable to gain redress from the firm directly, use indirect strategies to influence other powerful stakeholders to act against the firm?*

The next question concerns the nature of the issue itself. The fascinating aspect of this case is the gradual transformation during the course of a couple of years of an issue of water shortage experienced by the Adivasis into a nationwide debate on the ownership of water. The holding of the World Water Convention of 2004 in Plachimada illustrates the extent of international support and attention received by the struggle. Similarly, the state government's agenda for setting up an investigative tribunal was to examine the ecological damage in the region caused by Coca-Cola. Therefore the other research question central to this case is to examine how the issue originally involving dyadic relations between the firm and the stakeholder (the Adivasis) transformed into a 'social' issue. *How do stakeholder issues become social issues?* This is an important research question since firms find it significantly more difficult to deal with multiple stakeholders and social issues than with an individual stakeholder. Understanding this process can therefore provide useful insights to firms in managing their stakeholders.

Analyzing the Coca-Cola Controversy

Given the complexity of the case, I rely on a variety of research methods and traditions to analyze the Coca-Cola controversy. My research employs techniques from grounded theory (Glaser and Strauss, 1967) in that it combines both an exploratory and a theory-testing phase. Unlike classic grounded theory, my initial research is not used to generate new theory; rather, it suggests several existing theories that seem relevant to explain what occurred. I then use network analysis to examine the complexity of stakeholder relations and to understand how the Adivasis were able to develop new ties with other stakeholders. The grounded theory approach of Glaser and Strauss (1967) advocates using intensive field research on one or several cases to develop new theory, to test the theory in subsequent stages of the research, and to further develop and specify the theory as new data is gathered. My initial exploratory research on this controversy, and the timeline of the controversy (Table 8.1), suggests not that a completely new theory is needed, but rather that several existing theories could be adapted and combined to explain what has occurred. Specifically, I use elements from four theoretical traditions – stakeholder theory, social network theory, resource dependency theory, and social movements theory – to build a preliminary theoretical framework for exploring the Coca-Cola controversy in Plachimada from 2000–06.

According to stakeholder theory a firm's performance is affected by how it is able to identify and deal with the needs and demands of a wide variety of stakeholders. This includes internal stakeholders (such as employees), and external stakeholders (such as the government and the local community). This emphasis of stakeholder theory on dyadic ties, though useful,

Table 8.1   Timeline of the Coca-Cola controversy

March 2000	Coca-Cola plant (HCCBPL), commissioned in Plachimada, Kerala, India
Late 2000	HCCBPL begins distributing its sludge as fertilizer to local farmers
Late 2001	Water shortages first noticed by local Adivasis and attributed to the operations of HCCBPL. Demands to HCCBPL for water supply and jobs as compensation refused
April 2002	Formal anti-Coca-Cola agitation launched by the Adivasis and certain local activists
April 2003	Local governing body, the *Panchayat*, refuses to renew Coca-Cola's licence
June 2003	The Centre for Science and Environment finds that Coca-Cola products contain pesticide content higher than permissible levels. The Indian Parliament bans Coca-Cola products from its premise.
July 2003	*BBC Radio 4* report suggests that the sludge generated by HCCBPL has toxic content above permissible limits
December 2003	Single bench of the High Court of Kerala, rules that water belongs to the people and one entity (HCCBPL) cannot draw an indiscriminate share
Late December 2003	Following an appeal by HCCBPL, the High Court constitutes an expert committee to look into the groundwater situation and determine HCCBPL's rightful share for daily consumption. First such study in India
January 2004	Special delegation of the World Social Forum meets in Plachimada and passes the Plachimada Declaration against the privatization of water
March 2004	State government of Kerala asks HCCBPL to stop production temporarily in view of the severe drought situation in the state
March 2004	HCCBPL temporarily suspends production
March 2004	*Panchayat* again refuses to renew annual licence
April 2005	Based on the expert committee's report that HCCBPL's water consumption is within permissible limits, the division bench of the High Court of Kerala reverses the earlier judgment of the single bench, and holds that HCCBPL can resume operations conditionally
April 2005	The Adivasis and members of the anti-Coca-Cola agitation state that HCCBPL will not be allowed to resume operations at any cost
May 2005	*Panchayat* decides to approach the Supreme Court to appeal against the High Court's decision and grants only a temporary licence to HCCBPL

Table 8.1   (continued)

August 2005	The Kerala State Pollution Control Board (KSPCB) orders HCCBPL to shut down in view of the high toxic content of its waste and non-compliance with the board's directions
November 2005	Based on the report of the Groundwater Monitoring Committee, the state government of Kerala declares Plachimada a notified (high risk) area due to severe water shortage and over exploitation of groundwater resource
November 2005	High Court of Kerala rejects HCCBPL's petition against *Panchayat's* conditional issue of licence
May 2006	The coalition of Communist parties, wins the state election
June 2006	The new chief minister of Kerala, K. Achuthanandan, assures the government's proactive support to the delegates of the anti-Coca-Cola agitation
August 2006	Coca-Cola products banned in the state of Kerala, following the latest findings of the Centre for Science and Environment that they contain pesticides
August 2008	The Kerala government agrees to finance the legal expenses of the anti-Coca-Coca agitation's continuing legal battle against Coca-Cola in the Supreme Court for compensation
April 2009	The Kerala government sets up a 14 member panel to examine the controversy
March 2010	The committee holds Coca-Cola responsible for ecological damage in the region, and recommends damages of approximately $400 million.

does not fully capture the multiplicity of stakeholder interactions that may be present in a controversy such as this one. Organizations such as Coca-Cola are embedded in a web of dynamic relationships rather than in a 'vacuum of dyadic ties' (Rowley, 1997: 890).Multiple ties among stakeholders can have synergistic outcomes, and therefore firms need to be aware not just of dyadic ties with their most direct and obvious stakeholders but of the structure and dynamics of the web of ties – the full network – in which they must operate (Rowley, 1997; Rowley and Moldoveanu, 2003). By adding a social network perspective to the stakeholder perspective, my research contributes to improving the understanding of the 'complex array of multiple and interdependent relationships existing in stakeholder environments' (Rowley, 1997: 890).

Social network theory is commonly used to highlight and map communication ties between social actors. But some researchers using the network approach have applied it to resource exchanges and dependencies. In particular, imbalances in resource dependencies are used to explain the power of network actors. That is, network actors who possess resources needed by others will typically have considerable power over them (Frooman, 1999). I suggest that resource dependencies are crucial to understanding what happened in the Plachimada case. Indeed, a key issue is how the Adivasis were able to progress from a situation of relative exclusion and/or dependency on others' resources to one of having a central role in a coalition that had considerable resource control over Coca-Cola.

This raises the issue of agency and change. Network theory may imply structural determinism since it predicts that an actor's power is determined by its position in a network (Emirbayer and Goodwin, 1994; Stevenson and Greenberg, 2000), but social actors have some degree of intentionality and efficacy, and can transcend the constraints of their current position in a network by developing new ties (Emirbayer and Goodwin, 1994). This is precisely what the Adivasis did throughout the period included in this study.

Finally, to capture the common agreement among the key stakeholders to act against Coca-Cola, I employ the concept of 'frame alignment' from social movements' theory (Snow, Rochford Jr, Worden, and Benford, 1986). Frame alignment refers to the development of common understandings and definitions of the situation between various actors, and it is assumed to be crucial in explaining action and developing an effective coalition. Here I use the concept of frame alignment to explain the mutual understanding and considerable agreement on the Coca-Cola issue among multiple stakeholders which led ultimately to action against Coca-Cola.

DEVELOPING A FRAMEWORK TO EXAMINE THE TRANSFORMATION OF A STAKEHOLDER ISSUE INTO A SOCIAL ISSUE

In order to develop a preliminary theoretical framework that explains the transformation of a stakeholder issue into a social issue, I first offer a comprehensive definition of a social issue. Next, I discuss the potential for action of those aggrieved stakeholders whose issues are unlikely to be addressed at the firm level due to their peripheral (powerless) position in the firm's resource dependence and communication networks. I then identify the strategies these aggrieved stakeholders can adopt to overcome their network constraints, take their issue into the larger arena, and influence the other actors in the network against the firm. As the final step of the framework, I examine the conditions under which the cumulative action against the firm by other stakeholders is likely to transform the stakeholder issue into a social issue.

Defining Social Issues

Despite being studied over the decades, the concept of social issues still remains an ambiguous one. This could be because the word social lends itself to a multitude of interpretations (Clarkson, 1995b). The increasing interdependence between business and society over the years has only added to the complexity of this concept (Wood, 1991). The bulk of the relevant literature suggests that the public nature of the issue is one of the criteria in defining a social issue. Some of the early conceptualizations of social issues around consumerism, environment, product safety, occupational safety, and discrimination (Carroll, 1979); quality of life (Strand, 1983); and societal change in values and attitudes (Wartick and Cochran, 1985) take this view. These classifications, however, are at best illustrative.

A more specific definition is the use of two tests to identify a social issue (Clarkson, 1995b). Social issues are characterized by the presence of legislation and recognition at the institutional level of analysis as opposed to the firm level of analysis. The logic used here is the separation of the impact of a business on society in general from its impact on the task environment that comprises its day-to-day operations. Though this definition is concise and closely related to my research question, a deeper examination reveals its inadequacy for this study

Consider the criterion of legislation. Social issues need not involve legislation, and legislation often comes into force after the issue has become public in nature. Similarly, mere legislation does not render an issue social. The basis for examining legislation also remains unclear. Does a single piece of legislation against the focal firm make this a social issue? Or should the nature and the extent of the legislation be considered? Thus, the concept of social issue needs further clarification.

My framework views the transformation of a stakeholder issue into a social issue as the outcome of a successful influencing strategy to garner the support of other stakeholders. The level of analysis thus moves to that of an organizational field: the population of organizations that critically influence the focal firm's performance, such as suppliers, regulatory agencies, and consumers (Scott, 1995). Thus, I view an issue as social when it is moved from the firm level to the level of the firm's stakeholders. At the firm level, the interactions occur between the firm and a particular stakeholder, while at the organizational field level multiple stakeholders interact simultaneously with the firm.

However, the change in the level of analysis, though important, is again not sufficient to make a stakeholder issue a social issue. For example, consider discrimination, one of the illustrative examples of a social issue (Carroll, 1979; Donaldson and Preston, 1995). Though several sectors of society were aware of its existence and unfairness, it truly became a social issue only when these groups acted against discrimination. This included legislation by the government, voluntary hiring practices by firms, and organized protests by citizens. Therefore, action taken by the stakeholders constituting the organizational field is a crucial test of a social issue.

Based on the above discussion, my framework views legislation and regulation as actions taken by only one stakeholder group, the government, and thus not sufficient to make the issue social (Clarkson, 1995b). Legislation and regulation, more often than not, culminate from actions by other stakeholders. Consider the introduction of the Sarbanes Oxley Act (2002) following the spate of corporate financial scandals in the US. The Act came into force after a series of actions by multiple stakeholders, including stockholders, employees, and the media. The decline of public trust in accounting practices had already become a social issue before Congress stepped in and passed the Act. Thus, stakeholders not involved in the day-to-day functioning of the firm, outside of the firm's task environment, helped to transform the issue into a social issue.

The preceding paragraphs have delineated some of the characteristics that render an issue a social issue. However, to develop a specific definition of a social issue, it is important to also examine the meaning of an 'issue'. The closely related area of issues management (Buchholz, Evans, and Wagley, 1985; Heugens, 2002; Stanley, 1985; Wartick and Mahon, 1994) offers a specific definition of an issue as follows:

> An issue is (a) a controversial inconsistency based on one or more expectational gaps (b) involving management perceptions of changing legitimacy and other stakeholder perceptions of changing cost/benefit positions (c) that occur within or between views of what is and/or what ought to be corporate performance or stakeholder perceptions of corporate performance and (d) imply an actual or anticipated resolution that creates significant, identifiable present or future impact on the organization (Wartick and Mahon, 1994: 306).

Thus, the continual existence of an expectation gap between the stakeholder's desired and perceived firm performance, and the ability of this expectation gap to influence firm performance, is crucial in defining an issue.

Based on the preceding discussion, then, I define a social issue in my framework as (a) an expectation gap held by multiple stakeholders, between the desired performance and perceived actual performance of the focal firm that (b) requires the involvement of stakeholders outside the firm's task environment and (c) can, if action is taken by these stakeholders, affect the focal firm's performance. The next section discusses the framework to examine the transformation of a stakeholder issue into a social issue. The defining aspect of a stakeholder issue is that the expectation gap is held by a single stakeholder and the issue exists at the firm level of analysis.

Building a Preliminary Framework

Stakeholder mobilization

My research question is primarily concerned with examining how powerless stakeholders successfully act against a firm by garnering support from other powerful stakeholders. But what makes these powerless or marginalized stakeholders act in the first place? Existing research examining the causes of stakeholder action can be broadly divided into the interest-based perspective and the identity-based perspective (Rowley and Moldoveanu, 2003). The interest-based perspective, which accounts for the bulk of the studies (Frooman, 1999; Rowley, 1997; Savage, Nix, Whitehead and Blair, 1991), takes the view that stakeholders will act against the firm in order to protect their interests.

The second perspective, the identity-based perspective, focuses on the dynamics between stakeholders of a single type (Butterfield, Reed and Lemak, 2004; Rowley and Moldoveanu, 2003; Stevenson and Greenberg, 2000). Stakeholder characteristics, in particular commitment and solidarity (Ashforth and Kreiner, 1999), are considered crucial in explaining stakeholder action. The identity-based perspective thus emphasizes the factors that hold the stakeholder group together during the long process of mobilization.

Yet each of these perspectives alone is inadequate for fully explaining the comprehensive process of stakeholder mobilization. Although the interest-based perspective is fundamental in understanding stakeholder action, it cannot fully explain its origins. The cases of successful stakeholder mobilization are relatively few compared to stakeholder grievances. Even stakeholder groups with similar interests often have different degrees of mobilization. For instance, the Narmada Bachao Andolan protest against the construction of the Sardar Sarovar Dam in Gujarat, India, has now entered its twenty-fifth year and has succeeded in stalling the project considerably, while a similar anti-dam movement to save Lake Pedder in Tasmania in the 1970s proved unsuccessful, primarily due to mobilization issues.

The identity-based perspective can explain this differential aspect of mobilization, where some stakeholders diligently pursue lost causes despite their limited resources and support from others. However, the identity-based perspective on its own cannot explain the causes of stakeholder action, since interests are crucial in mobilization.

A combined use of the interest and identity-based perspectives (Rowley and Moldoveanu, 2003) can provide insights into both the initial and ongoing process of stakeholder mobilization. But the primary research question of my study – how marginalized stakeholders successfully take their issue into the larger arena – still remains unanswered. What strategies should they use? Should different strategies be used with different stakeholders?

A relevant area of research in answering these questions is the classification of influence strategies into direct and indirect, based on the type of resource dependencies between the firm and the stakeholder (Frooman, 1999). This classification, though simple and effective, again does not explain the factors contributing to the success of these strategies, a crucial aspect of my research question. For instance, can any stakeholder using an indirect strategy be successful? Or is the success of an indirect strategy dependent on the characteristics of the stakeholder? What is the significance of the stance of the other stakeholders towards the firm? Network theory, combined with an assessment of political opportunity structure (Stevenson and Greenberg, 2000) is another promising area of research to answer some of these questions, but the process of transformation of a stakeholder issue into a social issue still remains unanswered.

Thus, additional research streams need to be tapped into to explain this transformation process. The nature of the firm-stakeholder relationship needs to be discussed first, since it affects the ability of a stakeholder to exert control over a firm during firm-stakeholder conflict.

Building a stakeholder network

How are different stakeholders related to the focal firm? One scheme involves the use of stakeholder typologies, such as voluntary and involuntary (Clarkson, 1995a), primary and secondary (Carroll, 1979), strategic and moral (Goodpaster, 1991), high and low salience (Mitchell, Agle and Wood, 1997), and legitimate and non-legitimate (Donaldson and Preston, 1995). Another scheme is based on the characteristics of the firm-stakeholder relationship, such as resource dependence (Frooman, 1999), the nature of contracts (Jones, 1995), the moral responsibility of the firm (Clarkson, 1995b; Wood and Jones, 1995), and value creation for the stakeholders (Freeman, Wicks and Parmar, 2004).

The firm-stakeholder resource dependence relationship appears to be most relevant in examining the research questions in this study. A resource dependence is said to exist when an actor supplies a resource to another that is controllable, concentrated (in the hands of a few), non-mobile, non-substitutable and essential (Barney, 1991; Emerson, 1962; Jacobs, 1974; Pfeffer and Salancik, 1978). Stakeholders who control some crucial aspect of the firm's functioning are most successful in influencing the firm because of the latter's dependence on them (Pfeffer and Salancik, 1978). Thus, the power relationship between the firm and its stakeholder in times of conflict is a direct function of the resource asymmetry between them. This resource asymmetry not only can explain the type of strategy used by the stakeholder to influence the firm (Frooman, 1999), but can also be used to examine the likelihood of a stakeholder issue being settled at the firm level. Stakeholders who have power over the firm settle their grievances directly, and the firm is more likely to act promptly on these stakeholder's grievances.

On the other hand, stakeholders dependent on the firm may find it difficult to get the firm's attention. A firm in a superior position with respect to the stakeholder is 'somewhat impervious to stakeholder influence' (Frooman, 1999: 200). Such stakeholders stand a poor chance of having their issues settled to their satisfaction through direct contact with the firm. The only recourse available to them is to influence the firm through other stakeholders who directly control the firm's resources.

However, the success of such indirect attempts will depend not only on the relationship between these two stakeholders, but also on the relative importance of the aggrieved stakeholder and the firm to the new stakeholder. In other words, an aggrieved stakeholder would find it difficult to influence other stakeholders against the focal firm if they are more themselves dependent on the firm. Influencing other stakeholders would be easier if they are more dependent on the aggrieved stakeholder than the firm. Thus, the ability of a stakeholder to exert control over a firm can be better explained by examining its relationships with other stakeholders.

Network theory, by simultaneously conceptualizing multiple stakeholder relationships, provides a more complete picture of a firm's external environment (Rowley, 1997). Therefore, I consider the firm-stakeholder relationship as existing in a network of relationships. In this network, the ability of a stakeholder to establish alliances with other stakeholders and influence them to act against the firm will depend on the relative importance accorded to them compared to the firm by these stakeholders. Thus, the analysis moves beyond the triadic level (Frooman, 1999) to a complex web of interactions between the firm and its stakeholders. The influence strategies used by the stakeholder in this network will depend on its relative network power with respect to the firm, and this is discussed next.

Dynamics of network power and influence in networks
A stakeholder's ability to influence other stakeholders against a firm depends on the dynamics of power and influence in networks. Network power comprises domination and influence (Knoke, 1990). Domination

stems from resource imbalances in which one actor controls the behavior of another by offering or withholding some valued benefit or harm (Brass and Burkhardt, 1993; Knoke, 1990). Influence, on the other hand, arises in communication networks (Knoke, 1990) when one actor intentionally transmits information to the other in order to alter the latter's action. If an influence process is successful, the two actors should share common understandings.

Network centrality is commonly used to measure network power (Brass, 1984; Burkhardt and Brass, 1990). While analyzing resource dependence relationships, a high degree of centrality of an actor (number of ties to other actors) indicates a high level of dependence of others on it. The actor with greater power is usually the one chosen by others for resources (Brass and Burkhardt, 1993; Knoke and Burt, 1983), and thus a high centrality score also indicates that the actor is well connected in the network. In a firm-stakeholder conflict situation, for example, stakeholders with high centrality scores are able to use their existing ties with the other actors in the network to influence them against the firm. Stakeholders with low centrality scores, on the other hand, must first establish new ties (mobilize) to influence the other stakeholders.

Returning to my research question, a stakeholder low in centrality with respect to the firm in the resource dependence network would thus be low in dominance and would have to seek the support of other stakeholders. Since an existing communication tie is a precursor to influence (Knoke, 1990), the stakeholder's position in the communication network will affect its ability to influence the other stakeholders against the firm. A stakeholder with a low centrality in the resource dependence network might thus still be able to influence the firm if it has high centrality in the communication network. However, if a stakeholder has low centrality in both networks, it will have to undergo the laborious and time-consuming process of developing new ties.

In sum, aggrieved stakeholders peripheral in both the resource dependence network (dominance network) and the communication network (influence network) would find it difficult to influence the firm using their existing ties. This is the launching point for my proposed framework (see Figure 8.1 below). The distinction between existing ties and new ties is crucial in understanding the transformation of a stakeholder concern into a social issue. Forging new ties is a dynamic process and, if successful, can shift the stakeholder's' power in a network. Networks can be viewed as dynamic situations where actors are constantly involved in establishing new ties and in altering or abandoning existing ones, and where their influence and access to resources may be increasing or decreasing over time (Emirbayer and Goodwin, 1994).

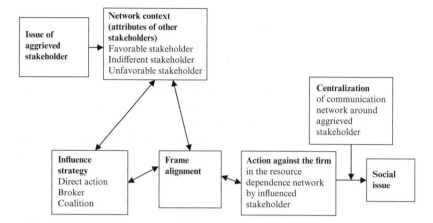

Figure 8.1   Preliminary framework to explain the transformation of a stakeholder issue into a social issue

The primary focus of my framework, then, is to attempt to understand how peripheral aggrieved stakeholders forge new ties in the stakeholder network and successfully influence other stakeholders to act against the firm. Forging new ties can be a public and drawn out process due to the efforts required to influence other stakeholders. It can also result in the involvement of multiple stakeholders against the firm, thereby shifting the level of analysis to the organizational field and thus facilitating the emergence of a social issue. In the following sections I describe each component of the framework in detail.

The network context

The success of a stakeholder in achieving its ends depends on the ties it is able to form as well as on the contextual factors in the network (Stevenson and Greenberg, 2000). While the structural position of an actor can explain the structural constraints and opportunities placed on the actor's behavior, contextual factors are important in assessing an actor's ability to capitalize on these opportunities or constraints. Though network studies often tend to neglect contextual effects (Stevenson and Greenberg, 2000), I feel that the strength of the case study method lies in its ability to intimately capture the contextual variables.

The network context consists of the attributes of the actors in the network as well as the structural characteristics of the network such as density and centralization. These jointly affect the outcome of stakeholder actions (Monge and Contractor, 2003). Each is discussed in the following subsections.

Actor Attributes

Among the widely used conceptualizations of context in the social move-ment literature are 'political opportunity' and 'opposition within the network'. Political opportunity refers to the political context that offers opportunities for action and openness to change (Gamson and Meyer, 1996; Knoke, 1990; Stevenson and Greenberg, 2000), while opposition within the network indicates the presence of contrary subgroups. It is important to recognize the latter, since mobilizing stakeholders often have to modify their strategies to counter opposition in the network (Gottlieb, 1983; Klandermans, 1992; Stevenson and Greenberg, 2000).

Based on the existing literature on social networks and social move-ments discussed previously, it seems that, ideally, the context variable should capture those attributes of the actors that the structural network cannot. For example, although a tie between two actors in a network indi-cates the presence of a communication link, it could either be positive or negative. Or, in another instance, the absence of a tie between two actors could be either because of their negative feelings towards each other, or because they are unaware of each other.

The nature of the tie between actors is important, particularly when considering influence strategies. The strategy to influence a favorable stakeholder would obviously be quite different from the strategy to influ-ence an unfavorable stakeholder, although both instances would be char-acterized by the presence of a tie if only the structural component were considered. Therefore, the context variable, in addition to indicating the presence or absence of ties, should also shed light on the nature of ties.

In my framework, the aggrieved stakeholder's goal is to influence the other actors against the firm. It is logical to assume that the aggrieved stakeholder will first assess the landscape and gauge the attitude of other stakeholders towards their cause, and then formulate their influence strat-egies accordingly. Since the focus here is on the aggrieved stakeholder's perspective, the perceived context, rather than the actual context, is con-sidered. Thus, depending upon the aggrieved stakeholder's perception of the attitudes of the other stakeholders towards their cause, a stakeholder can be classified as *indifferent, unfavorable* or *favorable* (Stevenson and Greenberg, 2000).

Network influence strategies

This research focuses on aggrieved stakeholders who occupy peripheral positions in the network. Thus, their ties with other stakeholders are either non-existent or very few. Their initial efforts would consist of attempts to establish ties with other stakeholders before influencing them to join in action against the firm. Influence occurs in communication networks, and thus the presence of a communication tie between two actors is the precursor to an influence strategy (Knoke, 1990).

Types of ties

Common influence strategies among network members are establishing direct ties, using brokers who are able to bridge structural holes, and forming coalitions comprised of highly cohesive ties between actors who then bargain collectively with other actors (Burt, 1987; Kilduff and Tsai, 2003; Monge and Contractor, 2003).

Direct ties are the easiest to form and are also the most cost effective (Stevenson and Greenberg, 2000) since they are usually forged with similar actors and do not require much effort on the part of the stakeholder. It is common in social movements for actors to join the mobilizing stakeholder due to the tendency to be drawn to similar actors (McPherson, Smith-Lovin and Cook, 2001).

Engaging a broker is an expensive strategy (Stevenson and Greenberg, 2000) because brokers usually receive compensation of some sort for their efforts. Brokers operate through their key positions in the communication network (Knoke, 1990), and thus possess the ability to connect two actors who are not communicating either due to some political or social barriers, or because of the lack of opportunity (Diani, 2003a). In other words, brokers help connect heterogeneous actors (Diani, 2003a), and are effective when the network has open spaces for actors with different perspectives to converge. Thus, the presence of a broker is likely to be crucial in helping an aggrieved stakeholder connect with other parts of the network.

Coalition building is the highest-cost strategy (Galaskiewicz, 1989). It is a public strategy, as actors pool resources to achieve their common goals (Hinckley, 1981). Pre-existing ties have been shown to influence coalition building, making it easier for central actors than peripheral actors to form coalitions. However, marginalized and powerless stakeholders, who need the resources of the network, often find coalition building a viable strategy (Stevenson and Greenberg, 2000). To exert influence, it is important to be part of the dominant coalition that controls the flow of information in the entire network (Brass, 1984). It can thus be assumed that aggrieved stakeholders may have to resort to coalition building to tap into network resources and influence indifferent or unfavorable stakeholders.

Examining the network context allows a reasonably accurate assessment of the influence strategies used by the aggrieved stakeholder. For example, a stakeholder is most likely to use direct strategies with favorable stakeholders. Direct ties are also likely to be used when the network has a high density, because a dense network indicates that the actors are well connected. In networks of high centralization, a stakeholder needs to be part of the dominant coalition in order to be influential (Knoke, 1990). If the dominant coalition is centralized around an unfavorable stakeholder, the aggrieved stakeholder will have to use a coalition strategy and reduced the centralization of the network. On the other hand, if the network is centralized around an indifferent stakeholder, a broker can be employed to connect the aggrieved stakeholder to the dominant coalition.

With respect to the research question of how a stakeholder issue is transformed into a social issue, it appears that such a transformation is more likely when the aggrieved stakeholder uses a broker or coalition, and also when the network has a high density and centralization. The use of brokers and coalitions, by their very definition, indicate the involvement of multiple stakeholders, and thus their employment is likely to shift the level of analysis to the organizational field.

Next, I examine how successful influence strategies can lead to frame alignment among stakeholders in a network.

Achieving frame alignment

The key aim in mobilizing a network is to create common understandings among actors (Knoke, 1990). The concept of frame alignment is useful in conceptualizing such common understandings (Stevenson and Greenberg, 2000). Goffman (1974) defines a frame as an interpretative scheme that actors use to perceive and understand situations. Common frames help actors to organize their experiences and guide their actions (Zavestoski, Agnello, Mignano and Darroch, 2004). Frame alignment thus involves deliberate measures by movement actors to create congruence in the ideology and interests of various actors around a common standard for collective action. Frame alignment has been found to be a necessary condition for movement participation (Knoke, 1990; Snow, Rochford Jr, Worden and Benford, 1986; Tarrow, 1994) and success (Diani, 1996; Snow et al., 1986; Stevenson and Greenberg, 2000).

Aggrieved stakeholders want to encourage other stakeholders to act against the focal firm. However, this will happen only if the other stakeholders first accept the aggrieved stakeholder's grievance against the firm as a genuine issue. How grievances are interpreted among a group of stakeholders is crucial (Snow, Rochford Jr, Worden and Benford, 1986). In fact, 'to enable action toward collective goals, movement members must align their frame of reference to a common standard' (Knoke, 1990: 71).

The frame alignment literature presents movement participation as a dynamic and interactional process, as it focuses on the steps that actors take to create such alignment (Snow, Rochford Jr, Worden and Benford, 1986). This dynamic aspect of the process of frame alignment makes it particularly attractive for the purposes of my investigation. Further, the antecedents of frame alignment identified by Snow and colleagues (1986) fit squarely with the network influence strategies identified in the previous section. For example, the concept of frame bridging (the linkage between two ideologically congruent but structurally unconnected frames) is similar to the influence strategy of bridging ties with favorable stakeholders. The concept of frame amplification (the clarification of a frame to the general public) is similar to the influence strategy used by the aggrieved stakeholder towards indifferent stakeholders. Frame extension (the efforts of the movement to seek wider participation) is comparable to coalition formation. Finally, the concept of frame transformation (change of frames to attract new and formerly unsupportive actors) is comparable to strategies used to influence unfavorable stakeholders.

Frame alignment is thus an indicator of the success of an influence strategy in my proposed framework. However, the importance of frame alignment lies in its role as a precursor to action: the ultimate goal of the aggrieved stakeholder (Knoke, 1990; Snow et al., 1986). I therefore use a narrow definition of frame alignment as 'the shared understanding among stakeholders of the need to act against the firm'.

Network centralization and action
This structure of the network is important because it influences, aids, and constrains the tie formation efforts of the aggrieved stakeholder with others in the network (Monge and Contractor, 2003). Network centralization is the structural attribute relevant in analyzing the Coca-Cola controversy.

Centralization is the extent to which one actor in the network is more connected to other network members than are the others (Monge and Contractor, 2003). Research on collective action indicates that mobilization is more likely to be successful if the concerned actor has a central position in a network (Coleman, 1973, 1986; Marwell and Oliver, 1993). A stakeholder who does not hold such a central position would find it extremely difficult to form an alternate center of power, and would have to engage in extensive mobilization activities to make its cause heard. On the other hand, a network with low centralization indicates that there is no single view prevalent in the network, and therefore the aggrieved stakeholder would find it easier to influence the other stakeholders and form its own center of power. Thus, the centralization of the network significantly affects the influence strategies used by the aggrieved stakeholder. For example, in the beginning of the Coca-Cola controversy the predominant view prevailing in the network was that of Coca-Cola's ability to bring greater economic development to the area, indicating a high level of centralization around Coca-Cola by virtue of cohesion around a single point (Scott, 1991).

Transformation of a stakeholder issue into a social issue

The final components of my framework represent the point at which a stakeholder issue transforms into a social issue. The test of a social issue, as defined previously, is a shift in the level of analysis of the issue to the organizational field, where there is widespread action taken against the firm by multiple stakeholders. I defined frame alignment as agreement concerning the need to act against the firm. However, action by one stakeholder against the firm does not render an issue a social issue. The key is for the aggrieved stakeholder to achieve frame alignment with multiple stakeholders. This is when network centralization becomes important.

A high degree of centralization indicates that one actor or group has a high centrality score compared to the others and controls the information in the network. Since the transformation of a stakeholder issue into a social issue depends on the extent to which the network shares the ideas of the aggrieved stakeholder, network centralization can effectively indicate the homogeneity of the network (Wasserman and Faust, 1994).

So, frame alignment, accompanied by a corresponding increase in centralization of the network around the aggrieved stakeholder, indicates the involvement and action taken by multiple stakeholders against the firm leads to the shift in the level of analysis to the organizational field level, and transforms the original stakeholder issue into a social issue.

Conclusion

Due to the increasing interdependence between business and society, and the subsequent increase in stakeholder litigation and activism, stakeholder activism is now acknowledged as a genuine managerial issue (Rowley and Moldoveanu, 2003). However this area continues to receive scant attention probably due to the primarily managerial focus of stakeholder theory (Donaldson and Preston, 1995; Jones, 1995). Research and practice would greatly benefit from deeper insights into the stakeholder side of the firm-stakeholder relationship (Frooman, 1999).

Managers lacking a clear understanding of the increasingly complex firm-stakeholder relationships could make decisions leading to stakeholder conflict. Several instances of organizational failure following stakeholder conflict, such as Star-Kist Tuna versus environmentalists (Frooman, 1999), GE versus environmentalists (Mitchell, Agle and Wood, 1997), Cargill in India (Kostova and Zaheer, 1999), and Coca-Cola in Kerala have been attributed to managers' inaccurate perceptions of their stakeholder environments. Even in less extreme cases firm-stakeholder conflict can have serious implications for a firm's performance and reputation (Johnson-Cramer, 2003). Understanding the process by which stakeholders get what they want is therefore crucial for effective management of firm-stakeholder conflict (Frooman, 1999).

My research therefore adds to this comparatively under-researched area of the stakeholder side of the firm-stakeholder relationship. By specifically focusing on the ability of peripheral stakeholders to overcome their network constraints through relevant influence strategies, this framework illustrates the power of dynamic networks, as is evident from the unexpected success of the anti-Coca-Cola agitation.

The resolution of social issues has a greater bearing on a firm's reputation due to their public nature (Fombrun and Shanley, 1990). Since most social issues originate from a stakeholder issue, understanding the key components of this transformation is useful to both firms and stakeholders alike. Firms should therefore constantly monitor stakeholder alignments and be on guard when coalitions are formed. For example, it was the formation of a coalition between the anti-Coca-Cola agitation and the *panchayat* that marked the beginning of Coca-Cola's serious woes. Similarly, marginalized stakeholders unable to redress their genuine grievances can gain significant insights from the framework to overcome their network constraints.

REFERENCES

Ashforth, B.E. and G.E. Kreiner (1999), 'How can you do it? Dirty work and the challenge of constructing a positive identity', *Academy of Management Review*, **24**: 413–34.

Barney, J. (1991), 'Firm resources and sustained competitive advantage', *Journal of Management*, **17**: 99–20.

Brass, D.J. (1984), 'Being in the right place: a structural analysis of individual influence in an organization', *Administrative Science Quarterly*, **29**: 518–39.

Brass, D.J. and M.E. Burkhardt (1993), 'Potential power and power use: an investigation of structure and behavior', *Academy of Management Journal*, **36**: 441–70.

Buchholz, R.A., Evans, W.D. and R.A. Wagley (1985), *Management response to public issues*, Englewood Cliffs, NJ: Prentice Hall.

Burkhardt, M.E. and D.J. Brass (1990), 'Changing patterns of change: the effect of a change in technology on social network structure and power', *Administrative Science Quarterly*, **35**: 104–27.

Burt, R.S. (1983), 'Network data from archival records', in Burt, R.S and M. Minor (eds), *Applied Network Analysis*, London: Sage Publications, pp. 158–74.

Butterfield, K.D., R. Reed and D.J. Lemak (2004), 'An inductive model of collaboration from the stakeholder's perspective', *Business and Society*, **43**: 162–95.

Carroll, A.B. (1979), 'A three-dimensional conceptual model of corporate performance', *Academy of Management Review*, **4**: 497–05.

Clarkson, M.B.E. (1995a), 'A risk based model of stakeholder theory', paper presented at the Society of Business Ethics Conference, Vancouver, Canada.

Clarkson, M.B.E. (1995b), 'A stakeholder framework for analyzing and evaluating corporate social performance', *Academy of Management Review*, **20**(1): 92–117.

Coleman, J.S. (1973), *The mathematics of collective action*, Chicago, IL: Aldine.

Coleman, J.S. (1986), *Individual interests and collective action: Selected essays*, New York: Cambridge University Press.

Diani, M. (1996), 'Linking mobilization frames and political opportunities: insights from regional populism in Italy', *American Sociological Review*, **61**: 1053–69.

Diani, M. (2003a), '"Leaders" or brokers? Positions and influence', in Diani, M. and McAdam (eds), Social Movements and Networks, New York, US: Oxford University Press, 105–23.

Donaldson, T. and L.E. Preston (1995), 'The stakeholder theory of the corporation: concepts, evidence and implications', *Academy of Management Review*, **20**: 65–91.

Emerson, R.M. (1962), 'Power-dependence relations', *American Sociological Review*, **27**: 31–41.

Emirbayer, M. and J. Goodwin (1994), 'Network analysis, culture and the problem of agency', *American Journal of Sociology*, **99**: 1434–54.

Fombrun, C. and M. Shanley (1990), 'What's in a name? Reputation building and corporate strategy', *Academy of Management Journal*, **33**: 233–58.

Freeman, R.E., Wicks, A. C. and B. Parmar (2004), 'Stakeholder theory and "the corporate objective revisited"', *Organization Science*, **15**(3): 364–69.

Frooman, J. (1999), 'Stakeholder influence strategies', *Academy of Management Review*, **24**: 191–205.

Frooman, J. and A.U. Murrell (2003), 'A logic for stakeholder behavior: a test of stakeholder influence strategies', Academy of Management best paper proceedings.

Galaskiewicz, J. (1989), 'Interorganizational networks mobilizing act on the metropolitan level', in Perucci R. and H. R. Potter (eds), *Networks of Power: Organizational Actors at the National, Corporate and Community Levels*, New York: de Grayter, pp. 81–96.

Gamson, W.A. and D.S. Meyer (1996), 'Framing political opportunity', in McAdam D., J.D. McCarthy and M.N. Zald (eds), *Comparative Perspectives on Social Movements*, Cambridge: Cambridge University Press, 273–90.

Glaser, B.G. and A.L. Strauss (1967), *The discovery of grounded theory: Strategies for qualitative research*, New York: Aldine de Grutyer.

Goffman, E. (1974), *Frame Analysis: An essay on the organization of experience*, New York: Harper Colophon.

Goodpaster, K. (1991), 'Business and stakeholder analysis', *Business Ethics Quarterly*, **1**: 53–74.

Gottlieb, B.H. (1983), *Social Support Strategies*, Beverly Hills, CA: Sage.

Heugens, P.P.M.A.R. (2002), 'Strategic issues management: implications for corporate performance', *Business and Society*, **41**: 456–68.

Hinckley, B. (1981), *Coalitions and politics*, New York: Harcourt Brace Jovanovich.

Jacobs, D. (1974), 'Dependence and vulnerability: an exchange approach to the control of organizations', *Administrative Science Quarterly*, **19**: 45–59.

Johnson-Cramer, M. (2003), 'Organizational-level antecedents of stakeholder conflict', unpublished dissertation, Boston University, Boston.

Jones, T.M. (1995), 'Instrumental stakeholder theory: A synthesis of ethics and economics', *Academy of Management Review*, **20**(2): 404–37.

Kenis, P. and D. Knoke (2002), 'How organizational field networks shape interorganizational tie-formation rates', *Academy of Management Review*, **27**: 275–93.

Kilduff, M. and W. Tsai (2003), *Social Networks and Organizations*, Thousand Oaks: Sage Publications.

Klandermans, B. (1992), 'The social construction of protest and multiorganizational fields', in Morris A.D. and C.M. Mueller (eds), *Frontiers in Social Movement Theory*, New Haven, CT: Yale University Press.

Knoke, D. (1990), *Political networks: The structural perspective*, New York: Cambridge University Press.

Knoke, D. and R.S. Burt (1983), 'Prominence', in Burt R.S. and M.J. Miner (eds), *Applied network analysis: A methodological introduction*, Beverly Hills, CA: Sage, pp. 195–222.

Kostova, T. and S. Zaheer (1999), 'Organizational legitimacy under conditions of complexity: the case of the multinational enterprise', *Academy of Management Review*, **24**: 64–81.

Marwell, G. and P. Oliver (1993), *The critical mass in collective action: A micro social theory*, Cambridge, UK: Cambridge University Press.

McPherson, J.M., L. Smith-Lovin and J.M. Cook (2001), 'Birds of a feather: homophily in social networks', *Annual Review of Sociology*, **27**: 415–44.

Mitchell, R.K., B.R. Agle and D.J. Wood (1997), 'Toward a theory of stakeholder identification and salience: defining the principle of who and what really counts', *Academy of Management Review*, **22**(4): 853–86.

Monge, P.R. and N.S. Contractor (2003), *Theories of communication networks*, New York: Oxford University Press.

Pfeffer, J. and G.R. Salancik (1978), *The external control of organizations*, New York: Harper & Row.

Rowley, T.J. (1997), 'Moving beyond dyadic ties: a network theory of stakeholder influences', *Academy of Management Review*, **22**(4): 887–910.

Rowley, T.J. and M. Moldoveanu (2003), 'When will stakeholder groups act? An interest- and identity-based model of stakeholder group mobilization', *Academy of Management Review*, **28**(2): 204–19.

Savage, G., T. Nix, C. Whitehead and J. Blair (1991), 'Strategies for assessing and managing stakeholders', *Academy of Management Executive*, **5**: 61–75.

Scott, J. (1991), *Social network analysis: A handbook*, Thousand Oaks, CA: Sage Publications.

Scott, R.W. (1995), *Institutions and organizations*, Thousand Oaks, CA: Sage Publications.

Shivarajan, S. and T. Halbert (2005), 'Coke in Kerala: a social network theory analysis', Academy of Management paper proceedings, Hawaii.

Snow, D.A., E.B. Rochford Jr, S.K. Worden and R.D. Benford (1986), 'Frame alignment processes, micromobilization, and movement participation', *American Sociological Review*, **51**: 464–81.

Stanley, G.D.D. (1985), *Managing external issues: Theory and practice*, Greenwich: JAI Press.

Stevenson, W.B. and D. Greenberg (2000), 'Agency and social networks: strategies of action in a social structure of position, opposition, and opportunity', *Administrative Science Quarterly*, **45**: 651–78.

Strand, R. (1983), 'A systems paradigm of organizational adaptations to the social environment', *Academy of Management Review*, **8**: 90–96.

Tarrow, S. (1994), *Power in movement*, NY: Cambridge University Press.

Wartick, S.L. and P.L. Cochran (1985), 'The evolution of the corporate social performance model', *Academy of Management Review*, **10**: 758–69.

Wartick, S.L. and J.P. Mahon (1994), 'Toward a substantive definition of the corporate issue construct', *Business and Society*, **33**: 293–311.

Wasserman, S. and K. Faust (1994), *Social Network Analysis*, New York: Cambridge University Press.

Wood, D.J. (1991), 'Social issues in management: theory and research in corporate social performance', *Journal of Management*, **17**: 383–406.

Wood, D.J. and R.E. Jones (1995), 'Stakeholder mismatching: a theoretical problem in empirical research on corporate social performance', *International Journal of Organizational Analysis*, **3**: 229–67.

Yin, R.K. (1994), *Case Study Research*, Thousand Oaks: Sage Publications.

Zavestoski, S., K. Agnello, F. Mignano and F. Darroch (2004), 'Issue framing and citizen apathy toward local environmental contamination', *Sociological Forum*, **19**: 255–83.

9. How can sustainable environmental stewardship enhance global competitiveness?

Irene Henriques

'A system must be managed. It will not manage itself. Left to themselves in the Western world, components become selfish, competitive. We cannot afford the destructive effect of competition.'

William Edwards Deming (2000) in *The New Economics for Industry, Government, Education*

According to Hill (2006), globalization refers to the moving away from an economic system in which national markets are distinct entities, isolated by trade barriers and barriers of distance, time and culture, and toward a system in which national markets are merging into one global market. This process has been facilitated by declining barriers to trade and investment and advances in transportation and telecommunications technologies which have decreased the perceived distances and cultural barriers. More firms, both large and small, are becoming international businesses with the help of the internet. Despite the trend toward globalization, countries differ in their cultures, political systems, economic systems, legal systems and level of economic development. International scholars argue that businesses that understand these differences are best able to gain a competitive advantage over their competitors (Dhanarj and Beamish, 2009; Delios and Henisz, 2003).

But where does the natural environment fit into this picture? From a purely economic perspective, the natural environment is the source of our natural resources which are inputs into the production process. This simplistic view, however, has been shown again and again to reduce a country's competitiveness when renewable and non-renewable resources such as oil and gas, fisheries, clean air and tropical forests are depleted (See Yale University's Environmental Performance Index at http://epi.yale. edu/Home). Long-run sustainable environmental stewardship as opposed to short-run decision making is needed. I define sustainable environmental stewardship as the ability of the firm to take responsibility for the environmental and social impacts of its operations on the carrying capacity of ecosystems (Sharma and Henriques, 2005). Ecosystems, however, do not respect borders. The latter suggests that the activities of firms and citizens in one country may impact the ecosystems of other countries (as is the case with global warming). Consequently, increasing the competitiveness of one country without taking into account the natural environment may have a disastrous impact on the whole. Rising environmental concern worldwide has increased institutional pressures from governments, environmental groups and community groups for greater environmental stewardship (Pew Research Centre, 2007). Sustainable environmental stewardship, however, is currently in its infancy and more research is needed to assess firms' environmental stewardship across different international settings.

The first step in taking responsibility is a thorough understanding of what the firm produces and the associated environmental impacts. Such an assessment is possible via the adoption of an environmental management system (EMS). In understanding the link between EMS and business performance, it is important to consider the motivations for adopting these management systems. Some scholars have used institutional theory to explain why organizations adopt EMSs and other proactive environmental strategies (Bansal and Roth, 2000; Hoffman, 1999; Bansal and Clelland, 2004). These authors suggest that organizations are motivated to increase their internal efficiency and external legitimacy, which can lead to competitive advantage. Other scholars have relied on the resource-based view of the firm to explain that complementary resources and capabilities lead to the adoption of proactive environmental strategies (Sharma and Vredenburg 1998; Darnall and Edwards, 2006; Aragón-Correa and Sharma, 2003) and improved business performance (Russo and Fouts, 1997). By implementing these strategies, these authors suggest that organizations are more likely to gain competitive advantage.

Darnall, Henriques and Sadorsky (2008) examined the relative contributions of institutional theory and the resource-based view of the firm to determine the motivations for EMS adoption, and the extent to which these two theories are associated more (or less) with improved business performance. While both institutional pressures and resources and capabilities may encourage EMS adoption and improved business performance, questions remain about whether organizations that are motivated mainly by their resources and capabilities benefit to the same extent as organizations that are driven to adopt an EMS mainly because of institutional pressures. These relationships were analyzed using OECD survey data from manufacturing facilities operating in Canada, Germany, Hungary, and the US. They show that facilities that are motivated to adopt more comprehensive EMSs because of their complementary resources and capabilities (and the tacit, behavioral, imperfectly imitative features that these capabilities may entail (Powell, 1995)), such as total quality management, export orientation, employee commitment and environmental research and development (as opposed to institutional pressures), observe greater overall facility-level business performance.

These results suggest that the first step towards environmental stewardship requires organizations to possess certain capabilities. In the case of facilities in Canada, the US, Germany and Hungary, the capabilities associated with total quality management, experience with the global market, employee commitment and empowerment to deal with environmental issues, and the availability of technological resources to address environmental concerns, provide the inputs from which sustainable environmental stewardship can start. But would this model apply in Japan?

Much research has examined Japan's innovative high-quality products (Powell, 1995; Hackman and Wageman, 1995; Ishikawa, 1998). The latter suggests that Japanese manufacturing firms may possess vast quality capabilities which may give them a competitive advantage in the environmental arena as well. On the institutional side, however, scholars of Japanese environmental politics have commented on the weakness of environmental movements in Japan (Broadbent, 1998; Schreurs, 2002) which may have the opposite effect.

Using the framework developed by Darnall, Henriques and Sadorsky (2008), I first summarize the hypotheses which are drawn from institutional theory and a resource-based view of the firm. I then examine and empirically test the relative contribution of each of these theoretical perspectives to a facility's overall business performance in Japan. Finally, realizing that Japan differs significantly from Western countries in its culture, political system, economic system and legal system, I compare the Japanese results with those obtained in Darnall, Henriques and Sadorsky (2008) to determine if these differences may have helped or hindered Japan's movement towards sustainable environmental stewardship.

THE MODEL – DARNALL, HENRIQUES AND SADORSKY (2008)

An environmental management system (EMS) consists of internal policies, assessments, and implementation actions that affect the entire firm and its relationship with the natural environment. Such systems are increasingly being recognized as comprehensive mechanisms for improving environmental and business performance (Coglianese and Nash, 2001). Darnall, Henriques and Sadorsky (2008) draw on institutional theory and the resource-based view to evaluate when a facility's EMS improves business performance. Below is a brief description of the model and the resulting hypotheses.

Institutional theory.   Related to the natural environment, institutional theory suggests that regulatory, market and social pressures constrain organizations' economic activities, and create opportunities for strategic advantage (Hoffman, 2000). For example, companies can preempt costly regulations or reduce the costs of future regulations by adopting an EMS. Similarly, market pressures may encourage companies to engage in proactive environmental strategies as customers become increasingly aware of the natural environment (Pew Research Centre, 2007). Environmental accidents have increased social pressures from environmental and community groups (Hoffman, 2000), as well trade associations (King and Lenox, 2000) and labor unions. Pressures from each of these groups therefore are expected to influence whether or not a facility adopts an EMS. Another type of institutional pressure is that imposed by shareholders (Henriques and Sadorsky, 1996). Adopting a more comprehensive EMS may be consistent with shareholders' growing interest in investing in environmentally responsible organizations. Shareholder expectations that firms and their facilities be environmentally responsible are increasing as they come to understand the financial liabilities associated with a poor environmental reputation. For example, previous studies have shown that firms with higher toxic chemical emissions (Konar and Cohen, 1997) and chemical spills (Klassen and McLaughlin, 1996) are penalized by lower stock prices.

Hypothesis 1: Facilities that endure greater institutional pressures adopt more comprehensive EMSs.

Resource-based view.   Companies respond to external pressures in numerous ways based on their access to resources and the complementary capabilities that have developed over time (Oliver, 1997). Prior research suggests that facilities with stronger complementary capabilities may adopt EMSs because doing so may create competitive advantage (Hart, 1995). For instance, firms with greater investments in environmental research and development generate more knowledge-based capital, which is critical to sustained competitive advantage (Ghemawat, 1986). Similarly, quality management systems require knowledge-based capabilities that facilitate proactive environmental management (Hart, 1995).

Quality management systems involve coordination among large numbers of people, especially line employees, in continuous-improvement efforts and thus serve as a basic foundation for EMS implementation (Sarkis and Kitazawa, 2000).

Additionally, a facility's export orientation may facilitate its EMS adoption decision because foreign customers are often unable to monitor the environmental performance of the facility or firm (Nakamura et al., 2001). As such, export-oriented organizations derive greater benefits from undertaking protective environmental actions (Nakamura et al., 2001).

Hypothesis 2: Facilities with greater resources and capabilities adopt more comprehensive EMSs.

EMS and business performance. Institutional research has shown how facilities can use EMSs to respond to institutional pressures, enhance external legitimacy, and create opportunities for improved business performance (Hart and Ahuja, 1996; Rivera 2002). The resource-based view of the firm suggests that environmental strategies that go beyond compliance with environmental regulations are associated with improved business performance because they create valuable organizational capabilities (Hart, 1995) that must be continually improved in order to generate a stream of innovations that lead to sustained competitive advantage (Sharma and Vredenburg, 1998).

Hypothesis 3: Facilities that adopt more comprehensive EMSs obtain positive business performance.

Some facilities, however, may struggle to adopt legitimate yet difficult-to-implement environmental practices, especially if they lack the complementary resources and capabilities to do so (Darnall and Edwards, 2006). Facilities in this case may want to signal that they are environmentally proactive when in fact they are not. In this case, an EMS represents a symbolic action that does little to improve a facility's internal efficiencies. Reacting to institutional pressures in this way may lead to some financial gain by increasing external legitimacy, at least in the short run. However, facilities that lack the complementary capabilities and resources to maintain their EMS over time (Darnall and Edwards, 2006) may forego competitive advantage opportunities (Barney, 1991).

Hypothesis 4: Facilities whose EMSs are driven mainly by their resources and capabilities (rather than institutional pressures) are more likely to obtain positive business performance.

DATA AND METHODS

To evaluate these hypotheses, I rely on data from a 12-page survey developed by the OECD Environment Directorate and university researchers from Canada, France, Germany, Hungary, Japan, Norway and the US The survey was sent to environmental managers in each of the seven countries' manufacturing facilities that had 50 employees or more. A total of 4176 facility managers (24.7 percent) responded to the survey. Facilities in Japan are the focus of this study. In Japan, over 4700 facilities were contacted of which 1499 facilities responded, resulting in a 31.5 percent response rate.

EMS adoption.   The comprehensiveness of an EMS was measured by factor analyzing a host of variables reflecting a facility's environmental actions. To develop this measure, I used OECD survey data that asked facility managers whether they had implemented nine different proactive environmental practices: a written environmental policy; environmental criteria used in the evaluation and/or compensation of employees; an environmental training program in place for employees; external audits; internal audits; benchmarking of environmental performance; environmental accounting; a public environmental report; and environmental performance indicators/goals. As expected, the results of the factor analysis yielded 1 factor.

Institutional pressures.   Stakeholders – including regulators, customers, community, labor unions, environmental interest groups and trade associations – impose coercive and normative pressures on firms (Delmas and Toffel, 2004). Managerial perceptions of these institutional actors are extremely important in influencing environmental practices (Henriques and Sadorsky, 1999). I assess regulatory pressures by using OECD data that asked environmental managers how important the influence of public authorities was on the environmental practices of their facility (regulator influences). Respondents indicated whether public authorities were 'not important', 'moderately important', or 'very important'. Facility managers were also asked the number of regulatory inspections they had received over the last three years (inspection frequency). Market pressures are measured using OECD data that asked facilities how important household consumers, commercial buyers, and suppliers were on the environmental practices of their facility (Cronbach's alpha = 0.70). Respondents indicated whether each external stakeholder group was 'not important', 'moderately important', or 'very important'. Additionally, four societal pressures are measured using the same scale to determine the importance of labor unions, trade associations, environmental groups, and community groups on the facility's environmental practice (Cronbach's alpha = 0.76). Ownership pressures are proxied by whether the parent company was listed on the stock exchange.

Resources and capabilities. To measure facilities' experience with quality management systems and health and safety management systems, I used OECD data that asked facilities whether or not they had implemented either management system. Managerial and non-managerial commitment to the environment is determined by asking facility managers to what extent they considered the influence of (1) management and (2) non-management employees on the facility's environmental practices. Respondents answered by indicating either 'not important', 'moderately important', or 'very important'. These items are combined and, using factor analysis, form a factor called 'employee commitment' (Cronbach's alpha = 0.90).

Business performance. As suggested by Cho and Pucik (2005), two measures for an organization's performance are employed: profitability and growth performance. Facility profitability is measured by using OECD data that asked environmental managers whether their facility profits had changed over the past three years. Respondents replied using a five-point scale indicating whether during the last three years revenue was 'so low as to produce large losses', 'insufficient to cover our costs', 'at break even', 'sufficient to make a small profit', or 'well in excess of costs'. Growth performance is measured using OECD data that asked managers how the facility's value of shipments changed in the last three years. Respondents replied using a five-point scale indicating whether they have 'significantly decreased', 'decreased', 'stayed about the same', 'increased' or 'significantly increased'. A factor analysis confirms the existence of a single scale, 'business performance' (Cronbach's alpha = 0.59). To control for size, the natural logarithm of the number of employees in a facility is used. Dummy variables are included to control for industry effects (the chemical industry was the omitted category). A data set with no missing observations resulted in a sample size of 1073 observations. Summary statistics for the variables are presented in Table 9.1.

RESULTS

EMS comprehensiveness is the dependent variable in models 1–4 (Table 9.2). Facility business performance is the dependent variable in model

Table 9.1 Correlations and descriptive statistics, Japan*

Variable	1	2	3	4	5	6	7	8	9	10	11	12	13
1 Business performance	1.00												
2 EMS comprehensiveness	0.15	1.00											
3 Regulator influences	0.04	0.25	1.00										
4 Inspection frequency	0.04	0.16	0.25	1.00									
5 Market pressures	0.08	0.24	0.44	0.04	1.00								
6 Social pressures	0.02	0.15	0.21	0.13	-0.01	1.00							
7 Ownership pressures	0.07	0.29	0.17	0.17	0.09	0.24	1.00						
8 Quality management system	0.12	0.33	0.17	0.10	0.13	0.12	0.14	1.00					
9 Health & safety management system	0.05	0.00	0.01	0.09	0.01	0.08	0.01	0.22	1.00				
10 Employee commitment	0.13	0.41	0.31	0.14	0.14	-0.08	0.09	0.24	0.04	1.00			
11 Environmental R&D budget	0.13	0.22	0.07	0.09	0.11	0.15	0.13	0.12	0.09	0.09	1.00		
12 Export orientation	0.11	0.27	0.04	0.01	0.13	0.06	0.06	0.19	0.05	0.10	0.09	1.00	
13 Facility size	0.14	0.45	0.22	0.21	0.19	0.30	0.42	0.28	0.06	0.15	0.24	0.22	1.00
Mean	-0.01	-0.08	2.02	2.08	0.26	-0.34	0.11	0.76	0.57	-0.21	0.11	0.19	4.90
Standard deviation	1.00	1.09	0.83	4.53	1.00	0.95	0.31	0.43	0.50	0.99	0.32	0.39	0.97

Note: *N= 1073

214

5. I used multiple ordinary least squares regression techniques to evaluate the reasons why facilities adopt comprehensive EMSs (models 1–4). Model 1, which includes only control variables (facility size and dummy variables for industry sectors), is the baseline model. Model 2 incorporates control variables and variables for institutional pressure. Model 3 contains control variables and variables for resources and capabilities. Model 4 includes control variables and variables for both institutional pressures and resources and capabilities.

To control for the potentially endogenous relationship between EMSs and business performance, I use a two-stage least squares estimate of the EMS variable to estimate model 5. This model includes control variables and the two-stage least squares estimate of EMS comprehensiveness. The values of the EMS variable are first computed on the basis of a regression model (model 4) and the predicted values from this regression are then included as a driver in the business performance equation.

Model 1 (the baseline model) is reported in Table 9.2 for comparison purposes only. The addition of institutional pressures to the list of explanatory variables (Model 2) improved the fit of the model significantly. Each of the estimated coefficients on the institutional pressures variables is positive and statistically significant with the exception of social pressures, which is insignificant. These findings support hypothesis 1, which states that facilities that endure greater institutional pressures adopt more comprehensive EMSs. Model 3 includes control variables and variables measuring facility resources and capabilities. Each of the estimated coefficients is statistically significant at the 1 percent level. Surprisingly, having a health and safety management system reduces the comprehensiveness of an EMS suggesting that such a system may be a substitute for a more comprehensive EMS. These results provide support for hypothesis 2, which states that facilities with greater resources and capabilities adopt more comprehensive EMSs.

Note that the increase in the value of R-squared between models 3 and 1 is 0.148, whereas the increase in R-squared between models 2 and 1 is 0.061, suggesting that resources and capabilities add more explanatory power in the determination of a more comprehensive EMS than do institutional pressures. To further explore this relationship, a non-nested one-tailed t-test for the change in R-squared value is used. The result of this test, t = 5.013 (p < 0.01), offers strong statistical evidence for the notion that EMS comprehensiveness is better predicted by resources and capabilities than institutional pressures.

Model 4 includes control variables and variables for both institutional pressures and resources and capabilities. The model fit is significantly improved over the model that includes variables for institutional pressure

Table 9.2 Regression analysis results, Japan[a]

Independent variable	Predicting EMS comprehensiveness[b]								Predicting business performance[c]	
	Model 1—Restricted model		Model 2—Institutional pressures		Model 3—Resources & capabilities		Model 4—Combined model		Model 5—Business performance	
	Coefficient	Std error	Coefficient	Std error	Coefficient	Std error	Coefficient	Std error	Coefficient	Std error
Regulator influences			0.138***	0.038			−0.004	0.037		
Inspection frequency			0.012**	0.006			0.010	0.007		
Market pressures			0.143***	0.031			0.122***	0.030		
Social pressures			0.007	0.032			0.050	0.031		
Ownership pressures			0.397***	0.085			0.373***	0.082		
Quality management system					0.354***	0.067	0.293***	0.069		
Health & safety management system					−0.150**	0.052	−0.141***	0.054		
Employee commitment					0.328***	0.026	0.314***	0.028		
Environmental R&D budget					0.329***	0.076	0.251**	0.078		

	b	SE	b	SE	b	SE	b	SE	b	SE
Export orientation					0.291***	0.068	0.314***	0.071		
EMS comprehensiveness									0.340***	0.070
Facility size	0.479***	0.025	0.346***	0.033	0.353***	0.028	0.265***	0.033	−0.030	0.047
Food	−0.752***	0.107	−0.701***	0.115	−0.526**	0.107	−0.471***	0.113	0.197	0.128
Machine	0.008	0.083	0.083	0.089	−0.077	0.078	0.002	0.002	−0.398***	0.097
Metal	−0.156*	0.091	−0.098	0.097	−0.170**	0.085	−0.104	0.088	−0.323***	0.103
Non-metal	−0.419***	0.168	−0.407**	0.174	−0.255	0.158	−0.220	0.167	−0.389**	0.193
Paper	−0.324***	0.121	−0.288**	0.130	−0.216*	0.121	−0.170	0.124	−0.138	0.130
Textiles	−0.376***	0.130	−0.262*	0.134	−0.172	0.121	−0.094	0.126	−0.240	0.160
Transport	0.136**	0.112	0.245**	0.118	0.010	0.114	0.125	0.116	−0.080	0.122
Wood	−0.219	0.201	−0.289	0.219	−0.193	0.222	−0.186	0.227	−0.651***	0.241
Constant	−2.312***	0.147	−2.066***	0.177	−1.894***	0.148	−1.532***	0.177	0.340***	0.177
R-squared	0.242		0.303		0.390		0.413		0.076	
Adjusted R-squared	0.237		0.294		0.383		0.403		0.067	
LR test[d]	677.54***		753.22***		1043.94***		1014.65***			

Notes:

a. N = 1073. Heteroskedasticity-robust standard errors are shown.

b. EMS comprehensiveness is the dependent variable in models 1 through 4.

c. Business performance is the dependent variable in model 5 and the two stage least squares estimate of EMS comprehensiveness is the independent variable of interest.

d. Likelihood ratio test of a model against a restricted model that includes a constant, facility size, and dummy variables for industry.

(model 2) and slightly improved over the model that includes variables for resources and capabilities (model 3). Moreover, not all estimated coefficients associated with the institutional pressure variables are positive and significant. Regulatory influences, inspection frequency and social pressures are insignificant while ownership pressures and market pressures are statistically significant, lending partial support for hypothesis 1. Each of the estimated coefficients associated with the resources and capabilities variables is positive and statistically significant with the exception of health and safety management system which is negative. These results lend additional support for hypothesis 2.

The fitted values from model 4 were used as an explanatory variable in model 5 to test the relationship between EMS comprehensiveness and business performance (hypothesis 3). The estimated coefficient on the EMS variable is positive and statistically significant providing evidence for hypothesis 3 – that facilities adopting more comprehensive EMSs obtain positive business performance. These findings, combined with the fact that resources and capabilities add more explanatory power in the determination of EMS adoption, suggest that facilities whose EMSs are driven mainly by their resources and capabilities (rather than institutional pressures) are more likely to obtain positive business performance (hypothesis 4).

DISCUSSION AND CONCLUSION

How do the results for Japan compare with those for Canada, the US, Germany and Hungary? Comparing the results for Canada, the US, Germany and Hungary (Darnall, Henriques and Sadorsky, 2008) with Table 9.2, we observe the following. In the institutional pressure model (model 2), social pressures in Japan do not have any impact on the comprehensiveness of a facility's EMS. In the resource and capability model (model 3), we observe that the existence of a health and safety management system appears to decrease the comprehensiveness of a facility's EMS in Japan while it had no impact on facilities in Canada, the US, Germany and Hungary. In the combined model (model 4), we observe the largest differences. More specifically, I find that in Japan the regulatory variables (influence and inspection frequency) are not significant while the existence of a health and safety management system appears to be a substitute for a more comprehensive EMS.

In the case of facilities in Japan, the capabilities associated with total quality management, experience with the global market, employee commitment and empowerment to deal with environmental issues, and the

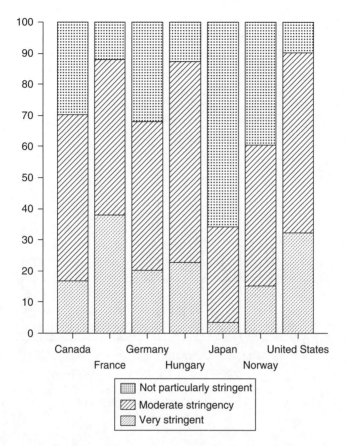

Figure 9.1   Relative stringency of environmental policy regime

availability of technological resources to address environmental concerns are the resource inputs from which sustainable environmental steward-ship can start. The existence of a health and safety management system, however, reduces the comprehensiveness of an EMS suggesting that it is a substitute capability rather than a complementary capability. Together there is strong support for the hypothesis that in Japan facilities with greater resources and capabilities adopt more comprehensive EMSs (hypothesis 2).

On the institutional side, however, we observe some significant differ-ences that may be attributed to differences in Japan's culture, political system, economic system and legal system. In this case, neither environ-mental regulation nor social pressures appear to affect the decision to

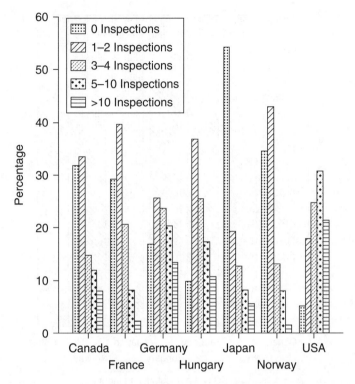

Figure 9.2   Frequency of inspections in last three years

adopt a more comprehensive EMS. Only market pressures and ownership pressures have the desired impact. What can explain such a difference? According to Schreurs (2002), the environmental institutional differences among Germany, Japan and the US are striking. Germany, for example, has a Green Party. The US has a large community of environmental NGOs that lobby Washington, DC. Japan, in contrast, has only a very small and weak community of environmental groups (Schreurs, 2002: 5). Schreurs (2002) also argues that Japan's politicians have not been champions of green issues and that its court system has been traditionally weak.

The institutional differences across countries can also be observed using two variables taken from the OECD database which measure respondents' perceptions of environmental policy stringency and the number of times the facility has been inspected over the last three years. Figure 9.1 depicts respondents' perceptions of the relative stringency of the environmental policy regime. Relative to the other countries in the survey, Japan had the lowest perceived stringency. Figure 9.2 depicts the average yearly frequency of inspections in last three years. Nearly 55 percent of all respondents in Japan had zero inspections (as compared to 7 percent in the US).

Despite the lack of social environmental leadership (government, environmental groups, and community), Japanese facilities have taken some steps towards sustainable environmental stewardship. Sustainable environmental stewardship requires continuous improvement. Pollution control and eco-efficiency are often the first activities that companies undertake. The next step towards sustainable environmental stewardship requires an organization to question the products and services they provide by addressing the recirculation of inputs and outputs in their operations, eco-design, eco-system stewardship and, if necessary, business redefinition (Sharma and Henriques, 2005). Institutional environmental pressures in Japan and worldwide will continue to mount. Table 9.3 provides some interesting data on the seven countries in our OECD database. Norway has the highest GDP per capita and the highest Environmental Performance Index ranking of the seven countries, while the US has the second highest GDP per capita and the lowest Environmental Performance Index ranking of the seven countries.

Table 9.3   Some OECD country comparisons

Seven OECD countries	2007 GDP per capita[a] (PPP international $)	2006 trade openness[b] (%)	2008 Environmental Performance Ranking[c]
North America			
Canada	35,729	70	12 (86.6%)
United States	45,790	28.2	39 (81.0%)
Europe			
Germany	33,154	84.7	13 (86.3%)
Norway	53,334	74.8	2 (93.1%)
France	33,414	54.9	10 (87.2%)
Hungary	18,679	154.8	23 (84.2%)
Asia			
Japan	33,525	30.9	21 (84.5%)

Notes:
a.   Source: World Bank, 2008. GDP per capita in purchasing power parity (PPP) current international dollars.
b.   Source: World Bank, 2007. Openness = (exports + imports)/GDP x 100.
c.   Source: http://www.epi.edu, Environmental Performance Index 2008 rank with score in parentheses.

Sustainable environmental stewardship is possible but it is only just beginning.

ACKNOWLEDGEMENTS

I would like to thank the organizers and participants of the 2009 CIBER Conference on 'Enhancing Global Competitiveness through Sustainable Environmental Stewardship' at the University of Connecticut (14–16 May 2009) for their helpful comments and feedback. I would also like to thank Perry Sadorsky for his helpful suggestions.

REFERENCES

Aragón-Correa, J.A. and S. Sharma (2003), 'A contingent resource-based view of proactive corporate environmental strategy', *Academy of Management Review*, **28**: 71–88.
Bansal, P. and K. Roth (2000), 'Why companies go green: a model of ecological responsiveness', *Academy of Management Journal*, **43**: 717–36.
Bansal, P. and I. Clelland (2004), 'Talking trash: legitimacy, impression management and unsystematic risk in the context of the natural environment', *Academy of Management Journal*, **47**: 93–103.
Barney, J. (1991), 'Firm resources, sustained competitive advantage', *Journal of Management*, **17**: 99–120.
Broadbent, J. (1998), *Environmental Politics in Japan: Networks of Power and Protest*, Cambridge: Cambridge University Press.
Cho, H.J. and V. Pucik (2005), 'Relationship between innovativeness, quality, growth, profitability, and market value', *Strategic Management Journal*, **26**: 555–75.
Coglianese, C. and J. Nash (eds) (2001), *Regulating from the Inside: Can Environmental Management Systems Achieve Policy Goals?*, Washington, DC: Resources for the Future.
Darnall, N. and D. Edwards, Jr. (2006), 'Predicting the cost of environmental management system adoption: the role of capabilities, resources and ownership structure', *Strategic Management Journal*, **27**: 301–20.
Darnall, N., I. Henriques and P. Sadorsky (2008), 'Do environmental management systems improve business performance in an international setting?', *Journal of International Management*, **14**(4): 364–76.
Dhanaraj, C. and P.W. Beamish (2009), 'Institutional environment and survival of overseas subsidiaries', *Management International Review*, **49**(3): 291–312.
Delios, A. and W.J. Henisz (2003), 'Political hazards, experience and sequential entry strategies: the international expansion of Japanese firms, 1980–1998', *Strategic Management Journal*, **24**(11): 1153–64.
Delmas, M. and M.W. Toffel (2004), 'Stakeholders and environmental management practices: an institutional framework', *Business Strategy and the Environment*, **13**: 209–22.

Deming, W.E. (2000), *The New Economics for Industry, Government, Education,* second edition, Massachusetts: MIT Press.

Ghemawat, P. (1986), 'Sustainable advantage', *Harvard Business Review,* **64**: 53–58.

Hackman, J.R. and R. Wageman (1995), 'Total quality management: empirical, conceptual and practical issues', *Administrative Science Quarterly,* **40**: 309–42.

Hart, S. (1995), 'A "natural" resource-based view of the firm', *Academy of Management Review,* **20**: 986–1014.

Hart, S.L. and G. Ahuja (1996), 'Does it pay to be green? An empirical examination of the relationship between emission reduction and firm performance', *Business Strategy & the Environment,* **5**: 30–37.

Henriques, I. and P. Sadorsky (1999), 'The relationship between environmental commitment and managerial perceptions of stakeholder importance', *Academy of Management Journal,* **42**: 89–99.

Henriques, I. and P. Sadorsky (1996), 'The determinants of an environmentally responsive firm: an empirical approach', *Journal of Environmental Economics & Management,* **30**: 381–95.

Hill, W.L. (2006), *Global Business Today,* fourth edition, Boston: McGraw-Hill Irwin.

Hoffman, A. (1999), 'Institutional evolution and change: environmentalism and the US chemical industry', *Academy of Management Journal,* **42**: 351–71.

Hoffman, A. (2000), *Competitive Environmental Strategy: A Guide to the Changing Business Landscape,* Washington, DC: Island Press.

Ishikawa, K. (1998), *What is total quality control? The Japanese way,* New Jersey: Prentice Hall.

Johnstone, N., C. Serravalle, P. Scapecchi and J. Labonne (2007), 'Project background, overview of the data and summary results', in N. Johnstone (ed.), *Environmental Policy and Corporate Behaviour,* Northampton, MA: Edward Elgar Publishing, in association with Organisation for Economic Co-operation and Development.

King, A. and M. Lenox (2000), 'Industry self-regulation without sanctions: the chemical industry's Responsible Care Program', *Academy of Management Journal,* **43**: 798–16.

Klassen, R.D. and C.P. McLaughlin (1996), 'The impact of environmental management on firm performance', *Management Science,* **42**: 1199–214.

Konar, S. and M.A. Cohen (1997), 'Information as regulation: the effect of community right to know laws on toxic emissions', *Journal of Environmental Economics and Management,* **32**: 109–24.

Nakamura M., T. Takahashi and I. Vertinsky (2001), 'Why Japanese firms choose to certify', *Journal of Environmental Economics and Management,* **42**: 23–52.

Oliver C. (1997), 'Sustainable competitive advantage: combining institutional and resource-based views', *Strategic Management Journal,* **18**: 697–713.

Pew Research Centre (2007), 'Rising environmental concern in 47-nation survey: Global unease with major world powers', The Pew Global Attitudes Project, Washington, DC: Pew Research Centre.

Powell, T.C. (1995), 'Total quality management as competitive advantage: a review and empirical study', *Strategic Management Journal,* **16**(1): 15–37.

Rivera J. (2002), 'Assessing a voluntary environmental initiative in the developing world: the Costa Rican certification for sustainable tourism', *Policy Sciences,* **35**: 333–60.

Russo, M.V. and P.A. Fouts (1997), 'A resource-based perspective on corporate environmental performance and profitability', *Academy of Management Journal*, **40**: 534–59.

Sarkis, J. and S. Kitazawa (2000), 'The relationship between ISO 14001 and continuous reduction programs', *International Journal of Operations & Production Management*, **20**: 225–48.

Schreurs, M.A. (2002), *Environmental Politics in Japan, Germany and the United States*, New York: Cambridge University Press.

Sharma S. and I. Henriques (2005), 'Stakeholder influences on sustainability practices in the Canadian forest products industry', *Strategic Management Journal*, **26**: 159–80.

Sharma, S. and H. Vredenburg (1998), 'Proactive corporate environmental strategy and the development of competitively valuable organizational capabilities', *Strategic Management Journal*, **19**: 729–53.

Index